Together Today

Together Today

Themes and stories for assembly

Robert Fisher

Bell & Hyman

Published in 1983 by
BELL & HYMAN LIMITED
Denmark House
37–39 Queen Elizabeth Street
London SE1 2QB

First published in 1981 by
Evans Brothers Limited

Reprinted 1983, 1985

Cover photograph by John Walmsley

ISBN 0 7135 1450 7

Typeset by CCC
Printed in Great Britain at the
University Press, Cambridge

Contents

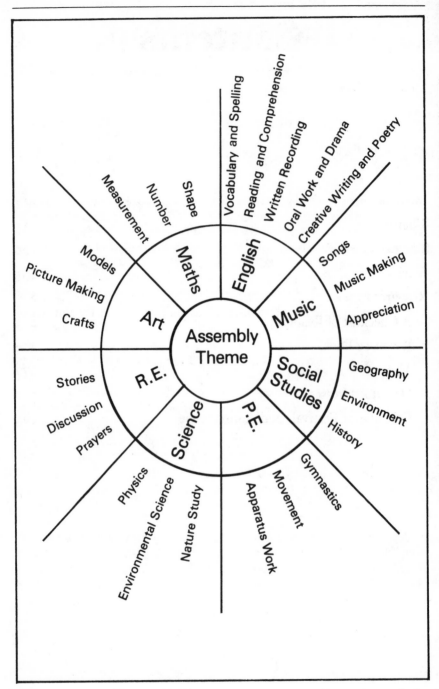

How an assembly theme can be related to all aspects of the curriculum.

Introduction

The assembly is a vital part of school life. For much of the day children work on their own, or in small groups, or in a class setting. An assembly is where the school gathers together as a community. It is a time for sharing common experiences and interests, and for cherishing individual worth. It is also a time when the school community may be related to the life of society, to the wider community.

Themes

The themes presented in this book act as meeting points for the school community. They provide opportunities for discussion and for a variety of shared experiences. They are guidelines only, to be altered or extended as the situation requires. They provide cores around which a complete assembly, or a series of assemblies, can be constructed. Children will be able to work out ways of presenting and extending the material themselves.

In the first section you will find over two hundred themes, linked to references. More will occur to you, and it is hoped that *Together Today* will provide a permanent framework for your notes and ideas. The diagram on page 6 shows how an assembly theme can be related to all aspects of the curriculum.

Stories

We are all aware of the impact of a well-told story. Children not only enjoy stories, but they need the imaginative enrichment which they can provide. Among those earliest recorded are teaching stories. These stimulate thought and illustrate questions of universal concern. Teaching stories such as the parables of Jesus are part of our cultural heritage, and should be part of the experience of all children. The stories in the second part of this book are plain and familiar tales, simply told for reading out loud, but the teacher's own experience will often be the best source of anecdote. Newspapers too will provide stories of immediate concern.

A story can be used to enrich a theme, or it may be told for its own sake. Children will like to write and read their own stories. But whatever the story its impact will be heightened by an element of drama. The storyteller might choose to *mime* the action of the story and mimic the voices of characters.

Children could be chosen to mime the story as it is told. *Props* are simply made. A square of cotton transforms a young girl into an old woman, a boy with a stick becomes an old man, and from a cardboard box anything might appear! *Sound effects* add colour and interest to any narrative. *Music* or projected images may be used to create a mood. Puppets will provide further dramatic opportunities. Themes or stories can be effectively illustrated through mime, music or movement. It is worth remembering that the art of drama originated as a form of religious worship.

The Bible

This provides a rich source of assembly material, in the form of stories and readings. Each major theme is illustrated by a Biblical reference, and in addition to the standard New English Bible there are many excellent versions suitable for children's use. Bible stories can be presented as they are, updated, or children can produce their own versions—often a fresh approach will provide new insights. Efforts should be made to include stories from all the major faiths so that children will gain in their understanding of non-Christian beliefs. Examples of such stories will be found listed under the themes of Judaism, Islam, Hinduism, Sikhism, Buddhism and Shintoism.

Music

The assembly is an ideal time to introduce children to good examples of classical and modern music. There is reference to a piece of music in each theme, and a list of music suitable for the assembly is given. There should be an opportunity to make music as well as listen to it. Use should be made of all instrumentalists, together with the school or class orchestras. Children may wish to accompany as well as to sing the wealth of hymn and song material that is available today.

Hymns and Songs

References are given to illustrate each theme. Suitable songs are to be found in a variety of hymnals and songbooks, though only one source will be given in the text. Children will be able to write hymns and songs themselves, the more gifted being able to set their own poems and prayers to their own music.

Poetry

'Poetry begins in delight and ends in wisdom' (Robert Frost). A poem may express something beautiful in itself, it may enlarge a particular theme, it may be read for the joy of its words, or simply for the fun of its humour. Delight should be the keynote. References to suitable poems are provided for each theme, with a source. Poetry can provide opportunities for choral speaking, for learning by heart, or for adaptation as prayers.

Prayers

The choice and use of prayers will clearly reflect the religious policy of the school. For many children the school assembly will be the only experience of communal worship. It is important therefore to use prayers which express in some way their needs, hopes and fears—as well as the multi-cultural background of most schools. Simple prayers have been given for each theme. Sometimes silent prayer can be more eloquent than words. Children should be allowed to *think* on themes themselves in a receptive and relaxed way. To listen, to be still, to experience oneself as a whole being—this too is a form of prayer.

Activities

Children learn through experience. The assembly can grow out of, as well as initiate, classroom work. Each theme concludes with a list of suggested activities. The creative life of the school will be fostered by the presenting and praising of good examples of creative work. The assembly should also act as a springboard for fresh endeavour.

Resources

In the third part of this book you will find a checklist of resources, and at the end there is a calendar of festivals and anniversaries which will suggest many opportunities for gathering together, and for celebrating. But the most important resources in any school lie in the teachers, the children and their parents. Assemblies should be seen as cooperative ventures in which all the school, children, teachers and parents can make their contribution. In this process there may be something for each of us to learn.

Themes

Abbreviations

Hymn Books

CP	Come and Praise (BBC)
FFC	Faith, Folk and Clarity (Galliard)
HJS	Hymns for Junior Schools (Oxford)
JHB	The Junior Hymn Book (Nelson)
MHB	Morning has Broken (Schofield and Sims)
ST	Singing Together (Oxford)

Poetry Books

BTP	The Book of a Thousand Poems (Evans)
CG	Common Ground (Faber)
CGV	A Child's Garden of Verses (Oxford/Puffin)
COL	Leonard Clark: Collected Poems (Dobson)
EBCV	Evans Book of Children's Verse (Evans)
FPB	A First Poetry Book (Oxford)
JV	Junior Voices I–IV (Penguin)
OBPC	Oxford Book of Poetry for Children (Oxford)
PBV	Puffin Book of Verse (Puffin)
PSA	Poems for the School Assembly (Blandford)
TD	Time's Delights (Hamlyn/Beaver)

Where full bibliographical information is not given for other books referred to in the Themes section, this will be found on pp. 274–76.

Allsorts

'It takes all sorts to make a world.' No two things in nature are exactly the same—everybody is different. The differences in people—physique, personality, abilities, speech etc. How every person is unique. All sorts within a school—the confident and the shy, those good at lessons, those good at sport, the well-behaved and the naughty. How each one has different sorts of people inside themselves: kind and cruel, generous and mean, friendly and unfriendly. The variety of the world—varieties of cars, houses, sweets etc. A variety show. 'Variety is the spice of life.' Sorting things into sets. What would it be like if everyone was the same? Making the most of our talents.

Story   Nail Soup p. 212

Bible   The Parable of the Talents (*Matt.* 25.14)

Music   *The Young Person's Guide to the Orchestra*   Britten

Poem   'Sing a Song of People' (*Assembly: Poems and Prose* p. 120)

Song   'The Family of Man' (CP no. 69)

Prayer   Dear God, please help us to remember
that we are all different.
Help us to make the best of our abilities,
so that working together and playing together
we may grow to be the sort of people
we would like to be.   Amen.

Activities   Discuss in what ways you are different from everybody else. Write a booklet 'About me', and find out as many facts as you can about yourself. Paint pictures showing everyone in your class or school. Compare profiles, fingerprints, palms of hands etc. Practise sorting into sets. Write descriptions of people—try guessing who they are.

Anger

What is anger? What people look and feel like when they are in a rage. How we all have a temper—good temper and bad temper. Does getting angry do any good? What makes you feel angry? How to control one's temper e.g. counting to ten. Who gets angry with you? Why? Does it do any good? Anger that is selfish—not getting one's way. Righteous anger—being angry about injustice. The anger of animals—roars, growls, hissing, spitting etc. 'Angry' as an adjective—angry clouds, waves, storm, wind etc. Seeing red.

Stories   The Death of Becket p. 162
The Quarrelling Quails p. 220
The Three Wishes p. 247

Bible   When Jesus Got Angry (*Luke* 19.45)

Music   *The Rite of Spring*   Stravinsky

Poems   'A Poison Tree'   William Blake (EBCV p. 152)
'Anger'   Yvonne Lowe, aged 8 (JV 1 p. 9)

Hymns   'When a Knight Won His Spurs' (CP no. 50)
'Heavenly Father, May Thy blessing' (CP no. 62)

Prayer   Dear God, help me to control my temper.
Rid my mind of selfish and angry thoughts,
make me gentle and unselfish,
and teach me the way of peace. Amen.

Activities   Discuss what happens to you when you get really angry. What makes you angry, and how you can control it. Find out what is meant by 'battered babies' and 'battered wives'. Act in group situations where someone gets very angry and does something which he or she is sorry for afterwards.

April Fools

The first day of April is All Fools' Day. It is a day for playing tricks on everybody. At midday all tricks stop. One favourite trick is to tell someone his shoelace is undone, and when they look down to shout 'April Fool!' In France April Fool's Day is called 'Poisson d'Avril'—April Fish Day. Here children will make a paper fish and try to stick it on the back of a grown-up, then shout 'See the April Fish!' Sometimes people will tell you to fetch something which is not there, this is called a 'fool's errand'. One explanation for these tricks goes back to when kings and lords had their own jesters or fools. Jesters wore caps, bells and clothes of many colours. They held a jester's stick, like a puppet, and pretended to talk to it. On 1st April jesters were given a holiday until midday, and so other people had to try to perform their tricks. It was sometimes called the Feast of Fools.

Stories   The Jester Who Fooled the King p. 193
Till Eulenspiegel p. 248
The Wise Fools of Gotham p. 266

Music   *Till Eulenspiegel*   R. Strauss
'The Fool on the Hill'   Beatles
The Perfect Fool   Holst

Poem   'God Must Have Smiled'   F. W. Harvey (*Readings* p. 13)

Hymn   'Give Me Joy in My Heart' (CP no. 43)

Prayer   Thank you, God, for our sense of humour,
for the ability to make others laugh,
and for the chance to laugh at ourselves. Amen.

Activities   Discuss practical jokes children have played, or had played on them. Make a jester's puppet stick. Practice being a jester, telling jokes, performing acrobatics. Find the joker in a pack of cards, (the Fool in Tarot Cards). Design your own joker or jester.

Artists

The joy that artists bring to the world through painting, drawing and modelling. The value of creating something for oneself. How art teaches us to look at things, the beauty of colour, texture and shape. The enjoyment of art exhibitions. What to look for in paintings. The talent of great artists. How taste in art differs—traditional and modern art. Where to see great works of art. The value of art works. Materials used by artists—oil paint, water colour, pastels, pencil, pen and ink, charcoal, clay, wood, stone, metal, glass etc. Types of artists—designer, sculptor, illustrator, painter etc. Where to find out more about artists.

Story The Two Painters p. 256

Music *Pictures at an Exhibition* Mussorgsky

Poem 'The Paint Box' E. V. Rieu (*A Puffin Quartet* p. 106)

Hymn 'All Things Bright and Beautiful' (CP no. 3)

Prayer Dear God, thank you for the artists of this world,
for the joy of painting, and for the beauty of
line and colour. Give us eyes to see what is beautiful
and hearts to love what is good. Amen.

Activities Hold an art exhibition. Exhibit as many different types of art as you can, using different kinds of materials. Mount or frame the exhibits, giving title and name of artist. Invite local artists to display examples of their work. Visit a local art exhibition. Ask students or artists to talk of their work and techniques. Display books, prints and projects on various artists. Try your own copy of a famous masterpiece or art work. Visit one of the great art museums e.g. National, Tate or Portrait Gallery. Show a film about a great artist. Discuss what art you like best and why.

Autumn

'Season of mists and mellow fruitfulness' (Keats' 'Ode to Autumn'). The days become shorter—the autumn equinox. Harvest time. What fruits do the trees bear? (Conkers, acorns, nuts, apples, pears, plums etc.). Autumn flowers—chrysanthemums, michaelmas daisies, dahlias. Wild fruits of the hedgerows—blackberries, hips, haws. The changing pattern of the weather—what this causes in nature. Leaves change colour and fall. Hibernation of animals. Migration of birds. How leaves feed the earth, plants rest after flowering.

Story   The Strange Treasure p. 241

Music   *In Autumn*   Grieg

Poem   'A Day in Autumn'   R. S. Thomas (TD p. 22)

Hymn   'Autumn Days' (CP no. 4)

Prayer   Dear God, thank you for the sights and sounds
of the changing seasons, for the fruits and flowers
of Autumn, for the beauty of falling leaves
and the sound of the wind in the trees.
For the joy of Autumn days, we thank you Lord.   Amen.

Activities   Make an autumn collection of flowers, fruits, and leaves changing colour. Paint an autumn frieze showing trees, birds and animals. Plant bulbs for winter flowering. Find out which trees are deciduous and which are evergreen. Find out why the days are getting shorter. Write a poem about autumn, (read 'Autumn for me is' by Helen Mackay, aged 9, *Weather and Seasons* p. 18 (Evans).)
For further material see: *The Autumn Book* James Reeves.

Bells

Bells in our life—alarm bells, door bells, telephones, school bells, fire alarm, clock chimes, Big Ben, cow bells, Church bells etc. Bell-shaped: why bells are shaped as they are. How they are made from bronze. How bells vibrate—effect of size on musical note. Church bells and bell-ringers. Belltowers and belfreys. Campanology. Types of bell—carillons, tubular bells, sleigh bells, ship's bell, Canterbury Bells, the Liberty Bell of 1776, Lutine Bell in Lloyds of London, Bow Bells. Types of ringing—peal, tolling, chiming. The tongue of a bell. What can be heard in a drowned village?

Story   The Bell of Atri p. 147

Music   *Tubular Bells*   Mike Oldfield
'The Bells of Moscow' in *1812 Overture*   Tchaikovsky

Poems   'Ring Out Wild Bells' from Tennyson's *In Memoriam CVI*
'The Bells of London' (*Young Verse* p. 47, BTP p. 52)
'The Bells'   E. A. Poe (PBV p. 29)

Song   'If I Had a Hammer' (CP no. 71)

Prayer   Dear Lord, help us
to ring out the old, and ring in the new,
ring out the false, and ring in the true,
with help from you.   Amen.

Activities   Make a collection of bells, compare their sounds, place them in order of musical scale, invent a tune with them. Invite a team of bellringers to visit the school. Visit a local church, inspect its bell tower. Find out about Big Ben. Quiz: which London bells are mentioned in the nursery rhyme 'Oranges and Lemons'? Construct a bell-circuit. What mathematical facts can you discover about a particular bell—height, weight, circumference, diameter etc.
See: *Ring Out!* (A Book of Bells) J. Yolen (Evans)
    'Belling the Cat' (Aesop's fable)

The Bible

What is the Bible? The Bible is a collection of books. How a 'bible' originally simply meant a book. A bibliography is a list of books. The two parts of the Bible, the Old and the New Testaments. The Old Testament as the history of the Jews, the New Testament as the life of Jesus. The number of books in the Bible: 39 in the Old Testament, 27 in the New Testament. (The importance of number 3; $3 \times 3 = 9$, $3 \times 9 = 27$ etc.). The type of books—history, poetry, wisdom and prophecy. The Four Gospels ('gospel' means good news), Matthew, Mark, Luke and John. Different translations of the Bible into English—King James I Bible of 1611, the New English Bible 1970. Swearing on the Bible—its use in the law courts. Bible lecterns in Church.

Stories Mary Jones and Her Bible p. 204
Ivan and the Hidden Bible Myrna Grant (Coverdale House)

Music *Jesu Joy of Man's Desiring* J. S. Bach
'Prepare Ye the Way of the Lord' from *Godspell*

Hymn 'Tell Me the Stories of Jesus' (MHB no. 32)

Prayer We thank you, Heavenly Father, for the gift of the Bible,
for the wonderful stories of Jesus,
and stories about the prophets of old.
Help us to read and learn from your great book
so that we may grow in knowledge, love and
understanding. Amen.

Activities Display a collection of Bibles old and new, large and small, English and foreign. Teach children how to look up Biblical references, to find chapter and verse. Compare illustrated Bibles, and discuss which illustrations are best. A Bible alphabet—can you find a name in the Bible for every letter? Make a 'Bible bookcase' (see *A Book of Bible Activities* by N. J. Bull (Hulton Educ.)). Listen to a record of Bible stories retold by David Kossoff.
For further information write to the British and Foreign Bible Society.

Bible Stories

The major stories of the Bible suitable for retelling in the school assembly, or as sources of inspiration for art, music and movement, or drama, or creative writing:

Old Testament		New Testament	
The Creation	*Genesis* 1	The Birth of Jesus	*Luke* 2
The Garden of Eden	*Genesis* 2	The Baptism	*Luke* 3,
			Matt. 3
Cain and Abel	*Genesis* 4	The Temptation	*Matt.* 4
Noah and the Flood	*Genesis* 6	Jesus in Galilee	*Matt.* 4,
			Luke 5
The Tower of Babel	*Genesis* 11	The Marriage in Cana	*John* 2
Lot's Wife	*Genesis* 13	The Miracles	see Theme
Abraham and Isaac	*Genesis* 17	Twelve Apostles Chosen	*Luke* 6
Esau and Jacob	*Genesis* 25	The Sermon on the Mount	*Matt.* 5
The Story of Joseph	*Genesis* 37	Jesus Preaches Forgiveness	*John* 8,
			Luke 7
The Birth of Moses	*Exodus* 1	Parable of the Sower	*Matt.* 13
Exodus from Egypt	*Exodus* 12	Jesus Calms the Storm	*Luke* 8,
			Mark 4
The Ten Commandments	*Exodus* 20	John the Baptist	*Mark* 6
Joshua and Jericho	*Joshua* 6	The Unmerciful Servant	*Matt.* 18
Samson	*Judges* 13	The Good Samaritan	*Luke* 10
David and Goliath	*I Sam.* 17	Labourers in the Vineyard	*Matt.* 20
Saul's Jealousy	*I Sam.* 18	The Prodigal Son	*Luke* 15
The Wisdom of Solomon	*I Kings* 3	The Rich Man and Beggar	*Luke* 16
Elijah and the Priests of Baal	*I Kings* 18	Zaccheus the Taxman	*Luke* 19,
			John 11
Naboth's Vineyard	*I Kings* 21	The Widow's Mite	*Luke* 21
Elisha Heals the Leper	*II Kings* 5	Parable of the Talents	*Matt.* 25
Jeremiah and the Fall of Jerusalem	*II Kings* 24	The Easter Story	see Theme
Daniel and Nebuchadnezzar	*Daniel* 3	The Coming of the Spirit	*Acts* 2
Belshazzar's Feast	*Daniel* 5	Stephen the First Martyr	*Acts* 5
The Lion's Den	*Daniel* 6	Conversion of Saul	*Acts* 9
Jonah and the Whale	*Jonah* 1	Paul's Journeys	*Acts* 13–28

Birds

What is a bird? The kinds of local birds that children might look for. The beauty of birdsong—listening to the dawn chorus. The wonder of flight—swooping, hovering, fluttering, gliding, soaring, diving etc. The place of birds in the cycle of creation—spreading seeds, consuming insects. Birds through the year—the miracle of migration, the homing instinct. The making of nests and use of birdsong in marking out territory. The conservation of birds—drinking trays, nesting boxes, seed in winter. Threatened species—the fate of the Dodo and the Great Auk. Man's use of birds—food and feathers. Bird sayings e.g. 'as proud as a peacock', 'up with the lark', 'swift as an eagle', 'taking a bird's eye view' etc.

Stories   The Birds of Capri p. 148
St Valentine and the Birds p. 230

Bible   Jesus said, 'Not one sparrow falls without the knowledge of the Father.' (*Matt.* 10.29)

Music   *On Hearing the First Cuckoo in Spring*   Delius
'Dawn' from *Peer Gynt*   Grieg

Poem   'Bird's Nests'   (EBCV p. 92)

Hymn   'All Things Which Live Below the Sky' (MHB no. 59)

Prayer   Little bird on lightest wing, who sings in every tree,
listen while our praise we bring: God cares for you and
me. Amen.

Activities   Display bird pictures, posters, identification charts and different types of feathers. Play a recording and learn how to identify birdsong. Visit a local zoo or aviary to study bird-types. Make a frieze or mobile of birds. Creative writing: describe your life as a bird. Show a film on bird life. Study birds' nests—could you make one? How fast can birds fly? What birds cannot fly? How many bird names can you write in five minutes? Send for information to The Royal Society for the Protection of Birds.

Birthdays

The wonder of birth and growth. The importance of birthdays—how we remember and celebrate our birth, and measure the passing of time. Human babies—their size, weight etc. compared to other animals. Differences between mammals, reptiles, insects and birds. Growth of the human baby, the need for food, shelter, love. How growth is a continuous process—you are growing all the time (hair, nails etc.). Spring as a time of birth—lambs, foals, chicks, and ducklings. The birth of pets. Ways of celebrating birthdays—cards, 'bumps', cake etc.

Story   The Ugly Duckling p. 257

Bible   The Baby Moses (*Exodus* 2.5)
The Nativity (*Luke* 2.1)

Music   'For Unto Us a Child Is Born' from Handel's *Messiah*

Poems   'Birth Days' (*Young Verse* p. 44, BTP p. 4)
'Prayer Before Birth'   Louis MacNeice (*Selected Poems* p. 74 Faber)

Song   'Happy Birthday to You'

Prayer   Thank you, God, for the gift of life,
for the wonder of birth, and new life in the world.
Help us to grow year by year, not only older
but wiser, not only bigger but better people.   Amen.

Activities   Children to collect and display photos and information of themselves as babies—when they started to sit up, to walk, speak, grow teeth etc. Draw a graph showing the birth months of your class or school. Investigate the births of animals, birds, mammals, fish, reptiles. Make a list of birthdays of famous people. Find out about birth signs (signs of the Zodiac). What is a centenary? How old are you in years, months, days, hours and minutes?

Bread

'Give us this day our daily bread' (Lord's Prayer). What does this mean?
The importance of bread as a food—the 'staff of life'. How bread is
made—the dough and the yeast. Types of flour used—white, wheatmeal,
wholemeal. Kinds of bread—French, farmhouse, cob loaves, pitta or
unleavened bread. The ways bread is used—what did Lord Sandwich
invent?—bread rolls, toast, fried bread, breadcrumbs, bread pudding,
stuffing etc.

Story   The Cargo of Wheat p. 155

Bible   Jesus said, 'I am the Bread of Life' (*John* 6.35)
The Miracle of the Loaves and Fishes (*Mark* 6, *John* 6)
'Cast thy bread upon the waters' (*Eccles.* XI.1)

Music   *Symphony No. 6* (*Pastoral*)   Beethoven

Poem   'This Bread'   Eleanor Farjeon (PSA p. 33)

Song   'Let us Break Bread Together' (FFC p. 4)

Prayer   Dear God, help us to remember that behind the loaf lies the
flour, and behind the flour is the mill. And behind the mill is the
wheat, the shower and the sun, and our Father's will.   Amen.

Activities   Grow your own 'cornfield'. Count the seeds on an ear of
wheat—compare findings. Make a collage of grains. Model shapes out of
dough. Make homemade bread or rolls. Visit a local bakery or flour mill, or
show a film on breadmaking. Investigate the growth of mould on stale
bread. Further information, charts and samples may be obtained from
large bakeries or from the Flour Advisory Bureau, 21 Arlington Street,
London SW1.

Buddhism

Buddhists follow a way of life called Buddhism. There are millions of
Buddhists living in the East, especially in Sri Lanka, Thailand, Burma and
Japan. There are some Buddhists in all countries. Buddhists go to
temples—you can visit a Buddhist temple in London. Some Buddhist
temples in the Far East have towers called pagodas. You can see a Chinese
pagoda in Kew Gardens. Many people have statues of the Buddha who
founded the Buddhist way of life. He is often shown seated in what is
called the lotus (or cross-legged) position. Buddhist monks shave their
heads and wear saffron-yellow robes. In Thailand and Burma many
Buddhists spend some time as monks practising the teaching of the
Buddha. Buddhists do not have to be vegetarian, but many choose to be.

Story   The Story of Buddha p. 153

Hymn   'Far Round the World' (MHB no. 26)

Prayer   The Buddha said:
Overcome anger by love,
Overcome evil by doing good,
Overcome greed by being generous,
Overcome lies by telling the truth. (*Dhammapada* 223)

Let us remember the life of the Buddha,
like him to live simply and to help others.   Sādhu!   (Amen.)

Activities   Display pictures or a statue of the Buddha. Find out what a
pagoda looks like and what sort of flower a lotus is. Find the symbol of
Buddhism—the wheel of life—on the flag of India. Show where Buddhist
countries are on the world map. Demonstrate sitting in the lotus position
(left foot on right thigh, right foot on left as in yoga). Make a series of
drawings showing the Buddha's life story. Light sticks of incense as they
do in Buddhist temples. Find out what meditation is. Discuss being a
vegetarian. Find out about the Buddhist festival of Vesak, which occurs at
the full moon in May, and the Kandy Perahera, which is held in Sri Lanka
at the full moon in July or August.

Bullying

What is a bully? Someone who fights, tries to frighten or teases others. A bully is always a coward, especially when he tries to pick on someone smaller than himself. Bullies can be boys or girls, any shape or size, at any age. Adults too sometimes bully one another. Rulers who bully people are called *tyrants*. What would you do if you were being bullied? Having the courage to stand up for yourself and for others. Some bullies are not bad e.g. Bully-beef, to bully off in hockey, the saying 'bully for you'.

Story   When Fingal Faced a Bully p. 261

Bible   David and Goliath (*I Samuel* 17)

Music   *Concerto for Piccolo*   Vivaldi

Poems   'Caring for Others'   Anon (PSA p. 134)
'Bad Sir Brian Botany'   A. A. Milne (*Young Verse* p. 78)

Hymn   'Heavenly Father, May Thy Blessing' (CP no. 62)

Prayer   Lord, make me gentle and unselfish;
help me to stand up for what is right,
and to care for others
as much as I care for myself.   Amen.

Activities   Discuss with children the experience of bullying or being bullied. Ask groups to act out situations in which bullying occurs, and to show how the problem is resolved. Write a story entitled 'The Bully'. Read about Flashman in *Tom Brown's Schooldays*—find examples of other bullies in fiction (see extracts and discussion points in *What do you Think?* by D. & C. Milman, p. 27 ff. (Blackie)).

Caring for Animals

Animal care at home—pets. The work of the R.S.P.C.A. Caring for animals in school (if any). Animals in zoos and safari parks. Care of animals in the wild—conservation and hunting. Threatened species and the work of the World Wildlife Fund. How we ourselves are part of the animal world. Our duty to protect animals. Author Robert Louis Stevenson once saw a dog being ill-treated. He stopped the owner, who told him 'It's not *your* dog.' Stevenson's reply was 'It's God's dog, and I'm here to protect it.'

Story   Androcles and the Lion p. 139
(See also the stories of Saints in the theme of Saints)

Bible   Noah's Ark (*Genesis* 6)
The Lost Sheep (*Luke* 15.4)

Music   *Carnival of the Animals*   Saint-Saens

Poem   'Caring for Animals'   Jon Silkin (EBCV p. 63)

Hymn   'All Creatures of our God and King' (words by St Francis CP no. 7)

Songs   'Who built the Ark?' (*Someone's Singing Lord* no. 44)
'The Animals Came in Two by Two' (ST no. 39)

Prayer   Hurt no living thing–
Ladybird nor butterfly,
Nor moth with dusty wing,
Nor cricket chirping cheerily,
Nor grasshopper so light of leap,
Nor dancing gnat, nor beetle fat,
Nor harmless worms that creep.
(*Christina Rosetti*)

Activities   Hold a Pet Show. Ask children how they look after their pets, and to tell any true stories about them. Invite a local R.S.P.C.A. inspector to come and talk. Send for information to the World Wildlife Fund. Discuss hunting, and killing animals for food.

Christmas Customs

What Christmas really means—the mass or festival of Christ. Why 25th December?—once the shortest day (old calendar) and time of sunworship; also the Roman feast of Saturn. Singing of carols (from 'carole', a French dance), thought to have been first performed by the angels at Bethlehem. Candles are lit in memory of the Star at Bethlehem. Use of evergreens— holly, ivy and mistletoe. Holly reminds us of the crown of thorns, red berries of the blood of Christ. The Christmas tree (trees were once worshipped) introduced to England by Prince Albert—the annual gift from Norway in Trafalgar Square. Nativity Plays and Miracle Plays. The making of a crib. Gifts given in memory of the Wise Men's gifts to Jesus— the Twelve Days of Christmas. Father Christmas or Santa Claus derived from St Nicholas. Christmas food, traditional boar's head, turkey, mince pies, pudding etc. Boxing Day is St Stephen's Day—tradition of Christmas boxes. Pantomimes, plays, circuses. Christmas decorations, and cards transferred from New Year Cards by Victorians. Christmas was once banned by Puritans. Christmas in other lands.

Stories   The First Christmas Tree p. 171
Silent Night—1914 p. 237

Music   *Fantasia on Christmas Carols*   Vaughan Williams

Poems   See the book of Christmas poems: *A Single Star*

Carols   *The Oxford Book of Christmas Carols*
Faith, Folk and Nativity

Prayer   O Lord, help us this Christmas time to remember
those less fortunate than ourselves, those who have no parents
or homes, those who are hungry, or ill, or alone.
Help us to help them.   Amen.

Activities   Learn carols sung in different parts of the world. Create a traditional carol with dance steps to the music. Read or enact *A Christmas Carol* by Charles Dickens. Make, design or print your own Christmas cards. Send cards or small presents to those in need. Make up a pantomime to show the younger children. Do a large frieze of a circus. Make Christmas decorations, candles, streamers, stars, snowflakes. Decorate a Yule log. Paint pictures of the presents given in the 'Twelve Days of Christmas'. Make a Christmas pudding or mince pies.
For further information see: *Christmas Customs and Folklore*   M. Baker
The Christmas Book   James Reeves

The Christmas Story

How the birth of the Messiah was heralded and awaited in the Old Testament. Prophets and prophecies. Palestine at the time of Christ's birth. The Four Gospels that tell the 'good news' (gospel) of the birth of Christ. Why Jesus was sent down to earth. The Christmas message. The Christmas story:

Bible An Angel Visits Mary (*Luke* 1)
The Journey to Bethlehem (*Luke* 2.1)
The Shepherds in the Fields (*Luke* 2.8)
The Coming of the Wise Men (*Matt.* 2.1)
The Flight into Egypt (*Matt.* 2)

Music 'For Unto Us a Child Is Born' from Handel's *Messiah*
The Christmas Oratorio Bach

Poems Christmas Poems (BTP p. 530–548)

Prayer O God, our Father, be with us all this Christmas.
Grant that as we keep the birthday of Jesus,
he may be born again in our hearts.
We thank you, Lord, for all the joy of Christmas
and for the gift of your Son, born to us at Bethlehem.   Amen.

Activities   Paint a frieze or collage of the nativity story. Make up a play of the events using your own words. How would it be covered by the news media today? Write a story from the viewpoint of a shepherd, a Wise Man, a stable animal, or King Herod. Find pictures or see a film, showing what Bethlehem is like. Perform a dance of the angels. Make a three-dimensional Star of Bethlehem. Discuss how a newborn baby should be looked after. Write a lullaby.

Clubs

What is a club? The clubs that there may be in your school. What clubs do children belong to out of school? The value of clubs—making friends, enjoying a sport or hobby, learning skills and abilities. Local clubs that children might join, Cubs and Scouts, Brownies and Guides, Boys' and Girls' Brigades, sports clubs, dancing classes, church choir, fan clubs etc. Membership badges and uniforms. Obeying the rules e.g. the scout promises on his honour to do his best, to do his duty to God and the Queen and to help other people at all times. How children can start their own clubs.

Story   The Story of Baden-Powell p. 142
Excerpts from *Jungle Book* by Rudyard Kipling

Music   A scout or guide song

Prayer   Dear God, we promise that we will do our best
to do our duty to you and to our Queen,
and to help other people at all times.
Help us to be prepared in all that we do
whether we are joining in with others
or whether we are just by ourselves.   Amen.

Activities   Ask children to talk about the clubs that they belong to and to demonstrate some activities that they do. Display uniforms, badges, equipment, books and information concerning these clubs. Invite a local club leader to talk about his club. Present the work of clubs in school. Talk about clubs in literature e.g. the Famous Five. Write a story about forming a club.
Read *Joining Things* Elizabeth Gundrey (Severn House)

The Commonwealth

The Commonwealth is a voluntary international association linking nearly forty independent nations which between them make up a quarter of the world. The Commonwealth was once called the British Empire. The Queen is head of the Commonwealth. Today Britain is just one of the member countries. Member countries come from all six continents and five oceans, and include different races, languages and religions. Some countries are rich, others poor, but all agree to help each other. The Commonwealth Institute is a centre for the study of all Commonwealth countries.

Stories Anansi the Spider (West Indies) p. 138
Ewongelema (Zambia) p. 168
The Impatient Jackal (India) p. 191
The Thorny Devil (Australia) p. 246

Music Steel band music from the West Indies, or other Commonwealth music

Poem 'Larrikin Language' W. T. Goodge (JV IV p. 22) (about Australian words)

Hymn 'Far Round the World' (MHB no. 26)

Song 'Family of Man' (CP no. 96)

Prayer Dear God, we thank you for the Commonwealth
of which our country is a member.
Help the peoples of the Commonwealth
to understand one another, to love one another,
and to bring peace to all nations. Amen.

Activities Compile a list of Commonwealth countries and locate them on a map. Display project work done on the Commonwealth countries, show costumes, flags and customs. Use facts about the Commonwealth as a basis for graph work and statistics. Investigate the history of the British Empire, explorers, colonists, independence. Visit the Commonwealth Institute, Kensington High Street, London W8 6NQ or the Commonwealth Secretariat, Marlborough House, Pall Mall, London SW1.

Courage

What is courage? The different types of courage—doing brave deeds (physical courage) and overcoming our private fears (moral courage). Examples of physical courage—the brave deeds of heroes, rescuing someone in danger etc. Examples of moral courage—telling the truth, being different from others, standing up for what is right. People whose job involves being brave e.g. firemen, lifeboat crews, miners, policemen, soldiers. How we all have fears. Common fears e.g. fear of the unknown, fear of the dark, strange noises. Awards for bravery, medals.

Stories Grace Darling p. 180
The Story of Prince Sana p. 217

Bible David and Goliath (*I Samuel* 17)
Daniel in the Lion's Den (*Daniel* 6)

Music *William Tell Overture* Rossini

Poems 'The Adventures of Isabel' Ogden Nash (*Young Verse* p. 72)
'The Daniel Jazz' Vachel Lindsay (JV II)

Hymn 'Fight the Good Fight' (MHB no. 12)

Prayer We pray for courage: courage to help others when
they are in danger, the courage to help ourselves
when we are afraid, the courage always to do
what we think is right. Help us to live brave and
cheerful lives. Amen.

Activities Discuss the times when children have been most afraid, and the bravest things they have done. Create a picture or frieze of people who have shown courage e.g. David and Goliath (true to relative sizes). Write a story about someone who is very afraid (of something real or imaginary) and show how they overcame their fear. Find out about jobs that involve being brave. Make a display of medals and military decorations.

Courtesy

Courtesy is something we give which costs nothing. Thinking of others—politeness and good manners. The magic words of 'please' and 'thank you'. Courtesy in school. Courtesy at home. Courtesy at the dinner table. Courtesy on the road. Courtesy on public transport. Courtesy in writing—Dear Sir or Madam, Yours sincerely. 'Thank you' letters. The history of manners—bowing, curtsies, lifting hats, salutes. Customs of greeting—handshaking, bowing (Japan), clapping in return (China), rubbing noses (Eskimoes) etc. Making strangers feel welcome.

Story   The Courtesy of Saladin p. 157

Bible   Jesus Washes the Feet of His Disciples (*Luke* 7)

Music   'The Entry of the Queen of Sheba' from *Solomon*   Handel

Poem   'Kind Deeds'   I. Watts (BTP p. 45)

Song   'Thank you' (FFC p. 3)

Prayer   Dear God, help us to be polite
and kind to all we meet.
Give us good manners and true courtesy
that we may welcome all who come
to see us, whether at home or at school. Amen.

Activities   Hold a Courtesy Week. Act out dramatic situations showing the effects of politeness and rudeness. Discuss how courtesy is shown in your school. Write an account of what you think good manners are. Why did men first start shaking hands. Find out how one says 'please' and 'thank you' in different languages.

Dance

What is a dance? The benefits of dancing—learning to move with rhythm, control and grace—the skills and exercise involved. Kinds of dance—disco, jive, modern, ballroom, tap, ballet, folk etc. National dances—Spanish flamenco, Scottish reels, Russian cossack, English morris, Hawaiian hula etc. Tribal dances for war, peace, rain and all celebrations. Dance music—minuet, waltz, ballet etc. Dance formations—ring, square, sets, pairs, conga, individual. Special dances—sailor's hornpipe, sword dance, maypole. Stories in dance—ballets, training for ballet, ballerinas, ballet dance steps. How things in nature dance—waves, windblown flowers, corn, butterflies etc.

Story   The Story of Swan Lake p. 242

Bible   David before the Ark (2 *Sam.* 6.14)

Music   Country dance or ballet music
'Polovtsian Dances' from *Prince Igor*   Borodin
Slavonic Dance No. 10   Dvorak
Johann Strauss waltz e.g. *Blue Danube*

Poem   'Joys of Dancing'   Ione Rowland (PSA p. 140)

Song   'Lord of the Dance' (CP no. 22)

Prayer   Dear God, thank you for the joy of dancing,
for the rhythm of our bodies,
and for the delights of music and movement.
Give us grace in all that we do.   Amen.

Activities   Hold a Festival of Dance, showing as many dance forms as possible. Make a study of dances around the world. Visit a ballet, or ballet school. Invite a ballet dancer or dance troupe to perform in your school. Study a painting that Degas did of ballet dancers.

Disaster!

There are many kinds of disaster in the world. What is a disaster? Some disasters are natural, some are man-made. Natural disasters are caused by changes in the weather and movement in the earth, such as flood and drought, great storms and typhoons, volcanoes and earthquakes. Some disasters are caused by the spread of germs and illness; these we call epidemics or plagues. Other disasters are caused by man; these include great fires (such as the Fire of London) and wars. When this happens people suffer in a variety of ways: their families may be killed; they may be driven out of their homes—these we call refugees. What disasters are in the news today? Many charities like Oxfam try to help in disasters. How can *we* help?

Stories   Grace Darling (Shipwreck) p. 180
        Hans of Harlem (Flood) p. 184
        The Village of Eyam (Plague) p. 259

Bible   The Escape of Moses from Egypt (Refugees) (*Exodus* 13)
        Jesus Escapes from Herod (Refugees) (*Matt.* 2.13)
        Jesus Calms the Storm (*Mark* 4.35; 6.45)

Music   'Four Sea Interludes': Storm sequence from *Peter Grimes* Britten
        Tannhäuser Overture Wagner

Poem   'The Boy Stood on the Burning Deck' (*Parlour Poetry* p. 140)

Hymn   'Eternal Father, Strong to Save' (JHB no 123)

Prayer   We pray for all those who have suffered in the disasters of this world, the sick, the homeless and the hungry.
        Help us to help them in all the ways that we can.   Amen.

Activities   Find out about some of the great disasters of the world e.g. the eruption of Vesuvius, the San Francisco Earthquake of 1906, the sinking of the Titanic, the Great Plague and Great Fire of London. Write an eye witness report of one of these events. Get project material from Christian Aid, Oxfam and Save the Children Fund. Discuss the small 'disasters' of your life.

Easter: Holy Week

Holy Week is the last week of Lent. It is the time when we prepare for Easter. The festival of Easter does not begin until Easter Day. During Holy Week we remember the events which led up to the Crucifixion of Jesus. We remember:

Bible   The Entry into Jerusalem (*Mark* 11.1, *Luke* 19.29, *Matt.* 21)
Cleansing the Temple (*Luke* 19.45)
Judas Plots to Betray Jesus (*Matt.* 26)
The Last Supper (*Mark* 14.12, *John* 13)
The Garden of Gethsemene: The Arrest (*Matt.* 26.47)
Peter Denies Jesus (*Matt.* 26.69)
Jesus before Pontius Pilate (*Matt.* 27.19)
The Crucifixion (*Matt.* 27.27)

Stories   Little Girls Are Wiser Than Men p. 200
The Mark on the Donkey p. 203

Music   Chorus from *St Matthew Passion*   Bach

Poems   'The Donkey'   G. K. Chesterton (*Rhyme* IV p. 118)
'He is Risen'   C. F. Alexander (TD p. 94)

Hymn   'There is a Green Hill Far Away' (MHB no. 77)

Prayer   We remember how Jesus rode into Jerusalem
ready to face the danger there. We remember how
he was betrayed and forsaken by his friends.
We remember how he suffered and died upon the cross.
Let us think of Jesus who died that we might live.   Amen.

Activities   Create an Easter Garden. Act out the happenings of Holy Week. Find out what happens on Maundy Thursday. Make Hot Cross Buns. Show a film, slides, or pictures of Jerusalem. Paint a frieze of the Crucifixion. Find out about the Turin Shroud.

Easter Festival

Easter Day is the most important day of the whole year for Christians. It is a time of great happiness and rejoicing. Jesus, who died for our sins on Good Friday, rose again on Easter Day and is alive for evermore. The Resurrection of our Lord on Easter morning. The message of Easter, that death is not the end of life, but the beginning of a new kind of life. Churches are filled with spring flowers and a Paschal Candle is lit as a symbol of the Risen Christ. It will burn for forty days until Ascension. In the old days people would buy new clothes and hats to wear to Church on Easter Day, viz. 'Easter bonnets'. Painted eggs were given as presents, symbolising new life. Chocolate eggs. Egg rolling contests. Simnel cakes. The sound of Easter bells.

Bible   The Resurrection (*John* 20.1)
Doubting Thomas (*John* 20.24)

Music   The 'Hallelujah Chorus' from the *Messiah*   Handel
Exultate Jubilate   Mozart
'Hosanna Hey Sanna' from *Jesus Christ Superstar*   Lloyd Webber

Poem   'The World Itself Keeps Easter Day'   J. M. Neale (TD p. 95)

Hymn   'Jesus Christ is Risen Today' (MHB no. 79)

Prayer   Heavenly Father, help us to remember the message of Easter:
that Jesus is alive and with us always,
that he brings to us new life and new hope.
Help us to keep the story of Easter in our minds
and the joy of Easter in our hearts.   Amen

Activities   Show a model of the empty tomb in the Easter Garden. Tell the story of the Resurrection from the point of view of Mary or Doubting Thomas. Paint Easter eggs, or dye them with onion skins. Light a Paschal candle. Make Easter cards. Hold an Easter parade of home-made hats, or bonnets.

The Elements

Traditionally there were four elements—earth, air, fire and water. It was thought that they were the basic elements of which the world was composed, and all matter would end up being of one of these elements. There was nothing *simpler* or more basic in nature (hence the word 'elementary' meaning simple, and 'elementary' schools). Nowadays we know there are many more chemical elements, but the four original elements can still be used as a means of simple classification. Could we live without any one of the four? Which is the most important? Elements as part of the study of chemistry. So what is an element of something?

Prayer   Praised be my Lord, for our Brother Sun,
Who caused all day his course to run.
For our Sister Moon, praised be my Lord
By stars in heavenly hosts adored.
For our Brothers, the Wind, the Cloud, and the Air
Whose blessings all your creatures share.
Praised be my Lord for Waters bright,
For our Brother Fire, for warmth and light,
To Mother Earth, your gifts you send,
O God our Father, and our Friend.   Amen.
(St Francis)

1. **Fire**   see theme on Fire

2. **Water**   see theme on Water

3. **Earth**   What is earth? What is it made up of? Why is it essential for life? Different types of soil, how climate affects soil. Life in the soil (the value of worms). The layers of the soil, the importance of compost and manure. Why fields lie fallow.
Story   The Troll's Share p. 250
Activities   Display elements of the soil e.g. sand, lime, compost, etc. Make a wormery to show the effect of worms on layers of soil. Collect advertisements of fertilisers, garden tools etc.

4. **Air**   The air we breathe. How long could you live without air (3 minutes). The use of oxygen in the body. Air pollution. Air pressure—pumps, tyres, gauges, Weather: high and low pressure areas—barometer. The power of winds—sailing, windmills, hurricanes.
Story   Daedelus and Icarus p.160
Activities   Test how long you can hold your breath. Show how a candle needs oxygen. Study a barometer, investigate hot air balloons. Listen to Bach's 'Air on the G string'.

Fashion

What is a fashion? Fashions in clothes, music, art, food, holidays, entertainment, children's games etc. Fashion is usually applied to clothes, to be 'in fashion', up-to-date, fashionable. How we like to be admired and not thought 'old fashioned'. How fashions change, the influence of designers, advertising, shops. How some things catch on, others do not, the recurrence of fashion. The history of fashion e.g. how few men wore trousers until the nineteenth century and few women until the twentieth. Strange fashions e.g. eighteenth-century wigs. Fashion in different parts of the world. Fashions of the future. Fashion puzzle—why do men's buttons do up on the right, women's on the left? The things in life that do not change.

Story   The Emperor's New Clothes p. 166

Bible   Joseph's Coat of Many Colours (*Genesis* 37.3)

Music   The latest record at the top of the hit parade

Poem   'Cotton'   Eleanor Farjeon (*Puffin Quartet* p. 30)

Hymn   'Everything Changes but God Changes Not' (HJS no. 2)

Prayer   We thank you, God, for the variety and colour
of our clothes, for fashions that change and
for all that is new. In a changing world help
us to remember those things that do not change,
our love for You, and our love for one another.   Amen.

Activities   Hold a fashion show complete with background music and commentary. Study and illustrate fashion through the ages. Display dolls showing traditional fashions from other countries. Visit an exhibition showing fashions e.g. the Victoria and Albert Museum, the Geffrye Museum. Design your own clothes, school uniform, sports wear and accessories. Discuss the fashions of the future.

Fire

The importance of fire for heating, lighting, and cooking. How fire was made before matches—flints, rubbing sticks. Fire as a protection against wild animals, and as a weapon of war. The fun of fires—bonfires, camp fires, fireworks. The dangers of playing with fire or lighting matches—how fires start—fire risks in the home—fire guards and precautions. What you should do if fire breaks out. The fire-fighting services. The importance of Fire Drill. How fire burns, melts, purifies. Distress flares, the Olympic Torch, fire-eaters, fire-ships, to fire, to be fired, have a flare-up, a flaming row etc.

Stories How Prometheus Brought Fire to Man p. 188
The Great Fire of London (see Pepys Diary, 2nd September 1666, in *The Illustrated Pepys* ed. R. Latham (Bell & Hyman) p. 120)

Bible Elijah and the Priests of Baal (*I Kings* 18)
Daniel in the Fiery Furnace (*Daniel* 3)
Tongues of Fire (*Acts* 2.1)

Music *Ritual Fire Dance* de Falla
The Firebird Stravinsky

Poems 'The Progress of the Fire' M. Baldwin (EBCV p. 196)
'Fire' James Reeves (PSA p. 35)
'Matilda' Hilaire Belloc (PBV p. 152)

Songs 'Fire Down Below' (ST no. 26)
'London's Burning' (Traditional round)
'The Fireman' (*Apusskidu* no. 33)

Prayer Dear Lord, thank you for the gift of fire.
Help us always to be careful with fire.
Let us remember the work of firemen who risk their lives
in saving others. Amen.

Activities Invite a local Fire Safety Officer to talk or show a film on the dangers of fire. Visit the local Fire Station. Practise a Fire Drill. Dramatise the outbreak of, and fighting of, a fire, with its aftermath. Discuss words which describe fire, then write a poem or description of one. Show the course of fire in music and movement—a fire dance. Show by experiment how fire needs oxygen.

Fireworks

5th November, Guy Fawkes Day, is the traditional time in England for letting off fireworks. Fireworks are set off in most countries at times of festival and celebration. Fireworks began long before Guy Fawkes. They were invented by the Chinese over two thousand years ago, setting off crackers to frighten away ghosts and evil spirits. The Crusaders brought the Roman Candle (then called 'Greek Fire') to this country after firing it from catapults during sieges in the Holy Land. Names of fireworks—Catherine Wheel, Sparklers, Volcano, Gold and Silver Rain, Rockets, Jumping Crackers etc. The danger of fireworks, especially bangers and rockets. The Firework Safety Code. Local organised displays are safer than bonfires at home. Taking care of pets and younger children. The work of the Fire Brigade.

Stories Guy Fawkes p. 182
    A legend of St Catherine the Martyr

Music *The Music for the Royal Fireworks* Handel
    Prélude 'Feux d'artifice' Debussy

Poems 'Fireworks' James Reeves (TD p. 104)
    'Please to Remember' Walter de la Mare (*Passport to Poetry* II
    p. 54)

Song 'Guy Fawkes' (Traditional song: see *Oxford Song Book* vol. II
    no. 57)

Prayer Thank you, God, for the colour and fun of fireworks.
    We pray that there are no accidents on bonfire night;
    that no children get burned, no animals scared;
    that we may all have a safe and happy time. Amen

Activities Demonstrate safe and dangerous ways of using fireworks. Make a frieze or collage of bonfire night. Write a poem or account of your own special bonfire night. Write a story about the Gunpowder Plot from the viewpoint of one of the conspirators, or enact a play. Make a graph of favourite fireworks. Investigate the chemical content of fireworks, show how rockets work.

Fishing

Fishing as a popular sport or hobby. People who fish are called anglers, the sport of fishing is called angling. Where you can fish—seawater and freshwater fishing (rivers, canals, lakes and ponds). What you need—rod and bait. Kinds of freshwater fishing—fly (for trout and salmon), float and ledger. Kinds of bait—bread, worms, maggots, fish. Kinds of fish—perch, bream, roach, pike etc. Fishing terms: casting, striking, bite, catch, reel, line, keep nets, tackle. Deep sea fishing—trawling, drifting, whaling. Shoals and schools. The food value of fish. The processing of fish—fresh, frozen, tinned, dried, smoked, raw (in Japan). Fish cookery. Fish on Friday?

Story The Day I Caught a Bus p. 161

Bible Jesus Calls the Fishermen (*Mark* 1.16)
Peter's Great Catch of Fish (*Luke* 5.1)

Music *The Trout Quintet* Schubert

Poem 'Fisherman's Lore' Anon (PBV p. 166)

Hymn 'When Lamps are Lighted in the Town' (JHB no. 11)

Prayer Let us think of the fishermen of the world, those
who fish in the sea, and those who fish by rivers and streams.
Let us help in keeping our waters clean for fish to live in,
for they too have a part to play in God's world.   Amen.

Activities Make a display of fishing tackle. Invite those who fish to recount their experiences. Interview local fishermen at work. Show on a large map of your area where fishing takes place locally. Collect pictures and posters showing fish. Show a film on deep sea fishing. Make a frieze showing different forms of underwater life. Quiz: How many names of fish do you know?

Flowers

The beauty of flowers. Why plants have flowers. How flowers grow—seeds and bulbs. What plants need to grow. Where they can be grown—the use of pots and windowboxes. The variety of flowers—indoor and outdoor plants, annuals and perennials. Wild flowers—why they should never be picked. The parts of flowers—petals, stamens, pollen, nectar etc. The scent of flowers. Flowers as symbols—rose, lily, poppy, etc. Flowers seen in the locality—parks, florists, gardens.

Stories The Forgotten Treasure p. 174
The Stolen Tulip p. 240

Bible 'Consider the Lilies of the Field' (*Matt* 6.28)

Music 'Waltz of the Flowers' from the *Nutcracker Suite*   Tchaikovsky
'The Floral Dance' (Cornish traditional song)

Poem 'Daffodils'   William Wordsworth (BTP p. 228)

Hymns 'Think of a World Without Any Flowers' (CP no. 17)
'Daisies Are Our Silver' (MHB no. 63)

Prayer Dear God, thank you for the beauty of flowers;
the flowers that grow wild in the fields, the
flowers of parks and gardens. Help us to see
what is beautiful, and to love what is good.   Amen.

Activities   Hold your own Flower Festival. Make a collection of pressed flowers. Exhibit flower drawings and paintings. Cultivate flower seeds in plastic containers. Display prints of famous flower paintings e.g. a Dutch still life; *Sunflowers* by Van Gogh. Collect a scrapbook of flower pictures. Make a graph of favourite flowers. Do a movement sequence of flowers growing, opening, dying. Visit a local nursery or park to study the flowers. Quiz: How many flower names can you write in five minutes?

Food

Why do we eat food? How food is essential for health, energy and growth. What goodness in food consists of—vitamins, protein, minerals, carbohydrates etc. How long could we live without food? (Answer: about a fortnight with water). What happens if you don't eat? Problems of malnutrition in developing countries. What is a famine? Problems in this country caused by eating too much. Dieting—good and bad diets, different diets around the world, getting a balanced diet. Is it right to kill animals for food? Factory farming. Vegetarians. The necessity of food for animals, both carnivores and vegetarians, and for plants. The work of cooks and chefs. Feeding the mind.

Stories   Food for Thought p. 173
Nail Soup p. 212

Bible   Famine in Egypt (*Genesis* 41.53)
The Loaves and the Fishes (*John* 6)

Music   'Food Glorious food' from *Oliver!*   Bart

Song   'Feed Us Now' (FFC p. 32)

Poem   'Beautiful Soup' (OBPC p. 12)

Prayer   Thank you, God, for food and drink,
help us to feed our bodies and our minds,
help us to think of those who are hungry,
and have not enough food to eat.
Help us, good Lord, to feed the world.   Amen.

Activities   Study the foods of the world. Display pictures and labels of different foods. Cook a meal, or prepare a menu for a week. Find out about nutritional needs, calories, carbohydrates etc. Send for posters and project material from Oxfam or Christian Aid.

Footsteps

What does it mean 'to follow in someone's footsteps'? The game 'Follow my leader'. How we all choose someone to follow, how we follow teachers, parents, older brothers and sisters. How Christians follow Jesus. Famous footprints; tracks in the sand—Robinson Crusoe; tracks in the snow—Good King Wenceslaus, the Abominable Snowman (Yeti). Setting foot for the first time e.g. moonlanding. The footprints or tracks of animals and birds.

Story Famous Footsteps p. 169

Music A march by a military band
Radetsky March J. Strauss

Poems 'The Footprint' James Reeves (*A Puffin Quartet* p. 81)
'The Hairy Toe' (JV II p. 65)

Hymn 'Onward Christian Soldiers' (MHB no. 13)
'O Jesus I Have Promised' (JHB no. 78)

Prayer Jesus, friend of the friendless,
helper of the poor, healer of the sick,
whose life was spent in doing good,
let me follow in your footsteps.
Make me loving in all that I say and do,
make me strong to do right,
gentle with the weak, and kind to all who are in sorrow,
that I may be like you, my Lord and master. Amen.

Activities Discuss in whose footsteps you would like to follow. Draw round and paint a collage of feet. Find out about the Abominable Snowman. Write a story about finding a footprint on a desert island. Study, draw or make plaster casts of animal or bird tracks. Movement—show different ways of stepping e.g. tightrope walking, going across stepping stones, tiptoes etc. Maths—measure feet, how many centimetres in a foot, measure by footsteps (pigeon steps).
Note: First words spoken on moon: 'That's one small step for a man, but one giant leap for mankind' by astronaut Neil Armstrong on 21st July 1969.

Forgiveness

'To err is human, to forgive divine.' (Alexander Pope). We all make mistakes, we all do wrong, we are all in need of forgiveness. How easy to forgive ourselves, how difficult to forgive others. The saying 'Forgive and forget'. Jesus was asked how often one should forgive others (*Matt.* 18.21)—what would be your reply? Giving people a second chance, a chance to make amends. What is a 'pardon'? When did Jesus say 'Forgive them for they know not what they do'? (*Luke* 23.34) What does 'Forgive us our trespasses' mean?

Story The Bishop's Candlesticks p. 149

Bible The Prodigal Son (*Luke* 15)
The Unmerciful Servant (*Matt.* 18.21)

Music 'The Lord's Prayer' from *African Sanctus* Fanshawe

Poem 'Little Things' J. Stephens (*Poems for Assemblies* p. 56)

Hymn 'The Lord's Prayer' (FFC p. 2)
'Heavenly Father, May Thy Blessing' (CP no. 62)

Prayer O God, our Father, grant us
The love which is always ready to forgive;
The love which is always eager to help;
The love which is always happier to give than to get.
And so grant that living in love, we may live like Jesus. Amen.
*(Dr William Barclay)**

Activities Discuss the problems of forgiving friends, and of forgiving enemies. What is a feud? Study a famous feud e.g. *Romeo and Juliet*, or write the story of a feud. Write a parable about forgiveness.

*From *Prayers for Young People* Dr William Barclay (Collins)
(Dr Barclay's prayer is reproduced here by kind permission of the publishers.)

Freedom

In this country we say that people are *free*. What is freedom? The opposite of freedom is slavery—the history of slavery. Other words for freedom—liberty and independence. In the U.S.A. they have Independence Day, the Statue of Liberty and a Liberty Bell. The United States and many other countries have had to fight for their freedom. The 'four freedoms' we enjoy—freedom of speech, of religion, from fear and from want—e.g. free speech at Speaker's Corner (Hyde Park), freedom of religion (many kinds of churches and other places of worship), freedom from fear (protected by police and armed forces), freedom from want (protected by the Welfare State). A freeman, freehold, freewheel, freehand, freestyle, freelance, (originally meaning knights who sold their services after the Crusades), a Free House, free trade, freedom of the city etc. Freedom of choice, what it is to have freewill.

Story   William Tell p. 264

Bible   'Let my people go'—The Story of Moses in *Exodus*

Music   *William Tell Overture*   Rossini

Poem   'The Pilgrim Fathers'   F. Hemans (BTP p. 451)

Songs   'Oh Freedom', 'Go Down Moses'   Negro Spirituals
'Die Gedanken Sind Frei' (all from FFC pp. 21 and 25)

Prayer   Dear God, thank you for giving me freedom,
freedom to be kind as well as selfish,
freedom to lie as well as to tell the truth,
freedom to be happy as well as to be sad.
Help me always to work for the freedom of others.   Amen.

Activities   Colour in on a world map the countries that are in what is called the Free World. Find out about the work of Amnesty International. Imagine you are a slave, write about your life and feelings. Find out about freedom fighters like Gandhi, Martin Luther King etc. What was Magna Carta?

Friends

What is a friend? What makes a friend special? Who your friends are—classmates, animals, policemen, teachers? The number of friends you have. Your best friend. The saying 'A friend in need is a friend indeed—what does it mean? What it is like to be without a friend, e.g. being new to a school or an area. How to make friends—joining clubs, having a pen friend. Words for friends—mate, pal, chum, buddy etc. Friends together—bunch, group, circle, crowd, gang etc. How you can have a friend in Jesus.

Stories The Bear That Spoke p. 143
The Two Friends p. 253

Bible David and Jonathan (*I Samuel* 18)
Ruth and Naomi (*Ruth*)

Music *Enigma Variations* (portraits of friends)   Elgar
'With a Little Help from My Friends' (*Sergeant Pepper*)   Beatles

Poem 'A Thank You for Friends'   R. Bennett (BTP p. 512)

Hymns 'Jesus Friend of Little Children' (MHB no. 37)
'There's a Friend for Little Children' (MHB no. 5)

Prayer Dear God, help us to remember those who might
be feeling lonely, help me to be a friend to others,
just as you are a friend to me.   Amen.

Activities   Make a list of the qualities of a friend: 'A friend is someone who . . . ' Make a pen-friend of someone living in another country, show in school some letters from pen-friends. Make up a play about a quarrel between friends—show how it is resolved. Describe your best friend. Look up John 15.13—'Greater love hath no man than this, that a man lay down his life for his friends.'—How does this apply to Captain Oates on Scott's last polar expedition?

Gifts

What is a gift? The times for giving gifts—birthdays, Christmas, weddings, Christenings, Mother's Day, anniversaries, leaving presents etc. The wrapping of gifts and the element of surprise. The hymn 'All good gifts around us are sent from heaven above'—what are the gifts from God? How we respond to gifts saying 'Thank you', and giving in return. The saying 'It is better to give than to receive.' 'Gifted' people—how everyone has special gifts, making the most of them.

Story   The Gift of Camels p. 177

Bible   The Gifts of the Three Wise Men (*Matt.* 2.11)
The Widow's Mite (*Luke* 21)

Music   'All Good Gifts' from the musical *Godspell*   Schwartz

Poem   'A Christmas Carol'   Christina Rossetti (PBV p. 257)

Songs   'Simple Gifts' (FFC p. 19)
'The Best Gift' (CP no. 59)

Prayer   Dear God, thank you for the gifts which you
have given us, help us to use them well. Jesus said,
'It is better to give than to receive.' Help us, Oh Lord,
to give cheerfully to others and to be grateful for
what we have been given.   Amen.

Activities   Make a display of holiday souvenirs and gifts received from other countries. Offer a brief history of each exhibit giving origin, date, to whom given etc. Make small gifts to give to younger children, friends, those in need etc. e.g. calendars, embroidered bookmarks, clay bowls. Collect unwanted toys as gifts for a local charity. Make a collage entitled 'All good gifts around us.' Design gift wrappings.

Gold

What do you think the most precious thing in the world is? Many people think it is gold. Why gold is so valuable—its colour, glitter, rarity. How it never rusts or tarnishes. How it is a soft metal and can be moulded into beautiful shapes. Gold coins, gold bars, gold fillings, gold nibs, rings and necklaces. The golden mask of Tutankhamun. Treasure dug up by archaeologists. The Gold Rush prospectors, gold mines, panning for gold. How it is measured into carats. Gold cups in sport and the medals: gold, silver, bronze. What is the Golden Rule? What does 'All that glisters is not gold' mean? Why is silence golden? Are you 'as good as gold'?

Stories   Midas and the Golden Touch p. 206
　　　　　 Salt Is Better Than Gold p. 233

Bible   The Golden Calf (*Exodus* 32)
　　　　 The Golden Rule (*Luke* 6.31)

Music   Theme song from the film *Goldfinger*   Barry

Poem   'Golden Glories'   Christina Rossetti (*Full Swing* p. 115)

Hymn   'Daisies Are Our Silver' (MHB no. 63)

Prayer   Dear God, help us to remember that the precious
　　　　　 things of life are not gold or silver,
　　　　　 but are our friends and our family,
　　　　　 our health and our understanding.
　　　　　 Help us to remember that it is not what we have
　　　　　 that counts, but what we are.   Amen.

Activities   Display in a careful setting some objects made of gold. Study golden treasures of the Egyptians, Greeks and Incas. Make your own golden jewellery out of papier mâché. Find out about goldmines, goldsmiths, the Gold Rush, El Dorado, Fool's Gold. What is a 'golden section' in maths?

Greed

What is a greedy person? It may be wanting more than you need, it may be wanting what others have got. What are people greedy for? Some are greedy for money, for food, for more toys and for possessions, for new clothes, for whatever is latest and best etc. Are you greedy? How we all have greedy thoughts sometimes. Why are people greedy? Sometimes a person is greedy when they are unhappy or unloved, sometimes a person is greedy because they are spoilt and always expect to have what they want. How a greedy person is only happy for a short time and may never feel satisfied but always want more. The greed of a miser. Being greedy with food may make you fat. Which animals are supposed to be greedy?

Stories The Three Wishes p. 247
The Greedy Dog; The Goose That Laid the Golden Egg
(Aesop's fables)

Bible Naboth's Vineyard (*I King* 21)

Music *The Thieving Magpie* Rossini

Poem 'Griselda' E. Farjeon (*Young Verse* p. 53)

Hymn 'Heavenly Father, May Thy Blessing' (CP no. 62)

Prayer Lord, make me gentle and unselfish,
take the greed from my heart,
make me happy with what I have got,
and not always wanting more. Amen.

Activities Discuss what things you are most greedy for. Make up a story or poem about a greedy boy, girl or animal. Draw or paint a picture of a miser. Find out what a glutton is.

Grumbling

What is grumbling? How some people go through their lives grumbling, grousing, groaning, moaning and complaining. The saying: 'Some people are never satisfied'—nothing is right for them, they never seem happy. Some grumbling is justified, when things go wrong. Do people grumble at you? Perhaps you have grumbles about other people. What do people grumble about? The weather, the prices, the traffic, the noise, the work they have to do, the people they live with, the government, the council and so on. It is right to complain if things go wrong when they should not, e.g. if you buy something from a shop which does not work. People who are always nagging are often discontented and unhappy—(nagging wives used to be put in ducking stools). Something that nags goes on and on e.g. a nagging pain. Does someone go on and on about you?

Story   The Old Woman in the Vinegar Bottle p. 213

Music   *Wasps Overture*   Vaughan Williams

Poems   'The Pessimist'   Ben King (OBPC p. 14)
        'Grumblers'   L. Clark (FPB p. 62)

Hymn   'Glad That I Live Am I' (JHB no. 7)

Prayer   Dear God, help me not to waste my time moaning
        and groaning and grumbling at people,
        but make me never afraid to protest at what is wrong,
        and to stand up for what is right.   Amen.

Activities   Discuss with the children who grumbles at them and whether they are justified. What complaints do the children have about the school, if any? Find out the opposite of a pessimist. Make up a conversation between an optimist and a pessimist. Make a model of a ducking stool. Who would you put in it?
Discuss:
    Two men looked through the prison bars:
    One saw mud, the other saw stars.

Hallowe'en

What is Hallowe'en? All Hallow's Eve when witches, devils and fairies were thought to have their annual holiday. How 31st October was regarded as the last day of summer. Old customs of making charms to ward off evil spirits e.g. pumpkin lanterns, bonfires, horseshoes. Hallowe'en parties—Bob Apple games. What is a superstition? Are you superstitious?

Stories   Hereward and the Witch p. 185
             Tam O'Shanter (see the poem by Robert Burns)

Music   *Tam O'Shanter Overture*   Arnold
           'In the Hall of the Mountain King' from *Peer Gynt*   Grieg
           Danse Macabre   Saint-Saens.
           'Witches Ride' from *Hansel and Gretel*   Humperdinck

Poems   'Hallowe'en'   Leonard Clark (TD p. 101)
           see the *Puffin Book of Magic Verse*, and many anthologies for
           witches' spells

Hymn   'Who Would True Valour See' (JHB no. 94)

Song   'There Was an Old Witch' (*Apusskidu* no. 17)

Prayer   Dear God, help us to live our lives free
            from fear and superstition. Give us the courage
            to stand up for what is true, and to follow
            what is good. For the sake of our Lord, Jesus Christ.   Amen.

Activities   Make Hallowe'en masks, lanterns, witches' hats. Paint a frieze showing silhouettes on All Hallow's Eve. Dress up a parade of witches, fairies and devils. Write your own spells. Perform a 'danse macabre'—use skeleton costumes and investigate ways of making artificial smoke. Discuss whether ghosts or evil spirits exist. Study superstitions. Tell your favourite ghost story.

Hands

What are hands for? What would it be like to have no hands? The sensitivity of fingers to touch. The structure of the hand—fingers, joints, palms, knuckles. Significant fingers—index finger, ring fingers, double jointed etc. Finger prints. The reading of palms. Measuring with hands, spans, heights of horses. Signs made with hands—hand signals, 'thumbs up', fist-shaking, beckoning, stopping, warning, waving, begging, clapping, praying etc. How the deaf speak with their hands. The expressions— handy, hamfisted, single-handed, light-fingered, to knuckle under, give a helping hand etc. What can you do with your hands? Handstands, playing an instrument, knitting, modelling, drawing etc.

Story   Feeling the Elephant p. 170

Bible   The Man with the Withered Hand (*Mark* 3.1–5)

Music   'He's Got the Whole World in His Hands'   Negro Spiritual (CP no. 19)

Poems   'This is the Hand'   M. Rosen (FPB p. 8)
'Hands'   P. Young (FPB p. 9)

Song   'One Man's Hands' (FFC no. 34)

Prayer   Dear God, bless my hands today,
and may the things they do
be kind and loving, strong and good,
hands that will work for you.   Amen.

Activities   Make up some 'feeling bags' containing different-shaped objects. What can you feel? Collect things with different surface textures. Make a collage of hands. Display a reproduction of Durer's *Praying Hands*. Try making some handshadow shapes. Movement—make up a dance of hands. Investigate handsizes. P. E.—find different ways of balancing on your hands. Take some fingerprints.

Harvest Festival

To celebrate the gathering of the harvest. The harvest of garden and field—flowers, fruits and vegetables. The harvest of corn, wheat, oats, barley. The harvest of fish from the sea. The harvest of the mines—coal, iron and oil. The harvests of other lands—rice, coffee, cocoa, dates, grapes, nuts etc. We think of all those who helped to bring the harvest home. Our harvest of offerings, may remind us of our own gifts—the *ears* of corn, the *eyes* of the potato, the *hand* of bananas, the *face* of flowers, and the growing *heart* of the cabbage. In the midst of plenty we remember too the poor and the hungry.

Story   The Strange Treasure p. 241
            The Troll's Share p. 250

Bible   The Creation (*Genesis* 1.9–10)
            Psalm 65 (latter half)

Music   *Symphony No. 6 (Pastoral)*   Beethoven
            The Creation   Haydn

Poems   'Harvest Home'   Leonard Clark (COL p. 16)

Hymn   'We Plough the Fields and Scatter' (JHB no. 16)

Prayer   Lord, you have said that while the earth remains,
            seedtime and harvest, and cold and heat,
            and summer and winter, and day and night,
            shall not cease. To you from whom come all good gifts,
            we offer you these our harvest prayers.   Amen

Activities   Collect and display harvest offerings. Distribute them with cards of harvest greeting to a local charity or to old folk in need. Study the harvests of other countries. What is a cornucopia? (Make your own cornucopia). Make or display a corn dolly. Visit a Church Harvest Festival display. Hold a barn dance.

Healing

What does it mean to heal someone? People who work at healing others—
doctors, nurses, dentists, psychiatrists etc. The National Health Service,
the different types of hospital. Doctors used to be men, and nurses women,
now they can be either. The work of a school doctor or nurse, e.g. checking
of head, feet, hearing, sight. The importance of ambulance men, the work
of the St John's Ambulance brigade. Types of illness—infectious and non-
infectious. First Aid, what to do in an emergency—the 999 service.
Cleaning wounds, bandaging, stretchers, X-rays, stitches etc. Common
complaints—'colds, coughs and sneezes spread diseases', travel sickness.
Prevention is better than cure. Keeping in good health.

Story   The Lady of the Lamp p. 199

Bible   The Nobleman's Son (*John* 4.46)
        The Sick Man (*Mark* 2.1)

Music   *Eine Kleine Nachtmusik*   Mozart

Poem   'Two Charms to Cure Hiccups' (JV I p. 48)

Hymns 'Lord of the Dance' (CP no. 38)
        'Feed Us Now' (FFC p. 32)

Prayer Lord Jesus, who healed the sick and helped all those in pain,
        look upon the sick today and make them well again.
        For all the strength and health we have, to thee we pray.
        Help us to heal the sick and ill, today and every day.   Amen.

Activities   Design posters for good health e.g. anti-smoking, cleaning
teeth, 'early to bed, early to rise' etc. Dramatise the story of Florence
Nightingale. Visit a local hospital, or ask a local doctor or nurse to talk
about their work. Study how disease is caused, and why injections are
given. Create a dance of 'good' and 'bad' germs.

Hearing

The joy of hearing. What it would be like to live in silence, to be deaf. How deaf people cope—sign language, lip reading. What it is to be 'hard of hearing', the use of hearing aids. How we can hear the slightest noise if we listen—can you hear a pin drop? How the ear works, why it is the shape it is, the ear drum. Sound waves and vibrations. Keeping the ears clean, cleaning out wax. The dangers of loud noise, sources of noise pollution. Hearing in animals, animals that are deaf e.g. snakes; animals with acute hearing e.g. dogs (who can hear whistles that we cannot). What we most like hearing, what we least like hearing.

Story   Beethoven p. 144

Bible   Jesus Cures the Deaf and Dumb Man (*Mark* 7)

Music   *Symphony No. 5*   Beethoven
            The Moonlight Sonata   Beethoven

Poems   'The Sounds in the Evening'   E. Farjeon (FPB p. 18–19)

> The wise old owl sat in an oak.
> The more he heard the less he spoke.
> The less he spoke the more he heard.
> Why can't we all be like that wise old bird?
>
> *Anon*

Hymn   'I Listen and I Listen' (CP no. 60)

Prayer   Dear God, thank you for the gift of hearing,
            for the song of birds and the sound of music,
            for laughter and happy voices.
            We remember those who are less fortunate than ourselves,
            those who are deaf and those who find hearing difficult.   Amen.

Activities   How could you communicate through sign language? Study and learn the way deaf people communicate by finger spelling. Tape record you favourite sounds. Quiz—can you recognise these sounds or voices. . . ? Study the hearing and the ears of animals. Investigate the effects of noise and sources of noise pollution. Draw a diagram of the ear. Make a survey of favourite sounds.

Hinduism

Hinduism is the religion of India. Many people in England whose families come from India still follow the Hindu religion. Hindus worship at temples. They believe that after death a person will be reborn—perhaps as an animal. Hindus are kind to animals, especially cows whom they regard as sacred. Many Hindus do not eat meat. They do not celebrate Christmas and Easter like we do, but have their own special festivals, songs and stories. Like Christians they are trying to find God, and to lead good lives.

Story   The Story of Divali p. 163
The Story of Rama p. 221

Music   Any piece of Indian music

Hymn   'Far Round the World' (MHB no. 26)

Poem   Let the earth and the water,
and   The air, and the fruits of my country,
Prayer   Be sweet, my God.
Let the homes and the markets,
The forests, and the fields of my country,
Be full, my God.
Let the promises and the hopes,
The deeds, and the words of my country,
By true, my God.
Let the lives and the hearts,
Of the sons and the daughters of my country,
Be One, my God.
                (Rabindranath Tagore)

Activities   Show India on a world map. Present project work on India. Invite a Hindu to tell, or be questioned, about his beliefs and practices. Show a film or slides on aspects of Indian life. Demonstrate the Hindu blessing (mark on forehead). Display a statue of the dancing Shiva. Investigate which words in the English language derive from Hindi e.g. verandah, char, kiosk. Copy some examples of Hindi or Sanskrit writing.

Hindu Festivals

Dussehra
Dussehra celebrates the victory of Lord Rama over the Demon King, Ravanna—the victory of good over evil. At this festival stories are told and plays performed based on the epic poem *Ramayana*. On the last day of Dussehra a huge effigy of the Demon King Ravanna is paraded and at sunset is burnt amid great celebrations.
(The Story of Rama p. 221)

Divali
Divali occurs about 20 days after Dussehra. Like Dussehra it is a festival of light in memory of the Lord Rama. Divali celebrates the return of Lord Rama to his kingdom after 14 years of exile in the forest. At Divali homes are filled with gaily coloured lights. People clean their homes and give each other presents, often new clothes. In India lamps are lit and traditional dances performed. Streets are decorated with lights and sparkling fireworks are lit.
Activities Decorate the hall with lights, lamps made by children, or night lights in small jars to represent the Divali decorations in Indian homes. Display Indian crafts, toys and musical instruments. Show saris.
(The Story of Divali p. 163)

Holi
Holi is a joyful festival which occurs during the full moon, usually in March. It is a fire festival and celebrates the coming of spring. Bonfires are lit to symbolise the triumph of good over evil, and rubbish is burnt to indicate that wrongdoing is forgiven and forgotten.
Spring is welcomed in by the throwing of colours. People put on bright clothes and spray each other with coloured water and powder. It is a time of goodwill when friends are visited and gifts exchanged.
For the legends of Holi see *Festivals and Saints' Days* by V. J. Green pp. 29–30

Rakshabandhan
Rakshabandhan is the festival for brothers and sisters. It falls on the full moon in the Hindu month Shravana (generally our July or August). It is a family festival involving a celebration between brothers and sisters, and between cousins. Rakshabandhan means a tie of security, and sisters tie them (popularly called Rakhi) on their brothers' wrists. Rakhi are made from coloured cotton or silk threads with little decorations. A brother in turn offers a gift to his sister.
See *Festivals and Saints' Days* p. 94.

Home

What is a home? Why do we need a home? Where people live—houses, flats, bungalows, caravans, chalets, tents, huts etc. The plight of the homeless, in this country and abroad. Special kinds of homes—a Children's Home, Home for the Elderly, Nursing Home, Battersea Dog's Home etc. Building a house—laying foundations, types of structure and roof, rooms needed. Kinds of animal homes—nests, hives, burrows, cages, dens etc.

Story   How Diogenes Found Happiness p. 186

Bible   The Houses Built on Sand and Rock (*Matt.* 7.24)

Music   'The Green, Green Grass of Home' Putnam
(Sung by Tom Jones)

Poem   'Home' Leonard Clark (COL p. 37)

Songs   'The Building Song' (CP no. 61)
'Lord of All Hopefulness' (CP no. 52)

Prayer   Let us close our eyes and think of our home.
Let us think of the love and happiness of our families,
of mothers and fathers, relatives and friends.
We remember those moments of joy and happiness which make life good.
May we bring joy and happiness to others,
in our homes and in our lives. Amen.

Activities   Display pictures, models and project work on different kinds of homes—homes through the ages, in different countries, homes of animals etc. Creative writing theme: 'Home is ... ' Visit a building site, or a special home in the district—record your impressions. Find out about the people involved in making a home—architects, surveyors, builders, plumbers, electricians, carpenters, interior designers etc. Design your own ideal home. Build a shanty home (staple old boxes together). How would you house the homeless? Find out about the work of Shelter.

Honesty

What does it mean to be honest? How no one is entirely honest, everyone has been guilty of telling lies. The different reasons why people tell lies. A 'white lie'. Are some kinds of lies worse than others? The courage needed to tell the truth. The saying, 'Honesty is the best policy'. Why this is so. Owning up—the story of George Washington cutting down the cherry tree. Honesty is also a purple flower with translucent pods.

Stories   The Story of Galileo p. 175
               The Boy Who Cried Wolf (Aesop)

Bible   The Son Who Lied (*Matt.* 21.28)
             Peter Disowns Jesus (*Mark* 14.66)

Poems   'What Kind of Liar Are You?' (JV III p. 53)
            'Matilda'   Hilaire Belloc (OBPC p. 30)

Hymns 'God Has Promised' (CP no. 31)
             'O Jesus I Have Promised' (JHB no. 78)

Prayer God, help us to speak the truth
            even when we do not want to,
            and help us to seek the truth
            in all that we say and do.   Amen.

Activities   Discuss whether it is ever right to tell lies. Ask the children if anyone has ever lied to them, and how they felt about it. Write a story or poem about a 'lie'. Make up some statements that are *true* and *false* (try finding some strange facts e.g. from the *Guinness Book of Records*) and test them on others. Illustrate the saying, 'Truth is stranger than fiction.' Practise sorting books into categories Fact and Fiction. Tell a tall story.

Hope

We all have hopes and fears. In every situation there is always hope—'hope springs eternal'. Behind every dark cloud there may be a silver lining. The hopes that we have for ourselves, and for the future. Times of hope, the New Year, Spring, all new beginnings. Is it better to travel hopefully than to arrive? Before Alexander the Great set out for Asia he divided up his kingdom among his friends. 'My lord,' one of them asked, 'what have you left for yourself?' 'Hope,' replied Alexander.

Story   Pandora's Box p. 215

Bible   St Paul on Hope (*Romans* 5)

Music   *New World Symphony*   Dvorak

Poem   'Time' E. Gore Booth (*Poems for Assemblies* p. 27)

Hymn   'Lord of All Hopefulness' (CP no. 52)

Prayer   O God, who has folded back the mantle
of the night to clothe us in the glory of the
day, chase from our hearts all gloomy thoughts
and make us glad with the brightness of hope.   Amen.
(Ancient Collect)

Activities   Discuss what hopes you have for the future, and how they might be achieved. Act out the story of Pandora's Box (do a dance of the spirits of evil in painted masks). Find out where the Cape of Good Hope is—why was it so named?

Inventions

What is an invention? Man as an inventive animal, who can use tools and imagination. How everything we use has been invented by someone. Inventors as scientists or engineers. The earliest inventions, the axe and the wheel. The history of invention, using the world's resources—wind, steam, electricity, oil, coal etc. The wonders of science, latest inventions. Problems of the future e.g. no oil for petrol, the need for new inventions. Inventors are original, they think for themselves, they solve problems. How we are nearly all able to invent something new—meals for cooking, games for playing, designs for machines etc. Patenting inventions. 'Neccessity is the mother of invention.' Being inventive.

Stories   Isambard Kingdom Brunel p. 192
           Daedelus and Icarus p. 160

Music   *Toy Symphony*   Mozart
         The Clock Symphony   Haydn

Poem   'The Secret of Machines'   Rudyard Kipling (*Selected Verse* p. 285, Penguin)

Hymn   'Come Let Us Remember the Joys of the Town' (JHB no. 95)

Song   'Wheels Keep Turning' (*Apusskidu* no. 24)

Prayer   Dear God, we thank you for the wonders of science,
           for all the men and women in the world who have invented
           things for our use.
           Help us to be inventive, and to think for ourselves.   Amen.

Activities   Hold an exhibition of designs and models of inventions that children have made. Study the great scientists and inventors of the past. Find out who invented the television, the telephone, the sewing machine, the sandwich and other everyday things. Visit the Science Museum. Movement themes: machines, mechanical toys, strange inventions, robots.

Islam

Muslims follow the religion of Islam. Most of the Muslims that live in England today come from Arab countries, or from Pakistan. Their churches are called mosques. On top of every mosque you will see a crescent moon, it is the symbol of Islamic countries (like the cross for Christians). Their name for God is Allah. Their day of worship is Friday, not Sunday. Muslims are supposed to pray five times a day, to wash before praying, and to bow down towards the direction of Mecca. Muslims have their own calendar which began in AD 622 on 16th July (1980 = 1400AH or After Hijira). Many Muslims are named Muhammad, after the first and foremost prophet of their religion. Muslims believe in God and in doing good to others.

Stories   The Beggar and the Fox p. 145
The Story of Muhammad p. 210

Music   Any Arabic music
'The Call to Prayer' from *African Sanctus*   Fanshawe

Hymn   'Far Round the World' (MHB no. 26)

Prayer   O Lord, grant us to love thee,
grant that we may love those that love thee,
grant that we may do the deeds that win thy love,
Make the love of thee dearer to us than ourselves
and our families, than wealth, and even than cool water.
(A prayer by Muhammad)

Activities   Display an Islamic prayer mat, a Koran and any project work on Arab countries. Find the crescent moon on flags of Muslim countries. Invite a Muslim to talk of his religion. Visit a mosque. Make a picture or model of a mosque with minarets. Paint Arabic patterns e.g. Altair designs. Study the history of numbers—why was the Arabic zero so important?

Muslim Festivals

Ramadhan   During the month of Ramadhan all Muslims must fast, having nothing to eat or drink between dawn and sunset each day. It is believed that during this time the prophet Muhammad received his first revelations from God, given to him by the Angel Gabriel.

After sunset each day during Ramadhan the family eats a satisfying meal. Some Muslims are allowed to miss the fast—young children, pregnant women, the very old, those who are travelling. Children are allowed to join the fast from the age of 8 onwards. The new moon announces the end of Ramadhan.

Eid-El-Fitr *(the feast of breaking the fast)*   At the end of Ramadhan is a great day of celebration. This is a party occasion, with visits to the mosque. Children are given sweets and dates, and new clothes to wear. In the mosque the Imam chants prayers, men and boys sit in one group, women and children in another. No one wears shoes in the mosque, out of respect to Allah.

For the rest of the 'Eid' there are parties, greetings cards are exchanged, and gifts are given to children. It is usually a holiday for all Muslims.

Muharram (*New Year*)   The Muslim calendar begins with the Hijra or migration of the prophet Muhammad from Mecca to Medina in AD 622, where he and his companions organised themselves into a religious community. Today greetings are exchanged and stories related about the prophet and his companions. At the end of 1980 it will be 1401 AH (After Hijra).

Eid-El-Adha   A three-day festival three months after Ramadhan, when the sacrifice of Abraham is commemorated. At the last moment God commanded him to substitute a ram for his son Ishmael and to let the boy live. In memory of this, sheep are roasted as the basis of great family feasts.

Meelad el Nabi (*Muhammad's Birthday*)   For Muslims the birthday of the Holy Prophet Muhammad marks the most important event in the history of the Muslim people. Muhammad is regarded as the greatest of the prophets. It was to him that God revealed his message, the Koran. Five times a day a Muslim should face towards Mecca, the birthplace of Muhammad, and say prayers. At least once during his lifetime a Muslim should make a pilgrimage to Mecca.

On Muhammad's birthday Muslims meet to hear the story of Muhammad, and remember in the words of the Koran that 'all believers are brothers'.

(See The Story of Muhammad p. 210)

Judaism

The religion of the Jews is called Judaism. Jews live in all countries of the world, but their homeland is called Israel. Their symbol is a six-pointed star called the Star of David. You can see it on the flag of Israel. Jews are called 'God's chosen people' in the Bible. They pray in synagogues and their day of rest is Saturday, which is called the Sabbath. Their religious teachers are called Rabbis, but any member of the congregation can lead the service. They often cover their heads when praying and sometimes wear small hats called skull caps. Their language is Hebrew. 'Shalom' in Hebrew means peace; Jews say this when they greet each other. The Old Testament is the story of the Jewish people. They worship God but do not believe Jesus was the son of God or the Messiah. Abraham, Moses, King David, Jesus and Mary were all Jewish. The Jews have suffered persecution (anti-semitism) throughout history. Many millions of Jews were killed by Hitler in the last war.

Stories   Anne Frank p. 140
The Crowded House p. 159
see Old Testament references listed under theme of Bible Stories

Music   *Psalm* 23 in a musical setting
Israeli folksong e.g. 'Hava Negila'

Bible   A Psalm of David e.g. *Psalm* 23 or 100

Hymns   'Oh God our Help in Ages Past' *Psalm* 90 (JHB no. 44)
'All People That on Earth Do Dwell' *Psalm* 100 (JHB no. 50)

Prayer   God be merciful to us, and bless us,
And cause your face to shine upon us,
That your way may be known to all nations upon earth.
Let the people praise you, O God.
Let all the people praise you.
(*Prayer based on Psalm* 67)

Activities   Invite a Jew to talk about his religion, ceremonies like Barmitzvah, the Sabbath and Kosher food. Draw a large map of Israel and study the history of the Jewish people from Abraham to the present day. Draw the Star of David—what mathematical facts can you find in your drawing? The Jewish calendar dates from 7th October, 3761 BC (the date of the creation of the world if the Bible is taken literally)—what year is it now in the Jewish calendar? What is a genesis and an exodus?

Jewish Festivals

Jewish New Year (Rosh Hashanah)   The Jewish New Year usually falls
in September or October. The festival celebrates the birthday of the
creation of the world. During services at the synagogue the *Shofar*, a ram's
horn, is blown. In Jewish homes at New Year a special cake is often baked
with honey in it, or special bread called 'challah' is dipped in honey. Honey
is a symbol of hope for sweetness in the coming year.

The large ram's horn trumpet is blown each day during the month
before Rosh Hashanah, at the festival itself, and finally ten days later at
Yom Kippur.

Yom Kippur (The Day of Atonement)   Yom Kippur is the holiest of all
holy days for the Jews—atonement means 'at one' with God. It is a sabbath
of fasting and rest. Adult Jews fast (neither eat nor drink) for 25 hours
(from before sunset until nightfall the day after) while they pray for their
sins and errors to be forgiven. Young children are not expected to fast, but
by the age of twelve children usually give up all their meals like the
grown-ups. The story of the scapegoat is told (*Leviticus* 16, 7*ff*), and the
leaders of the service are dressed in white. The Ark and the Scrolls of the
Law are also covered in white. (The Scrolls of the Law record the history
and laws of the Jewish people. They are kept in the Ark, which is a great
chest just like the one kept in the Temple in Jerusalem.) The day ends
with the sound of the Shofar.

The Feast of Tabernacles (Succoth)   The feast of Tabernacles is a
Jewish harvest festival. Tabernacles are shelters or huts built in the
wilderness which the Israelites lived in during the Exodus. Huts, or
tabernacles, the size of small sheds are often built in homes or gardens and
decorated with fruit, flowers and leafy branches. It is a joyful festival and a
time of thanksgiving like the Christian harvest festival. (See *Leviticus* 23.
39–43)

Chanukah (The Feast of Lights)   Chanukah celebrates the time over
2000 years ago when a Syrian king set up a pagan statue in the temple in
Jerusalem, until the Jews defeated him in battle and set about purifying the
temple. One of their first tasks was to relight the temple lamps. The Jews
remember this story every year at Chanukah. The Chanukah candlestick
(menorah) is displayed and each night an additional candle is lit until on
the last, eight candles are burning. Jewish children are often given
Chanukah presents. Story: 1 *Maccabees* 4. 36–59 (*Apocrypha*)

Jewish Festivals cont/d

Purim (The Feast of Lots)   Purim celebrates the deliverance of the Jews from the wicked Haman, the story of which is told in the Book of Esther in the Bible. On that day the Book of Esther is read in the synagogue and it is traditional for the children to bring rattles and hooters in order to drown the name of Haman whenever it is mentioned. There are fancy dress parades and parties and it is generally a most joyous festival.

Passover (Pesach or Feast of Unleavened Bread)   Passover is the oldest festival in the Jewish calendar. It is a feast celebrating the Jewish Exodus from Egypt over 3000 years ago. It is a spring festival and like Easter its date varies from year to year. Passover is a family festival. Before Passover the house is spring–cleaned, and on the eve of Passover a special meal is prepared. Each part of the meal is connected with the escape from Egypt. Unleavened bread is eaten in memory of that night when, in their hurry, they took bread which had not had time to rise. A roasted egg symbolises new life, a bowl of salt water symbolises the tears of the slaves. Bitter herbs (often horseradish) symbolise the bitterness of slavery. There are four glasses of wine for each person, and one for the unexpected guest. The Passover meal is what Jesus ate at the 'Last Supper'.

Pentecost (Shavuot or the Feast of Weeks)   Seven weeks after Passover comes Pentecost. It is the time in the Christian calendar called Whitsun. It is the festival of the summer harvest. Fruit and flowers decorate the synagogue, and wheat is harvested in Israel. Pentecost commemorates the giving of the Ten Commandments to Moses on Mount Sinai, and the story of Ruth is told.

Justice

What is justice? Treating people fairly. Justice in society—the work of the police and courts of law. Being just and fair to other people. The need to treat people equally—being equal in law. The symbol of Justice on the Old Bailey, in London, holding the sword and scales. Why is she blindfolded? How life is not always just or fair. The need to stand up for people who are being badly treated. What do you think is *unfair* at home or school? Are you always fair to other people?

Story   The Justice of Dick Whittington p. 197

Bible   The Justice of Solomon (*I Kings* 3)

Music   *Solomon*   Handel

Poem   'The Quarrel'   E. Farjeon (FPB p. 26)

Song   'If I Had a Hammer' (FFC p. 43)

Prayer   Dear God, help me to be fair to other people,
give me the strength to stand up for what is right
and to follow the path of justice
in all that I say and do.   Amen.

Activities   Study how the law works—the work of police, judges, and law courts. Display or draw a picture of the symbol of justice on top of the Old Bailey. Enact a court of law with defence, prosecution, accused, judge and jury. Debate some of the problems of justice e.g. what should happen to robbers, or murderers?

Keep Fit

Why should you keep fit? The enjoyment of health, strength and energy. The body is like a machine, it needs looking after and cannot be replaced. What you need for good health—exercise, rest and good food. How you get exercise in walking, running, playing games, sports, P.E., movement, dance etc. Jogging around parks. Sleep and rest. Not eating too much. Not smoking. The importance of breathing and posture. The benefits of fresh air. Health and beauty. How models and film stars must keep fit. Good exercise—skipping and swimming. The effect on muscles and growth. Tests of strength, endurance and flexibility. The aim of a sound mind in a healthy body.

Story   The Mirror of Truth p. 207

Bible   The Story of Samson (*Judges* 16)

Music   'Dem Bones' Negro Spiritual

Poem   'Thanksgiving for the Body'   Thomas Traherne (in *Poems, Centuries and Thanksgivings*, O.U.P.)

Hymn   'In Our Work and in Our Play' (MHB no. 46)

Prayer   Dear God, keep me fit in mind and heart,
in body and soul to play my part,
fit to stand and fit to run,
fit for sorrow and fit for fun,
fit for work and fit for play,
fit to face life every day.
Keep me fit in all I do,
Fit for me, and fit for you.   Amen.

Activities   Mount a gymnastic display. Try tests of strength, endurance, agility and flexibility. Practise complete relaxation. Try breathing exercises, and tests for good posture e.g. walk with books balanced on the head. Study pictures or models of the human skeleton. Identify muscles, lungs, bones etc. Train for the B.A.G.A. gymnastic awards.

Kings and Queens

We live in a kingdom. What is the United Kingdom? The Royal Family, our long line of kings and queens. Symbols of royalty—orb and sceptre, the Crown Jewels, the Palace. The Queen as our Constitutional Monarch. Other world leaders—Presidents and Republics. When were we a republic? Other kingly titles—Caesar, Kaiser, Czar, Khan, Pharaoh. The King's highway (King's Road in London), the King's Head (pubs), and the King's shilling. The king in chess (checkmate = *Shah mat* (Arabic) 'the king is dead'), in draughts and in cards. King sized. Other kings— kingfisher, king crab, kingcup etc, King of beasts, king of birds. The Three Kings (Magi), Christ the King, 'Thy Kingdom Come' (Lord's Prayer).

Story   King Alfred Learns to Read p. 198

Bible   The Book of *Kings* viz. King Solomon (*I Kings* 3)
Naboth's Vineyard (*I Kings* 21)

Music   The National Anthem
'The Entry of the Queen of Sheba' from *Solomon*   Handel

Poems   'Call Him a King?'   S. Tuck (PSA p. 136)
'Henry King'   Hilaire Belloc (*Selected Cautionary Verses*)

Hymns   'O Worship the King' (MHB no. 31)
'The King of Love My Shepherd Is' (CP 54)

Prayer   Dear God, bless our Royal Family
and all who take part in ruling our nation.
Help us to remember that we too
have a part to play in making our land
a better place to live in.   Amen.

Activities   Find out about the Kings and Queens of England—how many can you name? Draw the family tree of our Royal Family. Chart the latest royal tour. Visit a Royal Residence e.g. Windsor Castle. Examine the local pillar box—which royal emblem is on it? Should we have a monarchy? Would you like to be king or queen?

Knowledge

'If people don't know much, don't laugh at them, for each one of them knows something that you do not know.' (Gypsy saying)

The power of knowledge. The growth of knowledge, how we are continually acquiring knowledge from the day we are born until the day we die. Factual knowledge. Knowing the important facts of your life—address, telephone number, birthday etc. Knowing *how* to do things like swimming, cycling, telephoning, sewing, first aid etc. Where to obtain knowledge—parents, teachers, experts. Knowledge from books—dictionaries, encyclopedias, use of a reference library. Knowing yourself—your moods, why you have certain feelings, your abilities. Branches of knowledge—history, geography, biology, maths etc. To be knowledgeable, to be a know-all.

Story   The Salmon of Knowledge p. 231

Bible   Solomon Asks for Wisdom (*I Kings* 3)
            Proverbs 3.13–17

Music   *Academic Festival Overture*   Brahms

Poem   'I Wonder'   J. Kirby (FPB p. 122)

Hymn   'The Wise May Bring Their Learning' (CP no. 64)

Prayer   Lord, help me to know what is good,
            to love what is true. Help me to grow in knowledge,
            knowledge of you, knowledge of others,
            and knowledge of myself.   Amen.

Activities   Hold a general knowledge quiz. Display a collection of reference books complete with work or quiz sheets. Have a display of practical skills—gymnastic, musical, arts and crafts etc. Make a collection of Amazing Facts from reference books such as the *Guinness Book of Records*. Draw a tree showing the 'branches' of knowledge.

Light

Where does light come from? Natural sources are the sun, moon, stars and lightning. The moon's light is only reflected. Artificial light—fire, torches, candles, oil lamps, gas and electricity. Warning lights—traffic lights, lighthouses, belisha beacons, flashing lights on motorways, red lights, beacons and flares. Lights which advertise—neon signs. Lights which decorate—Christmas lights and illuminations. The Northern Lights, aurora borealis. The expressions 'to throw light on a subject', 'to see a red light', 'the light at the end of a tunnel', 'to shine' in something, to be enlightened etc. The effect of light on animals and plants. The speed of light. Festivals of light—Divali, Chanukah, Candlemas.

Story   Seeing the Light p. 234

Bible   Jesus said, 'I am the Light of the World, come follow me.' (*John* 8.12)

Music   'The People That Walked in Darkness' from the
Messiah   Handel
'Morning' from *Peer Gynt*   Grieg
The Moonlight Sonata   Beethoven

Song   'This Little Light of Mine' (FFC p. 15)

Poem   'Light'   John Morrison (PSA p. 22)

Hymn   'Give Me Oil in My Lamp' (CP no. 43)

Prayer   Eternal God, the light of the minds that know thee,
the joy of the hearts that love thee,
the strength of the wills that serve thee.
Grant us to know thee, that we may truely love thee,
so to love thee that we may fully serve thee
whom to serve is perfect freedom.   Amen.

Activities   Find out how fast light travels. What is a 'light year'? Make a model with flashing lights e.g. lighthouse. Study light through prisms, make a simple curcuit with bulbs and battery. Experiment to show how plants need light. What is a 'halo'?

May Day

A celebration of May Day. How in olden times 1st May was celebrated as the first day of summer. Many of these customs still exist—May Fairs, the May Queen (crowned with flowers), the Maypole danced round with plaited ribbons. Morris dances, the Hobby Horse, the Green Man, parades etc. May Day was once known as 'Robin Hood's Day' when adventures with the outlaws and Maid Marion were re-enacted. May Day carols in Oxford, (carol originally meant a song for dancing). The May tree. 'Ne'er cast a clout till May be out.' May Day as a national holiday for workers in many countries.

Story The Monster of Padstow p. 208
A Robin Hood story or ballad

Music 'Greensleeves' arr. by Vaughan Williams

Poem 'May Day Song' (GTP p. 274)

Hymns 'Sing All Ye Christian People!' (JHB no. 13)
The May morning hymn (*Oxford Song Book* 2 no. 19)
(as sung by the choir of Magdalen College, Oxford, on the top of the bell tower every first day of May at 6 p.m.)

Prayer This morning is the first of May,
The best in all the year,
So people all, both great and small,
I wish you joyful cheer.
Then take your Bible in your hand
And read the scriptures through;
And when the day of judgement comes
The Lord will remember you.
(Adapted from a May Day Carol)

Activities Compose your own May poem or carol—set it to music. Learn and perform a country dance e.g. Morris, stick, sword. Erect a be-ribboned Maypole, or create a frieze of Maypole dancers. Construct a hobby horse. Create a play from one of Robin Hood's adventures. Study famous May Days e.g. 1851, opening of Great Exhibition; 1926, eve of General Strike. Hold a May Fair.

Memory

Have you a good or bad memory? How memory can be trained. Why is memory so useful to us? How in the old days children were expected to memorise and quote from memory. What could *you* quote from memory—nursery rhymes, songs, poems? What was your earliest memory? What can you remember of last week e.g. what you ate or what you learnt? Aids to memory—mnemonics. Important things to remember e.g. full address and telephone number, family birthdays, days in a month. How the brain is like a computer, or memory bank. People who 'lose' their memory. 'In memory of', 'within living memory', a memento, a memoir, a memorial. Memorable times.

Story   Ewongelema p. 168

Music   Play a known piece of music—can the children remember the title, composer, or occasion played?

Poems   'I Remember, I Remember ...'   Thomas Hood (GTP p. 95)
            'A Memory'   D. Gibson (TD p. 20)

Hymn   'Come Let Us Remember the Joys of the Town' (JHB no. 95)

Prayer   O Lord, you know how busy
            I shall be this day.
            If I forget you,
            do not forget me.   Amen.
            (Sir Jacob Astley before the battle of Edgehill 1642)

Activities   Memory tests: 1. Uncover a tray of various objects for half a minute, how many can you recall? 2. 'I went to market and I bought a ...' Follow on, adding one item to the list until the chain breaks down. 3. Psychologists say on average we can remember only seven unrelated words. Test this finding. Visit and draw a local memorial statue. Write a story about someone who loses their memory. Write a poem entitled 'Memories'.

Milk

What is milk?* Animals that supply milk to their young are called mammals. Why do we drink milk? The food value of milk—calcium for teeth, vitamins, fat and minerals. Animals that supply milk—cows, goats, camels, reindeer, mares, buffalo, yak, llama etc. Milk products— evaporated, condensed, skimmed, powdered, cream, yoghourt, butter, cheese etc. How milk is processed—milking machines, dairy, pasteurisation, bottling, marketing. Does your family 'Drinka pinta milka day'? What is the 'milk of human kindness'?

Story   Louis Pasteur (1822–95) p. 202

Bible   Jael and Sisera (*Judges* 4–19)
            'A land flowing with milk and honey' (*Joshua* 5–6)

Music   *Horn Concerto No. 4*   Mozart

Poem   'The Cow'   R. L. Stevenson (PBV p. 46)

Hymn   'Let Us with a Gladsome Mind' (CP no. 8)

Prayer   Dear God, thank you for our daily milk,
            for the work of the milkman and the farmer,
            for cows and for grass we thank you, Lord.   Amen.

Activities   Make butter (by shaking creamy milk in a jar). Do a frieze showing stages of production from grass to table. Visit a dairy farm or the National Dairy Museum at Stratfield Saye. Send for information from the National Dairy Council (at the National Dairy Centre, John Prince's Street, London W1M OAP). Investigate the mathematics of milk e.g. a cow gives about 6000 pints a year—could one cow feed your school? Study the dairy producing countries of the world like New Zealand, Holland, Denmark, France and Ireland.

* Note: Milk is made up of 87% water, 5% milk sugar, 4% fat, $3\frac{1}{2}$% protein, $\frac{1}{2}$% minerals

Miracles

What is a miracle? A marvellous happening, which cannot be fully explained. The miracles performed by Jesus. The miracles of everyday life—dawn, springtime, birth, flight of birds etc. Today's 'miracles'—electricity, medicine, aeroplanes, television etc. Possible miracles to come—future inventions, space travel, peace, no more hunger etc. How miracles occur—faith healing. The miracles of Lourdes. The Royal Touch. The Miracle Plays of the Middle Ages.

The Miracles of Jesus

> The Marriage in Cana (*John* 2.11)
> Jesus Heals the Leper (*Mark* 1.40)
> Jesus Heals on the Sabbath (*Matt.* 12.10)
> The Invalid at the Pool (*John* 5.2)
> Jesus Restores Jairus' Daughter (*Mark* 5.22)
> The Feeding of the Five Thousand (*John* 6)
> Jesus Walks on Water (*Matt.* 14.22)
> Jesus Raises Lazarus (*John* 11)

Music   *The Miraculous Mandarin*   Bartok

Poems   *Miracles* an anthology   D. Saunders & V. Oliver (Evans)
'Miracles'   Walt Whitman (in the above)

Song   'Go Tell It on the Mountain' (CP no. 24)

Prayer   Thank you, God, for the miracles of this world,
for the miracles of nature and the miracles of invention,
for miracles that are large and miracles that are small.
Help us to remember that with you
everything is possible.   Amen

Activities   Discuss with children the nature of miracles and what they would call a miracle. Invite someone who has been to Lourdes to talk about their trip. Perform a miracle play. Write a class poem, like Walt Whitman's, about everyday miracles.

The Moon

What is a moon? The moon is a satellite of the earth. How long does it take to revolve around the earth? How 'month' derives from 'moonth' or moon period i.e. 28 days. How the moonlight is reflected from the sun. The phases of the moon, the new moon, the crescent moon, the full moon, lunar, lunatic (originally thought to be madness caused by changes in the moon, particularly a full moon). Gravity of the moon causing tides. The face of the moon always turned to earth. Distance away from earth. Conditions on the moon and moonlandings. Moonbeams. Honeymoon. Moonflower. A moonlight flit. Moonshine. A moonstone. To 'moon' around. The moon as symbol of Islam. The Chinese Moon Festival.*

Story   The Moon Festival p. 209

Bible   The Sun and Moon Stand Still (*Joshua* 10)

Music   *Clair de Lune*   Debussy
'By the Light of the Silvery Moon' (popular song)

Poems   'Flying'   J. M. Westrup (BTP p. 301)
'Silver'   W. de la Mare (BTP p. 280)
'Is the Moon Tired?'   Christina Rossetti (BTP p. 281)

Hymn   'All Creatures of Our God and King' (CP no. 7)

Prayer   Dear Lord, thank you for the beauty of the
moon that lights up our sky at night, and
help us to remember that we too have our part to play in your
creation.   Amen

Activities   Draw the phases of the moon, showing their time scale. Look up which phase it is in today. Find out about the moons of other planets. Find out about the moon goddess. Make a model of the moon, showing its craters and a moon landing. Draw a map of the moon. How high could you jump on the moon—Why?

* Note: The traditional Chinese Moon Festival occurs at the time of the autumn full moon in September. With gaily decorated lanterns the Chinese go to view the moon from hills and high places. The festival can still be seen in Hong Kong and Singapore.

Music

What is music? Sounds that please. The music of nature e.g. birdsong, running water, the sea, wind through trees, buzz of insects, hoofbeats etc. Music made by man, musicians. The history of music. Earliest instruments—the voice, the harp (from drawn bowstrings), the flute and the drum. Instruments of the orchestra—percussion, wind and string. Modern instruments—saxophone, electric guitars, steel drums etc. Instruments around the world—Eastern gongs, Indian sitar, Alpine horn, Jew's harp, African 'talking' drums, West Indian steel bands etc. St Cecilia the patron saint of music, her organ and her day (22nd November). Musical boxes. The Music of the Spheres. What is a 'musical'? Musical chairs. A music stool and a music stand. The expression 'to face the music'. Rhythm and melody.

Stories The Sorcerer's Apprentice p. 238
Till Eulenspiegel p. 248

Bible The Trumpets of Joshua (*Joshua* 6)
The Harp of David (*I Samuel* 16)

Music *The Young Person's Guide to the Orchestra* Britten

Poem 'Music' Leonard Clark (COL p. 47)

Hymns 'Praise the Lord in Everything' (CP no. 53)
'Sing a Glad Song' (MHB no. 8)

Prayer We thank you, Lord, for the gift of music,
for our ears to hear and our hands to play,
for composers of old and the tunes of today,
for sounds of nature, and for the music
that we play just for ourselves. We thank you, Lord. Amen.

Activities Study musical instruments. Open the back of the piano to show its 'works'. Learn how to identify the sound of instruments. Make up a class orchestra. Compose some music. Invite musicians to talk or play for you. Display a collection of instruments. Study the lives of great composers.

Stories in Music

Some programme music suitable for the school assembly:

Arnold, M.
Tam O'Shanter Overture the story of the drunken Tam's encounter with the devil, based on the poem by Robert Burns

Beethoven, L. van
Symphony No. 6 (Pastoral) sounds of the country-side, including storm and peasants merrymaking

Debussy, C.
Preludes impressions of mist, autumn leaves, moonlight, fairies, fireworks etc

Dukas, P.
The Sorcerer's Apprentice the story by Goethe, immortalised by Mickey Mouse in Walt Disney's *Fantasia*

Grieg, E.
Peer Gynt Suite music for Ibsen's play of Peer's travels and eventual return

Humperdinck, E.
Hänsel and Gretel Grimm's story converted into operetta, with a fine overture

Kodaly, Z.
Háry János Suite Hungarian music featuring a sneeze, a musical clock and the defeat of Napoleon

Mendelssohn, F.
A Midsummer Night's Dream incidental music to Shakespeare's play including the 'Wedding March'

Mussorgsky, M.
Night on a Bare Mountain a Witches' Sabbath
Pictures at an Exhibition an art gallery in music

Offenbach, J.
Orpheus in the Underworld the story of Orpheus and Eurydice

Prokofiev, S.
Lieutenant Kije story of an imaginary soldier, including the 'Troika', a snow sleighride
Peter and the Wolf the classic in children's music

Ravel, M.
Mother Goose Suite fairy stories including Sleeping Beauty and Beauty and the Beast

Rimsky-Korsakov, N.
Sheherazade stories from the Arabian Nights, includes a sultan, the sea, and Sinbad's ship

Rossini, G. A.
William Tell Overture story of the legendary Swiss hero

Saint-Saens, C.
Carnival of the Animals a grand zoological fantasy

Sibelius, J.
Swan of Tuonela a Finnish legend from the Kalevala

Strauss, R.
Don Quixote adventures of a quixotic knight
Till Eulenspiegel the legendary trickster

Stravinsky, I.
The Song of the Nightingale a Chinese fairy story

Tchaikovsky, P.
1812 Overture Napoleon's retreat from Moscow with 'Marseillaise' and cannon fire
Nutcracker Suite, Swan Lake etc. Ballet Stories

Walton, W.
Belshazzar's Feast Biblical story of the writing on the wall (*Daniel* 5)

Mystery

The world is full of mystery. Life is full of puzzles and problems. Scientists have found out many things, but there are a lot of mysteries still to be solved. We do not know how the world was created, or how to cure terrible diseases like cancer. A mystery is something we cannot explain. Historical mysteries—Stonehenge, hieroglyphics. Mysterious happenings—are there ghosts, or unidentified flying objects, can people foretell the future? Famous mysteries—the Loch Ness Monster, the Marie Celeste, the Yeti. Mystery novels and mystery writers e.g. Agatha Christie. The mystery plays of the Middle Ages.

Story   The Mystery of the Mary Celeste p. 211

Music   *The Surprise Symphony*   Haydn

Poem   'MacAvity the Mystery Cat'   T. S. Eliot (*Old Possum's Book of Practical Cats*, Faber)

Hymn   'Immortal, Invisible, God Only Wise' (HJS no. 5)

Prayers God moves in a mysterious way
His wonders to perform;
He plants his footsteps in the sea,
And rides upon the Storm.
                    (Cowper)

Help us, God, to be aware of the mystery
of this world, and help us to share
in its beauty and goodness.   Amen.

Activities   Investigate some of the world's unsolved mysteries—suggest your own solutions. Discuss whether there might be such things as ghosts or unidentified flying objects. Find out some authors of famous mystery stories. Write your own mystery story, or a poem entitled 'Mysteries'.

Names

'What's in a name? that which we call a rose
By any other name would smell as sweet.'

(Romeo and Juliet Act II Scene 2)

Why do we have names? Would you prefer a name to a number? Where
did your name come from? You have at least two names. Your surname is
your family name. Often these were named after jobs done by your family
many years ago e.g. Smith, Cooper, Baker. You also have at least one first
name, or Christian name, perhaps given you at Baptism the day you were
christened. Many of these also have meanings (give examples). Names
ending with son mean son of e.g. Richardson. Our names come from many
different countries—French, Greek, German, Jewish, Irish, Scots, Welsh
etc. Some countries put the family name first e.g. China. Nicknames. How
it is important to call people by their proper names, and how we should all
live up to our 'good names'.

Stories   Isambard Kingdom Brunel p. 192
          St Christopher the Bearer p. 225
          The Pot That Called the Kettle Black (Aesop)

Bible   When Saul Changed His Name (*Acts* 9)
          Adam Names the Plants and Animals (*Genesis* 2.19)

Music   *Variations on BACH*   Bach

Poem   'Boys' and Girls' Names'   Eleanor Farjeon (*Poetry and Life* II
          p. 9)

Hymns 'At the Name of Jesus' (CP no. 58)
          'All Hail the Power of Jesus' Name' (MHB no. 14)

Prayer   Dear Lord, help us to live up to our good names by being kind to
          others and always giving of our best.   Amen.

Activities   Find out where your name comes from or what it means.
Make a dictionary of names in your class. What is your name in French?
Survey the most popular names in the school. Quiz: Can you write an A–Z
of names (a name for every letter of the alphabet)? Make a list of famous
nicknames. Write an acrostic poem using your name and describing
yourself. Unscramble names whose letters have been jumbled.

Neighbours

Who is my neighbour? Neighbours in one's street, neighbouring schools, streets, districts, towns, counties, countries, continents, planets, stars etc. What is a neighbourhood? The neighbourhood of the school, Neighbourhood Associations. Jesus said, 'Love thy neighbour as thyself.' What is a good neighbour? Some neighbours can be unpleasant. What is a bad neighbour? Helping new neighbours. Neighbourliness. 'In the neighbourhood of' something.

Story   The Village of Eyam p. 259

Bible   The Good Samaritan (*Luke* 10.29)

Poem   'Neighbours'   Leonard Clark (COL p. 14)

Song   'When I Needed a Neighbour' (FFC p. 31)

Prayer   Dear God, thank you for our neighbours,
for those living both far and near.
Help us to be good neighbours, and to love
even those who are very different from us.
For the sake of our Lord Jesus
who taught us who our neighbours are.   Amen.

Activities   Spell the word 'neighbour'. Rewrite the story of the Good Samaritan in a modern setting, read it or act it out. Draw a map, to scale, of your neighbourhood. Discuss ways of improving your neighbourhood, send your plans and ideas to the local council or newspaper. Describe the neighbours that you have, and what sort of neighbour you are. Make a frieze of children from different lands joining hands round a map of the world.

Peace

Which is better, peace or war? The horrors of war—death, injury, fear, hatred, broken homes, etc. The two World Wars—Remembrance Sunday (Poppy Day). How the United Nations works for peace—meetings in New York, United Nations Day on 24th October. Peace between nations—peace treaties. Parts of the world without peace. Peace between people, make peace by ending rows, quarrels, arguments. Peace within people, to be at peace with oneself, peace of mind. To have no feelings of guilt, fear, worry or anger—feelings of peace. The ways people make peace—peace offerings, the pipe of peace. Peace words—pax (Latin), shalom (Hebrew)—'peace be with you'. A Justice of the Peace. The Peace rose.

Stories   Tulsi the Peacemaker p. 252

Bible   'Blessed are the Peace makers' (*Matt.* 5.9)
Swords into Ploughshares (*Isaiah* 2.4)

Music   *The Moonlight Sonata*   Beethoven

Poem   'The Peace Pipe'   H. W. Longfellow (PSA p. 125)

Songs   'Gonna Lay Down My Sword and Shield' (FFC p. 26)
'Strangest Dream' (FFC p. 26)

Hymn   'Peace Perfect Peace' (CP no. 53)

Prayer   Dear God, please help us to love one another,
help nations to be friendly, and help us play our part
in bringing peace to the world. May the peace of God be with us,
and stay with us, now and evermore.   Amen.

Activities   Study the work of the United Nations. Collect and contrast pictures showing scenes of peace and war. Display a Peace rose.

Perseverance

Few things in life worth doing are easy. To be successful in anything almost always requires hard work. The need for practice in learning a musical instrument, in training for sports, and in school work—practice makes perfect. What some find easy others find difficult, we need to persevere in different things. The saying, 'If at first you don't succeed try, try again'. Always do your best, you may achieve anything if you are really determined.

Story   Robert the Bruce and the Spider p. 223
           The Tortoise and the Hare (Aesop)

Bible   The Persistent Neighbour (*Luke* 11.5)

Music   'Keep Right on to the End of the Road' (Scottish song)
           Heroic Polonaise No. 6   Chopin

Poems   'Try Again'   E. Cook (BTP p. 481)
           ' The Mouse That Gnawed the Oak Tree down'   Rachel Lindsay (JV II p. 6)

Songs   'Jesus Good above All Other' (CP no. 23)
           'We Shall Overcome' (FFC p. 25)

Prayer   O Lord God, when thou givest us thy servants
           to endeavour any great matter,
           grant us also to know that it is not the beginning,
           but the continuing of the same until it be thoroughly finished,
           which yieldeth the true glory.   Amen.
                (Prayer of Sir Francis Drake)

Activities   Show the skills of the children in art, handicrafts, music, dance, gymnastics, sports etc. Discuss any difficulties they have had and how they were overcome.

Prayer

What is a prayer? The kinds of prayer—prayers that ask, prayers that thank. How every religion has its own form of prayer. People who have no religion may pray when danger threatens. How to pray, prayers said together, spoken out loud or spoken 'inwardly', and prayers said when one is all alone. Some people never pray, others say that prayers are always answered (but not always as we expect them). Special prayers: The Lord's Prayer, grace before meals, seasonal prayers etc.

Story Varenka p. 258

Bible Jesus Teaches Us the Lord's Prayer (*Matt.* 6.5)

Music 'The Lord's Prayer' from Fanshawe's *African Sanctus*, or other sung version

Song 'Standing in the Need of Prayer' (FFC p. 3)

Hymns 'Father Hear the Prayer We Offer' (JHB no. 98)
'Praise My Soul' (MHB no. 26)

Prayer He prayeth well, who loveth well
Both man and bird and beast.

He prayeth best who loveth best
All things both great and small;
For the dear God who loveth us,
He made and loveth all.
(From the *Rime of the Ancient Mariner* by Coleridge)

Activities Display a reproduction of *Praying Hands* by Durer. Collect and display children's prayers, prayer books etc. Discuss the meaning of the Lord's Prayer. Find out about praying in different religions. What is a prayer mat, a prayer wheel, a praying mantis?

Pretending

What is pretending? Trying to be, or playing at being, something one isn't. The good and bad sides of pretending. People who pretend to be cleverer than they are ('know-alls', 'bigheads'). Those who pretend they don't know e.g. when doing something wrong. Pretending to have done something you have not—boasting or bragging. People who tell 'tall stories', pretend to be ill when they should be working—skiving. People who pretend to themselves, who think they are something when they are not e.g. 'I am the greatest'. Pretending things are not what they are—fakes and forgeries. The good side—pretending for fun, using one's imagination, play acting (pretending with scenery, props and costumes). Telling jokes and funny stories—actors, clowns, fancy dress, impersonations, use of wigs, magic tricks, optical illusions etc. Pretence in nature, camouflage, the 'eyes' on peacocks' tails, moths' wings etc.

Stories   The Quack Doctor p. 218
             Tall Stories (JV IV p. 30)

Bible   Jacob and Esau (*Genesis* 27)

Music   *Flight of the Bumble Bee*   Rimsky-Korsakov

Poem   'Closet'   J. Thurman (FPB p. 119)

Prayer Dear God, please help me to be honest
            and never to pretend to be something I am not.   Amen.

Activities   Try to impersonate the sounds of animals, or voices of famous people. Study the theatre, learn the arts of make-up and disguise. Practise making sound effects, record them. Discuss whether you think spying is a good or bad thing. Read the stories of Baron Munchausen, find out about Mandeville's Travels, make up your own 'travellers tales'. Who was the Young Pretender?

Pride

The two kinds of pride—true and false pride. True pride is being proud of what is good, of one's achievements, one's school and one's country. The false pride of arrogance, boasting, bragging, being puffed up with conceit, a prig or a snob. What do you pride yourself on? The old saying 'pride before a fall'. As proud as a peacock, a pride of lions.

Stories   The Tinkling Medals p. 249
The Emperor's New Clothes p. 166
King Canute and the Waves (Legend) in *A Child's History of England* by Charles Dickens (Everyman)

Bible   The Pharisee in the Temple (*Luke* 18.9)

Music   *Pomp and Circumstance March No. 1*   Elgar

Poem   'The Mountain and the Squirrel'   R. W. Emerson (BTP p. 477)

Hymn   'Simple Gifts' (FFC p. 19)

Prayer   Take from us, O God, the pride which
makes us think that we are always right.
Help us to be ready to see the points of view of others,
and give us the courage to admit our mistakes.   Amen.

Activities   Discuss the things that you are proud of in your life—your abilities, your work, your family. Act out a story about what happens to some very boastful person.

Reading

The importance of reading in our lives. Reading for pleasure and for information. What do you read for pleasure—story books, comics, newspapers, magazines, library books, letters, postcards, your own writing? Reading for information—signs, labels, instructions, reference books etc. What is literacy? The problems of children who have no opportunity to go to school, the problems of illiteracy. Where you can find books to read, in school, in bookshops, the local library. What is your favourite reading book?

Story   King Alfred Learns to Read p. 198

Bible   Philip Teaches the Ethiopian to Read (*Acts* 8.27)

Music   *Academic Festival Overture*   Brahms

Poem   'The Land of Story-Books'   R. L. Stevenson (CGV p. 83)

Hymn   'Black and White' (CP no. 67)

Prayer   Dear God, we thank you for the gift
of books and the joy of reading.
Help those who are learning to read
and those who find reading difficult.   Amen.

Activities   Hold a Book Exhibition of books to buy, or of favourite reading books. Write book reviews. Make a survey of favourite authors. Invite a children's author to talk about their work. Study the making of books, binding, illustrating and printing. Visit a printer's to see a printing press in action. Try typing or printing your own stories. Produce a class newspaper.

Rules

What are rules? What are the rules of your school? Which are the most important rules? What would your school be like without any rules? The rules of society—laws and regulations. Rules of the road—the Highway Code, road signs, traffic lights. Rules in public parks, and swimming pools. Rules in buildings—No Smoking, Exit, Entrance, 'Shoplifters will be prosecuted'. Notices—'Private', 'No Trespassing', 'No entry'. Rules of games. Those who make sure rules are kept—referees, umpires, judges. How religions provide rules for living.

Story   The Sorcerer's Apprentice p. 238

Bible   The Ten Commandments (*Deuteronomy* V)
The Sermon on the Mount (*Matt.* 5–7)
The Golden Rule (*Matt.* 7.12)

Music   *The Sorcerer's Apprentice*   Dukas

Poem   'Whole Duty of Children'   R. L. Stevenson (PBV p. 142)

Hymns 'Saviour Teach Me Day by Day' (MHB no. 2)
'We Build Our School on Thee O Lord' (JHB no. 120)

Prayer Dear God, help us to obey those rules
which make for a good life. Help us to play
fairly in our games and guide us in thinking
for ourselves what is right. Now and evermore.   Amen.

Activities   Make up your own list of rules for a good life, for home or for school. Discuss your rules with others. Draw as many signs as you can showing particular rules. Have a quiz on the signs of the Highway Code. Invent a board game, say what the rules are.

Saints

What is a saint? Who chooses people to be saints? How a saint is a Christian person who has been canonised, or chosen, by the Church for having lived a very holy life. Anyone who is very kind and good may be described as 'a saint', or a 'saintly' person. In St Paul's day all Christians were called saints. Later special Christians, like martyrs, were chosen. Many Christian boys and girls are named after saints. Churches, cathedrals, schools, hospitals, and towns may be named after saints. Many days of the year are saint's days, when we remember particular saints. Patron saints are said to protect particular places or groups of people. 1st November is All Saint's Day. Do you know anyone today who might be called a saint?

Stories and Legends	St Andrew p. 224, St Christopher p. 225, St Columba p. 226, St David p. 227, St George p. 228, St Patrick p. 229, St Valentine p. 230
Bible	St Stephen the First Christian Martyr (*Acts* 6–8)
Music	'When the Saints Go Marching in' Negro Spiritual
Poem	'Saint Christopher' E. Farjeon (*Young Verse* p. 50)
Hymn	'For All the Saints' (JHB no. 61)
Prayer	Lord, make me an instrument of thy peace. Where there is hatred let me sow love, Where there is injury, pardon; Where there is doubt, faith; Where there is despair, hope; Where there is darkness, light; Where there is sadness, joy. *(Prayer of St Francis)*

Activities   Collect books, prints and pictures of saints. Find out what places in your locality are named after saints. Study maps to find places named after saints e.g. San Francisco. What English kings were called saints? What dog was named after a saint. What football club is called the Saints? Were you born on a Saint's day?
See: *Saints, Birds and Beasts*, Ed. M. Mayo (Kaye and Ward).

St Andrew of Scotland

St Andrew is the patron saint of Scotland, his festival day is 30th November. He lived in Galilee at the same time as Jesus, a fisherman, chosen to be a disciple along with his brother Simon Peter. It was Andrew who found the boy with the loaves and fishes with which Jesus fed the multitude. Andrew travelled widely, as far as Russia, founding many churches. He became the patron saint of Russia, as well as of Scotland. Andrew was crucified on an X-shaped cross after converting the wife of a Roman Senator. The relics of St Andrew were brought to Scotland, and buried at St Andrews. His flag is St Andrew's cross, a white diagonal on a dark blue ground, now part of the Union Jack. Scots have reunions and celebrations on his day. Dinner traditionally starts with piping in the haggis, and ends with Highland dances and Scottish reels.

Stories   St Andrew p. 224

Bible   Andrew is Chosen by Jesus (*Matt.* 5.18)

Music   'Scotland the Brave', or other Scottish melody
The sound of bagpipes

Poem   'My Heart's in the Highlands'   R. Burns (OBPC p. 14)

Song   'Loch Lomond' (ST no. 93)

Prayer   Lord, as we celebrate the festival of St Andrew,
we ask you to bless the people of Scotland,
bring joy to their lives and peace to their hearts.   Amen.

Activities   Display the Scottish flag. Locate St Andrews on a map of Scotland. What sporting event is St Andrews famous for? Perform a Scottish reel or sword dance. Find out all you can about Scottish traditions—clans, tartans, kilts, haggis etc. Ask Scots children to show their tartans and national costume. Show a film or slides of Scotland. (30th November is also the start of Advent: make an Advent calendar.)

St David of Wales

St David is the patron saint of Wales, and St David's Day is celebrated on 1st March. St David lived in the sixth century; he was a great preacher much loved by his people. The leek is always connected with St David—what is a leek? The leek became one of the emblems of Wales. Some Welsh people wear leeks on St David's Day but more often they wear the flower of Wales—the daffodil. The daffodil often appears on coins or stamps. The daffodil was the sacred flower of the Welsh Druids. They called it 'The Flower of the Sun'. It was first brought to Wales by Spaniards who traded it for Welsh coal. A cathedral in Wales is called St Davids in memory of the saint. Many Welsh people are called David, after their saint—this is sometimes shortened to Davy or Taffy.

Story   St David and the Leeks p. 227

Bible   David, Chosen to be King of Israel (*I Samuel* 16.11–13)

Music   'Cwm Rhondda' or other Welsh melody

Poem   'There Were Three Jovial Welshmen'   Anon (OBPC p. 24)

Song   'Men of Harlech' (ST no. 91)

Prayer   Lord, as we celebrate the festival of St David,
we ask you to bless the people of Wales,
bring joy to their lives and peace to their hearts.   Amen.

Activities   Display the emblems of St David—leeks and daffodils, and show the flag of Wales with its dragon. Can anyone speak some words of the Welsh language? Locate on a map St David's in Cardiganshire. Find out all you can about Wales. Who were the bards, what is an Eisteddfod? Show a girl, or doll, dressed in Welsh national costume. Who is the Prince of Wales? Learn and sing a Welsh song.

St George of England

St George is the patron saint of England and 23rd April is St George's Day. His special flag is a red cross on a white background, and his flower is the rose. Many churches are dedicated to St George, the most famous of which is the Queen's own St George's chapel at Windsor. The Queen's scouts hold a service there on the Sunday nearest to St George's day. St George is the patron saint of soldiers. Not much is known about the real St George. He was probably a soldier in the Roman Empire of the third century, who was martyred by the Emperor for being a Christian. There are many stories about St George overcoming the forces of evil. Evil was thought to take many forms in the old days—one of them being the dragon. St George's Day is also the day on which England's greatest playwright, William Shakespeare, is said to have been born and on which he died (1564–1616).

Story   St George and the Dragon p. 228

Music   'Land of Hope and Glory'   Elgar
'I Vow to Thee My Country'   Holst

Poem   St George and the Dragon   Anon (*Common Ground* p. 160)

Hymn   'And Did Those Feet in Ancient Time' (JHB no. 121)

Prayer   Lord, as we celebrate the festival of St. George,
we ask you to bless the people of England,
bring joy to their lives and peace to their hearts.   Amen.

Activities   Display the flag of St George. Perform a Mummer's Play of St George and the Dragon. Find out where St George's Channel is. Look up the George Cross and the Order of the Garter. Study dragons—in the Far East, in the sky (Dragon constellation), Viking dragonships, the Welsh Pendragon, the 'dragons of evil' inside us etc. Find out more about William Shakespeare.

St Patrick of Ireland

St Patrick is the patron saint of Ireland, and his special day is 17th March. His emblem is the three-leaved clover, called a shamrock. Irish people like to wear a sprig of shamrock, or at least something green, on St Patrick's Day. Ireland is a very green country, so it is called the Emerald Isle. St Patrick's cross is a red diagonal on a white background, and can be seen as part of the Union Jack. Patrick was born about AD 389 and was said to be over one hundred years old when he died. Many legends are told about his life. One tells how the shamrock first became the emblem of Ireland when Patrick picked it to show how the Trinity could be Three in One, just like the small three-leaved plant. Patrick was buried at Downpatrick, Co. Down and many Irish people visit his grave on 17th March.

Stories   St Patrick p. 229
Legends of St Patrick

Music   A traditional Irish song or melody

Song   'Cockles and Mussels' (ST no. 64)

St Patrick's Prayer
Christ be with me, Christ within me,
Christ behind me, Christ before me,
Christ beside me, Christ to win me,
Christ to comfort and restore me,
Christ beneath me, Christ above me,
Christ in quiet, Christ in danger,
Christ in hearts of all that love me,
Christ in mouth of friend and stranger.   Amen.

Activities   Display some shamrock and St Patrick's cross. Draw a map of Ireland, show Ulster and Eire, and Downpatrick where St Patrick was buried. What is Gaelic? Find out all you can about Ireland, its chief products, the Potato Famine etc. (17th March is also traditionally the day when Noah set sail in his Ark.)

St Valentine's Day

St Valentine's Day is held on 14th February. Valentine was a priest who lived in Rome around AD 300. He was beheaded for giving shelter to Christians who were being persecuted. His death came at the same time the Romans celebrated the festival of love (the Lupercalia), and at the same time that birds started mating. So Valentine became known as the patron saint of lovers (and birds). An old superstition says that the first unmarried man a girl sees on St Valentine's Day will be her future husband. On this day messages of love were sent. These later became Valentine cards. Old Valentine cards were decorated with turtle doves and love birds. They often had verses inside them. Sometimes flowers were mentioned, as in 'Roses are red, violets are blue, carnations are sweet and so are you.' Valentines are usually sent without a name, so that anyone who receives one has to guess who it is from.

Story St Valentine and the Birds p. 230

Bible The Song of Solomon 1.15

Music *A Midsummer Night's Dream* Mendelssohn
Romeo and Juliet Overture Tchaikovsky

Hymn 'God is Love' (CP no. 56)

Prayer Dear God, help us to love other people,
as You have loved us. Amen.

Activities Make your own Valentine card (using card, coloured tissue, doilies etc). Make a posy of real or paper flowers. Design a Welsh Love Spoon out of card or balsa wood. Find out who was the Greek god of love. Act a famous love story. Create a mobile of girls chasing boys chasing girls. Write a definition of Love.

The Sea

How two-thirds of the earth's surface is covered by sea. Why is the sea salt? Getting salt from the sea—Maldon sea salt. 'Harvest of the sea' fish. Harvest under the sea—oil and gas. What are the great oceans of the world? Inland seas—Black Sea, Dead Sea. Life in the sea—seaweeds, coral, fish, whales, and dolphins etc. How fish feed on plankton, live in schools, shoals. Mythical life—mermaids, monsters, Atlantis, underwater cities, gods, Neptune. Wrecks, divers, submarines. Dangers underwater— shark, octopus, stingray etc. Depth of the sea—fathoms, deepest oceans, the Bermuda Triangle. Sea birds—kinds of gull, puffins, albatross, flying fish. The life of the sea shore—rock pools, shells, seaweed, crabs, shellfish. How life started in the sea, waters covered the land, evidence of fossils. How waves occur, tides and the pull of the moon. Pollution in the sea.

Story   Why the Sea Is Salt p. 262

Bible   Jonah and the Whale (*Jonah*)
Jesus Walking on the sea (*Matt.* 14.22)

Music   *La Mer*   Debussy
Fingal's Cave (*Hebrides Overture*)   Mendelssohn

Poems   *Sea and Shore* an anthology   D. Saunders and T. Williams (Evans)

Hymn   'Eternal Father, Strong to Save' (JHB no. 120)

Prayer   Dear God, be good to me, the sea is so wide
and my boat is so small.
(*Prayer of the Breton fishermen*)

Activities   Display pictures, posters and project work on the sea. Paint a frieze of life underwater. Write poems about sea creatures, a story about discovering Atlantis. Sing a sea shanty, dance a hornpipe. Collect fossils. Explore a seashore. Listen to sea sounds. See a film of underwater exploration. Investigate sea legends. Discuss beachcombing.

Seeing

The miracle of sight. What it would be like without sight, being blind. How blind people use other senses. How blind people cope—the use of the white stick—guide dogs, talking libraries, Braille. How people can 'see' with the mind's eye. How the eye works—parts of the eye, pupil, iris etc. Care of the eye—danger of pointed sticks, throwing things at people etc. Glass eyes. Aids to seeing—glasses, monocles, lorgnettes, microscopes, periscopes, telescopes etc. Seeing at night—cats. Animals that are blind— mole, bat. Seeing beauty, and ugliness, around us.

Story   The Story of Braille p. 152

Bible   Healing the Blind Man (*Mark* 8)

Music   *Concierto de Aranjuez*   Rodrigo (the blind composer)

Poem   'Colours'   Christina Rosetti (*Young Puffin* p. 68)

Hymn   'Let Us with a Gladsome Mind' (CP no. 19) written by the blind John Milton

Prayer   O Lord, open my eyes to see what is beautiful,
my mind to know what is true,
and my heart to love what is good.
For the sake of Lord Jesus Christ.   Amen.

Activities   Blindfold a child—can he identify different objects on a tray? Draw a diagram of the eye. Study the eyes of animals (have a picture quiz). Collect and contrast pictures showing beautiful and ugly sights (eyesores). Discuss 'seeing' words—glimpsing, inspecting, viewing, glancing etc. Make a graph of the colour of eyes. How many times do you blink in a minute? Tape children's stories for local blind people. Find out the facilities for local blind people. Invite a blind person to school with his guide dog. Visit a blind school. Obtain information from the Royal National Institute for the Blind.

Selfishness

What does being *selfish* mean? We are all selfish at times. What would the world be like if everyone were selfish all the time? The need to give and take, to think of others. People in need—the old, the sick, the lonely, the hungry, those less fortunate than ourselves. The work of charities, those who have dedicated their lives to helping others, like Mother Teresa. The more you give to others the more you shall receive.

Stories   The Selfish Giant p. 235
'Scrooge', from *A Christmas Carol* by Charles Dickens excerpted in *The Christmas Book* by James Reeves (Heinemann)

Bible   The Rich Man and the Beggar (*Luke* 16)
'It is more blessed to give than to receive' (*Acts* 20.35)

Music   *Toy Symphony*   Mozart

Poem   'Let Me Today Do Something' (*Poems for Assemblies* p. 182)

Hymn   'Heavenly Father, May Thy Blessing' (CP no. 88)

Prayer   Forgive us, O Lord, for every unkind thought,
every selfish act and every hurtful word.
Help us, O Lord, to be gentle and unselfish,
and to think of others before ourselves.   Amen.

Activities   Choose a charity and discuss ways of raising money for it. Donate unwanted toys to local children in need (consult your local Social Services Department). Discuss how the rich countries could help the poor countries of the world. Write a story about how a selfish person saw the error of his ways. What is a dog in the manger? (See Aesop's fable.)

The Senses

The senses can provide an ideal theme for one assembly or for a series of assemblies. What are the five senses? How do we use them? Why do we have them? Could we live without them? Which are the most important? What do people mean by a sixth sense? How could we test to see if it works?

1. **Seeing**   see theme on Seeing

2. **Hearing**   see theme on Hearing

3. **Feeling**   see theme on Hands for the sense of touch

4. **Tasting**   How we taste with our tongues. The taste buds on different parts of the tongue. Types of taste: bitter, sweet, sour, hot etc. The pleasures of tasting—favourite foods. The dangers of tasting—strange plants, pills, sucking toys etc. Relationship of taste to smell.

Stories   Food for Thought p. 173
　　　　　Salt is Better Than Gold p. 233

Activities   Try tasting various things blindfold—what do you think they are? Try tasting the same thing on different parts of the tongue. Describe what you have tasted. Study the tongues of animals. Investigate poisons. For further material see theme on Food.

5. **Smelling**   The sense of smell. Pleasant smells—scents and perfumes. Unpleasant smells. The work of the nose—keeping it clean. Smelling danger—smoke, gas, stale food, petrol etc. Animal scents.

Poems   'Digging'   Edward Thomas (Blackwell's Poetry Cards)
　　　　　'Smells'   Christopher Morley (Blackwell's Poetry Cards)

Activities   Try smelling different scents—identify and describe them. Make a survey of good and bad smells. Discuss smelling salts, 'to smell a rat', being 'on the scent' of something. Find out what makes flowers smell.

Sharing

We all belong to a community, to a family. Every day we join with others to work, to play, to learn, to eat and drink together. People in a community care about each other. We try to care for each other by sharing and helping in all we do. We share the work of our community by doing different jobs and working together. We help and share things in our families with our mothers and fathers, brothers and sisters. All the families on earth make up one community. All over the world people are working, using their skills, sharing their gifts and helping others to live. What do we receive from others? What have we to share?

Story   The Wise Man of Ireland and His Cake p. 267

Bible   The Feeding of the Five Thousand (*John* 6)
The Fellowship in Jesus Christ (*Acts* 2)

Music   'Wedding March' from *A Midsummer Night's Dream*   Mendelssohn

Poem   'Working for People'   J. Morrison (*Assemblies* p. 23)

Song   'The Family of Man' (CP no. 69)

Prayer   We thank you, O God, for all your blessings.
Help us to share them with others, knowing that
in doing so we are serving you.
For the sake of our Lord Jesus Christ.   Amen.

Activities   Find out which products we receive from other countries, show where the countries are on a large map. Discuss ways in which rich countries can share their wealth with poorer countries. How should a family share the work of running a home? Study problems of sharing (dividing) in maths.

Shintoism

Shinto is a Japanese religion. A Shinto place of worship is called a shrine. Japanese people go there to pray and to be married just like we go to church. Instead of believing in one God, Shinto worshippers believe in many gods and goddesses. There are Shinto shrines to each of the nature gods. The most important shrine, at Ise, is dedicated to the Sun Goddess. The shrine contains a mirror, some jewels and a sword. The emperors of Japan claimed to have descended from the Sun Goddess. Japan is called the Land of the Rising Sun. There is a big red sun in the middle of their flag. A Japanese prays to his gods by giving thanks for all the good things in his life. They have many festivals. One of the traditional festivals of Japanese children is kite-flying. Many of the paper kites you see in shops today were made in Japan.

Story The Goddess of the Sun p. 179

Music Any piece of Japanese music
Overture of *The Mikado* Sullivan

Poems Japanese Haiku (JV II pp. 17 and 46)

Hymns 'Far Round the World' (IHB no. 30)
'In Christ There Is No East Or West' (CP no. 66)

Prayer Dear God, we ask for your blessing on the children of Japan.
Keep them safe from danger,
and help them to grow up strong and good.   Amen.

Activities   Display project work done on Japan. Show its position on a world map. Make and fly some kites. Practise origami. Write your own haiku. Collect pictures and objects of things made in Japan. Find out about ikebana, bonsai and tying a kimono.

Sikhism

Sikhs are people who follow the Sikh religion. There are more than 80,000 Sikhs in the U.K. Sikh men are easily recognised by the turbans they wear. They originally came from India or Pakistan. All Sikh men take the name Singh, as a sign of brotherhood. Singh means lion e.g. Singapore means Lion Port. The Sikh religion follows the teachings of Guru Nanak (1469–1539). Guru Nanak's birthday is a holy day for Sikhs. It is celebrated in November. Guru means wise man. There are ten gurus in the Sikh tradition. Sikhs always wear a steel bangle on their right wrist (a symbol of God, reminding the wearer to do no wrong with his hand). They do not cut their hair—men coil it inside their turbans, boys wear a bun. Their religion tells them to *work* hard, to *worship* God and to live in *charity* with others. The boys are taught to be as proud and brave as lions (Singhs).

Story How the Guru Chose Five Lions p. 187

Music Indian music or Punjabi folksong

Hymn 'Far Round the World' (JHB no. 30)

Prayer Let us think of these words of Guru Nanak:
'To love God you must first learn to love one another.'

Activities Invite a Sikh, or members of a Sikh family, to talk about themselves and their religion. Show how a turban is tied. Draw a map to show where Sikhs come from. Display the kara (steel bangle) worn by Sikhs, together with other Sikh clothes and jewellery. Find a picture of the beautiful Golden Temple of Amritsar. Find out more about Guru Nanak. Visit a Sikh temple.

Sleep

One third of our lives is spent asleep. The function of sleep—how everything in nature needs rest. Different bedtimes. How the body and brain are still at work—dreams and nightmares. Sleepwalking, talking in one's sleep, snoring. Sleeping positions—movement in the night. Rapid eye movements. How to get to sleep, lullabies, counting sheep. Types of sleep—slumbering, dozing, nodding off, sleeping like a log or top, having a cat nap or forty winks. Sayings: 'Let sleeping dogs lie'; 'To sleep the sleep of the just'. The Sandman, a railway 'sleeper', a 'sleeping' partner. Bed clothes. Animals asleep—eyes shut, open; standing on one leg etc. Hibernation.

Stories   Rip Van Winkle p. 222
The Seven Sleepers p. 236

Bible   Jacob's Ladder (*Genesis* 28)

Song   *The Cradle Song*   Brahms

Poems   'Poem'   Susan David (JV II p. 32)
'Ned'   E. Farjeon (*Young Verse* p. 67)

Songs   'All Through the Night' (Welsh Trad.)
'Golden Slumbers' (ST no. 72)

Prayer   Matthew, Mark, Luke and John
Bless the bed that I lie on,
Before I lay me down to sleep
I pray the Lord my soul to keep.
          (*Anon*)
see 'Before Sleeping' (TD p. 84)

Activities   Discuss children's experience of going to bed, being in bed and waking in the morning. Write or record their dreams and nightmares. Make up a lullaby. Set it to music. Make a graph of times children go to bed. Study the ways animals sleep. Write a story about waking up forty years from now. Create a modern version of Sleeping Beauty.

The Solar System

What is the Solar System? What are the planets which revolve around the sun? The order of the planets—Mercury, Venus, Earth, Mars, Jupiter, Saturn, Uranus, Neptune and Pluto. How the planets orbit the sun, variations in the length of a year (one complete orbit). Moons, asteroids and meteors. How planets have the Roman names of Greek gods. Description of the planets, temperature, distance from earth, how they all revolve. Possibility of seeing Venus in the night sky. Discovery of the planets by astronomers—possibility of another small planet? Space flights to planets. The uniqueness of our planet.

Stories   Mercury and the Axe p. 205
The Story of Galileo p. 175

Music   *The Planets*   Holst

Poem   St Francis' Song of the Creatures (*Poems for Assemblies* p. 36)

Hymn   'Can You Count the Stars that Brightly' (MHB no. 39)

Prayer   Heavenly Father, thank you for the beauty
and the wonder of your creation, for space
and planets and the sky.   Amen.

Activities   Make a mobile showing the orbit of the planets around the sun. Paint your own impressions of the different planets. Collect as much information as you can about each planet. Show the relative sizes of the planets compared to the sun. Study the Greek myths of the gods whom the planets were named after. Write a story about inter-planetary space travel. See a film about the Solar System or visit a planetarium.
See also the themes on the Sun, Moon and Stars.

Sports

The world of sport. Sporting seasons, summer sports and winter sports. Sportsmen and sportswomen. Being 'a good sport', fair play. The importance not of winning or losing but of playing the game. International sports—the Olympic Games every four years, when is it next? Athletics—track and field events, relays—outdoor and indoor events. Great sporting events and trophies. Sports stadiums—White City, Wembley, Wimbledon etc. Animals in sport—horseracing, showjumping, greyhounds, hunting. History of sports—the cruel sports of old e.g. bullbaiting. Sports around the world—baseball, cricket, skijumping etc. Sporting records. Sports at school.

Story   Atalanta's Race p. 141

Bible   Run to Win (*1 Corinthians* 9.24)

Music   *Skater's Waltz*   Waldteufel

Poem   'Confessions of a Born Spectator'   Ogden Nash (EBCV p. 242)

Hymn   'In Our Work and in Our Play' (MHB no. 46)

Prayer   Thank you, Lord, for the world of sport,
for the times that we win and the times that we lose.
Help us always to play fairly,
and in whatever we do to try our best.   Amen.

Activities   Display any medals, cups or certificates won by children in sports. Make up a running commentary or write a report on a real or imaginary sporting occasion. Find out about the original Olympic Games. Visit a famous sporting occasion, or sports team in training. Invite a local athlete or sportsman to be interviewed on their training and experiences. Study sports records. Draw the symbol of the Olympic Games.

Spring

The warming of the earth and the growth of seeds. The Spring Equinox, March winds and April showers. Spring flowers—daffodils, crocuses, hyacinths. Trees in spring—catkins, sticky buds etc. Birds and nests. Spring festivals, sowing the seed. Spring cleaning. Spring lambs. Trees in blossom.

Story   The Selfish Giant p. 235

Bible   Sowing the Seed (*Luke* 8.5)
'For, lo, the winter is past . . .' (*Song of Solomon* 2.11–12)

Music   *The Rite of Spring*   Stravinsky
On Hearing the First Cuckoo in Spring   Delius

Poems   'Spring'   T. Nashe (OBPC p. 102)
'Spring'   Oscar Wilde (TD p. 115)

Hymns   'Hark! A Hundred Notes are Swelling' (MHB 49)
'Sing, All Ye Christian People' (JHB no. 13)

Prayer   Let us give thanks for the miracle of spring,
for the beauty of spring flowers and their many colours,
for the wakening of the earth after its winter sleep,
for the growth of new life everywhere.
We thank you, God.   Amen.

Activities   Hold a Spring Festival. Make a collection of spring flowers, catkins, bulbs etc. Paint a spring frieze showing March winds, blossom on trees, young lambs etc. Write a Spring poem. Plant various seeds in plastic containers. Invent a Spring dance to show how nature comes to life.
For further material: *The Springtime Book* James Reeves

Stars

What is a star? Why do they shine and twinkle at night? Groups of stars—galaxies and constellations. Why the stars change position in the night sky—the movement of the earth. How the Greeks saw pictures in the sky and named the stars accordingly, e.g. the Plough, the Great Bear. The Pole Star. Shooting stars (small meteors) and starlight. Size of stars—dwarf and large, age of stars, and distances in space. Collapsed stars—black holes. The sun as a middle-aged star. Stargazers—the work of astronomers, radio telescopes. Star shapes. Stars on flags—the stars and stripes, the Red Star. Stars and luck—'Thank your lucky stars'. Film stars. Starfish. Asterisks. The Star of Bethlehem. The Star of David. The Star Chamber. Being 'starry-eyed'.

Story   The Dolphin and the Lyre p. 164

Bible   The Star of Bethlehem (*Matthew* 2)

Music   *Also Sprach Zarathustra*   R. Strauss (Theme from the film *2001*)
Theme from the film *Star Wars*   Williams
Variations on a Nursery Song ('Twinkle Twinkle')   Dohnányi

Poems   'Twinkle Twinkle Little Star . . .' (Traditional)
'I Stood and Stared'   R. Hodgson (TD p. 25)

Hymn   'Can You Count the Stars' (MHB no. 39)

Prayer   Dear God, thank you for every star in the sky.
Help us to remember that though there may
be very many, each one is an important part of your
creation.   Amen.

Activities   Observe the stars through a telescope at night. Make a star chart showing the major constellations. Find a chart of the sky at night at this time of year. Visit the London Planetarium. Maths—construct three-dimensional star shapes. What countries have stars on their flags—which constellation is on the flag of New Zealand?

Summer

The summer season lasts from the summer solstice on 21st June to the autumn equinox in September. 21st June is the longest day of the year. Midsummer Day is 24th June. The Druids held a service at Stonehenge on this day and bonfires were lit to drive away evil spirits. British Summer Time is when clocks are put forward one hour so that we can enjoy more sunlight. Summer flowers, trees and insects. Summer holidays. Summer sports. *A Midsummer Night's Dream* by Shakespeare.

Story   Why Summer Days Are Longer p. 263

Bible   *Psalm* 74 16–17

Music   *Fantasia on Greensleeves*   Vaughan Williams
              Flight of the Bumble Bee   Rimsky-Korsakov

Poem   'Summer'   Christina Rossetti (TD p. 121)

Hymns   'It Fell upon a Summer Day' (MHB no. 19)
              'Summer Suns Are Glowing' (JHB no. 15)

Prayer   Dear God, thank you for summertime,
              for the joy of long summer days
              and for the warmth of the summer sun.
              For the fullness of fruit and flower
              we thank you Lord.   Amen.

Activities   Make a survey of where people are spending their summer holidays. Display holiday resort brochures. Visit Stonehenge or Avebury, make a model of it, find out where the stones came from and describe how they may have been transported. Act, or tell the story of *A Midsummer Night's Dream* (Shakespeare).

The Sun

Why is the sun so important for us? Light and warmth. The sun is our star, a ball of fiery gases. Solar energy and the effect of sunspots. Sun-worshippers, traditional belief in a sun god, temples to the sun (Aztec, Incas, Stonehenge). The chariot of the sun in Greek myth, Apollo the sun god, Druids. The sun dance of American Indians. Japan—the Land of the Rising Sun. Our response to the sun—suntan, sunburn, sunglasses, sunblind, sunshade, sunshine roof, sunhat and sunstroke. The beauty of sunrise and sunset. How sunrise and sunset alter through the seasons. The Midnight Sun. Sundials. Sunday as the Lord's Day and first day of the week. Sunflowers. Sunbeams. Sundown in the tropics—'Make hay while the sun shines'. The sun's eclipse. How one day the sun will die.

Story The Wind and the Sun p. 265

Bible The Day the Sun Stood Still (*Joshua* 10)

Music 'Here Comes the Sun' Beatles

Poem 'Summer Sun' R. L. Stevenson (CGV p. 100)

Hymns 'Jesus Bids Us Shine' (MHB no. 34)
'I Love the Sun' (MHB no. 55)
'Summer Suns are Glowing' (JHB no. 15)

Prayer Prayer of St Francis p. 38
Dear God, we thank you for the warmth
and light of the sun. Help this little light
of mine to shine and bring warmth to the world. Amen.

Activities Find out as many facts about the sun as you can—how big, how hot, how far away etc. Make a model of a sun temple. Paint a sunset. Study and compare sunshine records, hours of sunshine in different parts of the country. Explain how the position of the sun affects day and night, the changing seasons. Make a sundial. Create a sun dance.

Talking

How there is a time for talking and a time for listening. The gift of speech. How we talk—the voice box, vocal chords, the vibrations of sound, use of tongue and mouth. People who cannot talk—the dumb, losing one's voice, cutting out tongues. The pleasures of conversation. The use of speech— news, stories, information, warnings, instructions etc. Talking too much, gossip, telling tales, being a chatterbox. Courtesy—always to listen to whoever is speaking to you. Clear speech, sounding vowels and consonants, ends of words, not mumbling. Giving a talk, lecture, speech. Special talkers—orator, spokesman, lecturer. Describing talk—speak, shout, whisper, scream, gabble, gasp, murmur, bark, roar, hiss etc.—'talking the hind legs off a donkey', 'through your hat'. Talking birds—parrots and budgerigars. Recording talk—'walkie talkies'. Talking to oneself.

Story   The Talking Turtle p. 243

Bible   The Tower of Babel (*Genesis* 11)
           Talking in Tongues (*Acts* 2)

Music   'Happy Talk' from the musical *South Pacific*
           Rodgers & Hammerstein

Poem   'English'   E. Farjeon (PSA p. 82)

Song   'Old Woman, Old Woman' (*Apusskidu* no. 10)

Hymn   'Thank you' (FFC no. 3)

Prayer   God be in my head and in my understanding,
          God be in my eyes and in my looking,
          God be in my mouth and in my speaking,
          God be in my heart and in my thinking.   Amen.
                        (*Book of Hours* 1514)

Activities   Record children's conversations. Play *Children Talking* (BBC Records). Demonstrate different ways of talking—mumbling, lisping, whispering etc. Try lip-reading. Make up a conversation between two interesting characters. Hold a talking competition—nonstop for one minute on any given or chosen subject.

Teamwork

Why is it better to work in a team than all by yourself? Co-operating with others, the fun of working together, 'many hands make light work'. How one stick alone will easily break, but five put together are unbreakable. Pulling together, the links of a chain and not being 'a weak link'. What happens to a chain with a weak link? Team games and sports. Special teams—school teams, Olympic teams etc. People in a team—captain, vice captain, members, reserves, manager, coach or trainer. Team colours, badges, uniforms, mottos. Quiz teams. Teams of horses, teams of workmen, team teaching. 'Teaming up' with someone. Great feats of teamwork—Great Wall of China, Pyramids, Hadrian's Wall, Stonehenge etc. How the workers in a school are like a team.

Stories   The Two Metre Chopsticks p. 254
Unity is Strength (*Fables of Aesop*, Penguin, p. 177)

Bible   Jesus Chooses Twelve Apostles (*Luke* 6.12)

Music   *Classical Symphony*   Prokofiev
(The orchestra as a team of musicians)
'The Eton Boating Song'   Drummond

Poem   'For Want of a Nail' (*Assembly: Poems and Prose* p. 127)

Song   'One Man's Hands' (FFC p. 34)

Hymn   'Far Round the World' (MHB no. 26)

Prayer   God bless our school, that working together
and playing together, we may learn to serve You,
and to serve one another, for Jesus' sake.   Amen.

Activities   How many team sports do you know? Study how different team games are played, team colours, badges etc. What is unity, united, a union? Play some team games. Work together on a large project e.g. knitting squares to make a blanket for Oxfam.

Teeth

The importance of dental care—regular brushing, healthy foods (milk for calcium), visits to the dentist. The growth of teeth—the twenty 'milk teeth', the 32 permanent teeth—the 'wisdom teeth' of adults. Harmful foods—sweets and sugar. Tooth decay and bacteria. False teeth. Tusks for ivory. The teeth of animals e.g. carnivores, cows, snakes, rodents. The teeth of a comb, 'tooth and nail', 'armed to the teeth', 'in the teeth of danger', 'dent du lion'—dandelion.

Story The Dragon's Teeth p. 165

Poems 'Oh I Wish I'd Looked after My Teeth' Pam Ayres (*I Like this Poem*, Puffin)
'Teeth' Spike Milligan (*Silly Verse for Kids*, Puffin)

Song 'The Building Song' (CP no. 61)

Prayer Dear God, help me to take care of my teeth,
teach me good habits so that I may grow in health. Amen.

Activities Design posters which promote care of the teeth. Make a magazine collage of smiles. Count your teeth. Make graphs of how often people clean their teeth, visit the dentist, favourite toothpaste etc. Study and draw animal skulls or jawbones. Display an ivory carving. Play tunes through teeth by using comb and paper.

Further information may be obtained from the Health Education Council or leading toothpaste manufacturers.

Thinking for Yourself

An important part of growing up is learning to think for yourself. The world is full of wonder, you should always be asking questions, always trying to find out. No one knows all the answers, there is always something new to learn. Never be afraid to ask. All finding out begins with the asking of questions—Why? How? When? Asking at home, asking at school, where to find answers. How we need to work out for ourselves what is right and wrong. The brain as a tool for our use.

Stories   Thinking for Yourself p. 244
The Boy Who Always Asked Questions p. 150
The Miller, the Son and the Donkey (Aesop)

Bible   'All that is true ...' (*Phil.* 4.8)

Music   *Children's Overture*   Quilter

Poems   'King John and the Abbot of Canterbury' (BTP p. 478)
'I Wonder'   J. Kirby (FPB p. 122)
'Who?'   J. Catermill (FPB p. 123)

Song   'Die Gedanken Sind Frei' (FFC p. 25)

Prayer   Dear God, help us to think for ourselves,
give us the courage to always ask questions
and guide us in finding the right answers.   Amen.

Activities   Start a Question Box in which children can write down any questions that puzzle them. Play some games which involve logic e.g. *Mastermind*. Make a large drawing of a question mark and try some question games e.g. 'I Spy', 'Twenty Questions'. Find a picture of Rodin's famous sculpture 'The Thinker'. Collect puzzles, riddles, mazes and brain teasers.

Travel

What is a journey? Why do people travel? Travel for exploration and discovery—'Travel broadens the mind'. Famous travellers who have found new worlds. Holiday travel—holiday destinations at home and abroad. Travel agents. Travelling to sell things—ice cream van, milkman, commercial travellers etc. Routine journeys—ways of coming to school. History of travel—by land, sea and air. Travel in the future. Departures and destinations—'to travel hopefully is better than to arrive'. The journey of life.

Stories   St Christopher the Bearer p. 225 (Travel on land)
              Columbus and the Egg p. 156 (Travel by sea)
              Daedelus and Icarus p. 160 (Travel by air)

Bible   Paul's Journey to Rome (*Acts* 27, 28)

Music   *Sheherazade*   Rimsky-Korsakov

Poem   'Travel'   R. L. Stevenson (PSA p. 18)

Hymns   'Travel On' (CP no. 42)
           'The Journey of Life' (CP no. 45)
           'As Jacob with Travel Was Weary One Day' (JHB no. 81)

Prayer   Wherever I go by night or day,
            I know I'm safe along the way,
            Because the Lord is there;
            In the sky and on the sea,
            I know that God is there with me,
            For God is everywhere.   Amen.

Activities   Study the history of travel and display project work. Discuss where children have travelled—look up timetables, maps, routes, work out distances travelled, average speeds etc. What games can you play on journeys? Show film or slides of a school journey or any other journey. What will be the transport of the future?

Trees

'The tree which moves some to tears of joy is, in the eyes of others, only a green thing which stands in the way' (William Blake).

The beauty of trees in parks and gardens, woods and forests. The value of trees: for *man* in providing timber (wood to burn, and to make things with), giving oxygen to breathe (largely produced by the great rainforests of Brazil), coal for our use, fruit and nuts, rubber, planted for beauty, to screen ugly sights and provide shade; for *animals* as homes, e.g. squirrels, birds; and *insects* for them to feed off. How trees grow from seeds, e.g. acorns. Telling the age of trees from bark rings, the yearly growth of bark. The work of roots, sap, leaves. Evergreen and deciduous trees. Famous trees, e.g. Oak Apple Day, and famous forests, e.g. New, Sherwood. Local trees. The effect of tree diseases, e.g. Dutch elm disease. How to plant your own tree or sapling. The work of the Forestry Commission.

Story   Johnny Appleseed p. 194

Bible   The Man Who Hid in a Tree (*Luke* 19)

Music   *Dumbarton Oaks*   Stravinsky
Finlandia   Sibelius

Poems   'Trees'   Walter de la Mare (PSA p. 79)
'The Pines'   M. Mahy (FPB p. 78)
'Trees'   Sara Coleridge (BTP p. 233)

Songs   'The Ash Grove' (Welsh trad: ST no. 70)
'The Tree in the Wood' (Trad: ST no. 73)

Prayer   Let us think of the beauty and strength of trees,
Let us think of the acorn that grows into an oak,
Let us remember how great things can grow
out of small beginnings.   Amen.

Activities   Display pictures and posters of trees, and the fruits of trees. Collect leaves and bark from different trees, make leaf rubbings, sketch tree shapes. Plant seeds from trees. Visit a wood or forest. Make a survey of trees in your area.

Quiz: How many names of trees do you know? What is a family tree?

Water

Where does water come from? Why is it so valuable? Water for plants and animals. The water cycle—evaporation and condensation. The effects of flood and drought. The uses of water—washing, cleaning, cooking, drinking, swimming, fishing etc. How water is purified and pumped to our homes. Power from water—waterwheel and hydro-electric dams. Baptism—holy waters, e.g. Jordan, Ganges. 'Washing one's hands' of something, e.g. Pontius Pilate. Scientific facts—H_2O, what dissolves in, absorbs, floats on water. Effects of boiling and freezing.

Story Hans of Harlem p. 184

Bible Noah and the Flood (*Genesis* 6–9)

Music *The Water Music* Handel
'Singing in the Rain' Freed & Brown (sung by Gene Kelly)
'Kyrie' from *Noye's Fludde* B. Britten
The Raindrop Prelude Chopin

Poem 'Water' J. R. Crossland (BTP p. 446)

Hymns 'Water of Life' (CP no. 2)
'Little Drops of Water' (MHB no. 48)

Prayer Dear Lord, thank you for the wonderful gift of water,
for the rain which makes things grow,
for rivers and streams, great lakes and small pools,
help us also to grow in thy love.   Amen.

Activities Draw a large diagram of the water cycle. Visit your local waterworks, discover how water is purified. Measure rain with a rain gauge and plot a rainfall graph. Experiment to see what dissolves in, absorbs and floats on water. Experiment to show how plants need water. Show the surface tension on water. Demonstrate condensation and evaporation. Discuss water words—moisture, dampness, drench, soak, soggy, saturated, drowned etc.

Winter

The resting time of nature. Why the weather gets colder and days get shorter. The effects of cold on growth—how freezing preserves life, the seeds and roots in the earth. Winter flowers—Christmas roses, snowdrops, winter jasmine. The shapes of trees in winter. Animals and insects in winter. Winter in different parts of the world. Winter weather—frost, ice, snowflakes. The temperature. Keeping warm and fit in winter. Looking after and feeding birds.

Story   How Winter Came to Earth p. 190

Music   'Winter' from Vivaldi's *Four Seasons*

Poems   'The North Wind Doth Blow' (OBPC p. 97)
           'Winter the Huntsman'   Osbert Sitwell (TD p. 137)

Hymn   'The Snow is Falling Fast' (JHB no. 49)

Prayer   Dear God, thank you for the joys of winter,
           for snow and wind and sparkling frost,
           for glowing fires and indoor games,
           for the warmth of clothes,
           and for the shelter of homes on stormy nights.
           For the glitter of snow and frost,
           we thank you, Lord.   Amen.

Activities   Display winter pictures. Keep weather records on changes in rain, temperature and wind. Investigate the effects of salt on ice. Look at snowflakes through a microscope or make snowflake patterns. Study what winter is like in other parts of the world—in the Far North, the Sahara, Australia. Follow a winter nature trail.
For further material see: *The Winter Book* E. Gundrey

Writers

What is a writer? A writer is someone who writes. In school we are all in our different ways writers. Why do we learn to write? The importance of communication over long distances, writing, and the pleasures of receiving letters and postcards. Communication to many people—books, newspapers, plays and poems. Famous writers of the past. Favourite authors today. People who make a living by writing—authors, playwrights, journalists. Writing in other languages, translation. The history of writing—hieroglyphics. The printed word, varieties of magazines and newspapers. Typewriters, shorthand, codes. Word puzzles and the fun of words.

Story   Hans Andersen (1805–75) p. 183

Bible   The Writing on the Wall (*Daniel* 5)
The Letters of St Paul (e.g. *1 Corinthians* 13)

Music   Play a piece of classical music, let children write their impressions, then read them to the music

Poem   'The Land of Story Books'   R. L. Stevenson (CGV p. 83)

Song   'Black and White' (CP no. 67)

Prayer   Dear God, thank you for the gift of writing,
for stories and poems and letters and cards,
for the great writers of past and present.
Help us to share in the joy of writing.   Amen.

Activities   Arrange a display of handwriting and written work. Collect varieties of printing from books, papers, comics, magazines, labels, adverts etc. Produce a class or school magazine. Find examples of writing from other countries—Chinese, Arabic, Hindi, Hebrew, hieroglyphics. Do book reviews, and discuss your favourite authors. Invite an author in to discuss or read from his or her work. Visit a local newspaper or printing works.

Themes in Brief

Accident! Safety first. The use of First Aid. How to summon the Emergency Services. Safety in the home, at school and on the roads. Danger spots: building sites, railway lines, pylons and waterways. Safety by the seaside. Accident statistics. Cycling proficiency tests. See the journal *Safety Education* published by ROSPA.

Adverts Survey the different forms of advertising. Create your own adverts for good causes. Investigate the claims of various adverts. Do you believe all you read?

Ancestors Who are our ancestors? The making of family trees. The origin of names and surnames. Immigration through the ages—Celts, Romans, Anglo Saxons, Normans, Jews, the Commonwealth etc. How we used to live. Our original ancestors—Adam and Eve?

Babies What you were like as a baby—size, weight, hair, colour of eyes, care needed? The human baby compared with other animals. A baby's needs. Gifts to the newborn and naming (christening). Babies around the world. Music: *Cradle Song* (lullaby) by Brahms. Bible: The Nativity (*Luke* 2.1) Moses as a baby (*Exodus* 2).

Beauty 'A thing of beauty is a joy forever' (Keats). What is beautiful? Beauty in nature. Explore the lines of the hymn 'All things bright and beautiful'. Beauty in art. Beauty in literature—Black Beauty, Beauty and the Beast. Beauty sleep, beauty spot, beauty parlour. Beauty being 'skin deep'.

Being Disabled What it means to be disabled or physically handicapped. How some are handicapped from birth, others by disease, some by accident and some in war. Providing facilities for the handicapped. Caring for the handicapped. The need for inoculation against polio. The work of the Spastics Society.

Bones Parts of the skeleton (backbone, jawbone, funnybone, wishbone etc). Vertebrate and invertebrate animals. Boney expressions: 'a bone to pick', 'make no bones', 'bone dry', 'bone idle', 'to feel in one's bones', 'a boneshaker' etc. The negro spiritual 'Dem bones'.

Building   What is being built in your area? How is it being built? The people involved—architects, surveyors, builders, carpenters, plumbers, electricians etc. The need for foundations. (cf. The House Built on Sand *Matt.* 7.24). Constructing models. Building materials. Buildings that are 'protected', (conservation areas). Song: 'The Building Song' (CP no. 61).

Character   How would you describe yourself? Qualities of character, good and bad. What makes you different from everybody else? Different types: eg. introvert and extrovert. Famous characters in fiction. The character you would like to be.

Charity   Giving to others. Those who need help at home and abroad. Anagram of Christianity = 'It's in charity'. The Widow's Mite (*Luke* 21). Discuss the saying 'Charity begins at home'.

Cheating   The cheater was originally an 'Escheater', the king's tax collector. What do we mean by cheating? The need for rules in games, in school and in society. 'Cheats never prosper' (except in the cardgame called 'Cheat').

Cheerfulness   The power of laughter and smiles—they're catching! Having a sense of humour. Learning to laugh at ourselves, not taking our small troubles too seriously. Songs: 'Pack up your troubles', 'If you're happy' (*Ta-ra-ra boom-de-ay*, Black).

Churches   Survey the churches in your neighbourhood, which saints are they named after? The architectual features of the church, denominations and kinds of clergy. The major church services. Who goes to church? The history of the Church. Churches in different religions.

Circus   History of the circus, travelling players, gypsies. Circus stories. The training of animals. High wire acts—skill and co-operation. Jugglers and gymnasts. The universal clown. Song: 'The Clown' (*Apusskidu* no. 35) See the anthology *Strolling Players*   Z. & I. Woodward (Evans).

Colour   The spectrum, colours of the rainbow, how they merge into white. Primary and secondary colours. Colours in nature (camouflage). Favourite colours, colour schemes. Being colour blind. The symbolism of colours, colour signals, national colours. See: *Colours* by N. J. Bull (Burke Books) Poems: *Colours* an anthology by D. Saunders and T. Williams (Evans). Music: *Colour Symphony* Bliss. Song: 'Sing a Rainbow' (*Apusskidu* no. 5)

Communication Learning to talk and read. Non-verbal communication—looks, mime. gesture, signals. Animal communication, territorial behaviour. Means of communication: printed word, postal service, mass media, telephone, newspaper, T.V. etc. Communication satellites. Mind reading.

Conscience The voice of conscience, have you ever heard it? Where it comes from—our sense of right and wrong. The difference between a clear and guilty conscience. To have something on one's conscience. To be conscientious.

Conservation The need to preserve our national heritage. The conservation of nature and wildlife, parks, open spaces, the Green Belt. The conservation of old buildings, traditional crafts, the best of the past. Study the conservation needs of your area. World Wildlife Fund and The National Trust.

Countryside Follow the Country Code—guard against all risk of fire, fasten all gates, control dogs, keep to paths across farmland, leave no litter, protect birds and animals, and pick no wildflowers. Further information from The Countryside Commission. Story: The Town Mouse and the Country Mouse (Aesop)—which are you?

Creation The creation of the world, theories of the origin of the universe. The Genesis story. How we can all be creative, creative writing and creative arts, the importance of originality. How man has created the world he lives in. Poem: 'The Creation' by J. W. Johnson (*Rhyme* IV).

Diaries The fun and value of keeping a daily record of events. Printed diaries, specialist diaries, and the information to be found in a diary. Famous diaries: Samuel Pepys, Ann Frank. Illustrated journals e.g. *The Country Diary of an Edwardian Lady* by Edith Holden (M. Joseph and Webb & Bower). The school diary or log book.

Dragons The mythical monsters or serpents. Dragons in myth: Cadmus and the Dragon's teeth, Beowulf and Grendel, St George, St Romain and Gargouille (hence gargoyles) Viking Dragon ships, Chinese raindragons and dragon dances, the Welsh Pendragon. The dragons of evil inside each of us.

Dreams Dreams and sleep (rapid eye movements). The quality of dreams, dreams in colour, nightmares, dreams of falling, sounds. Daydreams. Famous dreams: Jacob's Ladder, Pharaoh's dreams, Nebuchadnezzar, Alice in Wonderland, Coleridge's 'Kubla Khan' etc. What dreams have the children had?

Eggs Which came first, the chicken or the egg? Easter eggs, decorated eggs, free-range and battery eggs. Egg sizes, shell, white and yolk. Eggs in cookery. Testing for freshness. Sayings: 'bad egg, good egg', 'teaching grandmother to suck eggs', 'all the eggs in one basket', to 'egg on', 'as sure as eggs is eggs'.

Elections What is an election? How people vote, what they vote for, the meaning of democracy, candidates and secret ballots. General elections, by-elections and local elections. Ballot or show of hands, which is better?

Energy Where do we get our energy? From eating plants and animals. How the energy of the sun is transformed into sugars and starches. Traditional sources of energy: coal, natural gas and oil. The need to conserve energy. New sources of energy: nuclear power, solar, water and wind power. Saving energy at home.

Escape Man's need to get away when he feels trapped. Holidays and rescues. Famous escapes e.g. Icarus, Ulysses, St Paul, Charles II, Bonnie Prince Charlie, Captain Blood, World War II POWs, The Berlin Wall and the plight of refugees. Ways of escape, fire escape, ejector seats.

Europe Our continent, its history and geography. The countries of the Common Market, what EEC stands for. The language, culture and products of each country. Holidays in Europe—costume dolls and toys.

Evil What is evil? What do you think are the evils of this world—hunger, disease, poverty? Evil thoughts, what are they, who has them? The three monkeys—see no evil, speak no evil, hear no evil.

Explorers How we all explore our environment. Man's curiosity in discovering the world. Famous explorers—exploration in space, exploration underwater, modern explorers. What you need for an expedition.

Fables The history and nature of fables—animal stories with 'morals'. Famous writers of fables: Aesop, La Fontaine, Krylov, the fables of India etc. Sayings that derive from fables e.g. 'dog in the manger', 'crying wolf', 'wolf in sheep's clothing' etc.

Fair Play Sportsmanship and playing to the rules. Is it the game not the winning that counts? What does being 'fair' mean? What is not fair in your life? What is not fair about the world?

Faith To have faith in someone, religious faith, faith-healing, a faithful person, 'Yours faithfully', faithful animals. 'Defender of the Faith' (Henry VIII)—see F.D. on coins. Biblical link with hope and charity (*I Cor.* 13.13).

Fears   What are you most afraid of? Fear of the dark, fear of the unknown. Fears that are real, fears that are unfounded. Ways to conquer fear—the use of prayer. Song: 'I Whistle a Happy Tune' (*Apusskidu* no. 3) Bible Story: Jesus Calms the Storm (*Luke* 22) Poem: 'The Bogus-Boo' J. Reeves (FPB pp. 22–23).

Flight   Man's dream of flying—birdman, Icarus, angels, witches, Superman etc. The beauty of flight, birds and butterflies. Symmetry and streamlining—darts, flying fish, arrows. Propellers, winged seeds and boomerangs. Kites, balloons and parachutes. Flying machines—aeroplanes, helicopters and hovercraft. Space flight, and our spaceship earth.

Football   'Match of the day'—our football team, the history of football, match reports, competitions, laws of the game, pitch measurements, supporters' clubs. Song: 'Shoot! Shoot! Shoot!' (*Apusskidu* no. 28).

Foundations   The foundation of your school—laying foundation stones. Learning as the foundation for life. Foundations in building, the Leaning Tower of Pisa. The man who built his house on sand (*Matt.* 7.24) A 'time capsule' (box of objects typical of our own time and culture) in the foundations, what would you include?

Games   The games people play, indoors and outdoors. To 'play the game', gamesmanship, to be 'fair game', game-birds, gamekeeper. How games have developed e.g. history of chess. Inventing new games. The use of rules. Olympic Games.

Gardens   Survey local gardens, size, design and plants grown. The school garden, outdoor and indoor. Famous gardens: Garden of Eden, Kew Gardens, Gethsemene, Hanging Gardens of Babylon etc. Market, botanical and zoological gardens. Make a miniature garden. Garden pests, garden tools. Have you been 'led up the garden path'?

Gossip   See how quickly rumour spreads—line up a class of children and whisper a message along the line and see how different a message becomes by the end.

Growth   The growth of living things. What plants need: air, light, warmth etc. Our need for food and love. Measuring growth and charting development. Interesting growths—crystals, mould etc. Record growths (see *Guinness Book of Records*) When you die what will continue to grow?

Heroes and Heroines   Who is your hero? Famous heroes of the past: King Arthur, Robin Hood, the Greek Heroes. Heroes of today; sportsmen, popstars, TV or film stars. Awards for bravery, rescue work. Heroes and heroines in literature.

Hobbies   What is a hobby? Hobbies that involve making things, collecting things, playing games or sports. Hobbies are indoor or outdoor, pursued by oneself or shared with others. Also to 'get on one's hobby-horse'.

Holidays   Holidays derived from Holy Days. The Holy Days of the Year—Christmas and Easter. Types of holiday—travel, seaside, adventure, country etc. Special holidays—Bank Holidays, May Day, New Year's Eve (Scotland), Saint's Days (Catholic countries), national holidays (e.g. US Thanksgiving). Show holiday souvenirs, share holiday experiences.

Hunting   All animals need to hunt for their food. The difference between carnivorous and herbivorous animals. Man the hunter and the animals he hunts: fox, deer, rabbits, whales etc. Are blood sports cruel? Hunting horns, trophies, customs. The 'happy hunting grounds'.

If I Ruled the World   What improvements would you like to see in the world? What would you like to get rid of? What would schools be like? The men who tried to rule the world—Alexander, Napoleon, Hitler etc. Listen to the song 'If I Ruled the World' sung by Harry Secombe.

Insect Life   What is an insect? An insect's body, (head, thorax and abdomen), six legs. Habitats, life cycles and varieties. Harmful insects, disease carriers, (e.g. mosquitoes) and crop destroyers (e.g. locusts). Useful insects e.g. bees, silkworms. The danger of insecticides. Aesop's fable: The Ant and the Grasshopper.

Into the Future   The future belongs to the young. What will life be like in the year 2000? What hopes have you for a better world? What are your ambitions? Predictions and prophecies. Science fiction. Time machines.

Jealousy   We are all selfish in different ways, and envious of what others have got. Jealousy in families, jealousy among friends cf. the biblical story of Joseph and his brothers. Have you ever been 'green with envy'?

Joy   We all get joy in different ways, the joy of simple pleasures, the joy of surprises and of special occasions. Joy the girl's name, joy-rides. Song of praise: 'Give Me Joy in My Heart' (MHB no. 17). Negro spiritual: 'Shout for Joy' (FFC p. 5). Poem: 'Joys' J. R. Lowell (BTP p. 289).

Keep Britain Tidy   How to keep the environment cleaner, tidier and more beautiful. Where rubbish goes, rubbish that can be recycled (compost, glass, rags and paper); the problems of plastic and glass not rotting—do we need all that plastic wrapping? Britain has been called the dirtiest country in Europe—how can we change this?

Knights Knights of old and the meaning of chivalry. Armour and coats of arms. Lady knights (dames). The knighting ceremony. Famous men who have been knighted. Famous dames. The House of Lords, Knights of the Garter, Knights of the Round Table, Don Quixote. Hymn: 'When a Knight Won His spurs' (CP no. 50).

Laziness Lazybones, being slothful (the sloth—a South American mammal). Giving one's best. The saying 'If a job is worth doing, it's worth doing well'. Fable: The ant and the grasshopper (Aesop). Poem: 'Don't Care' (OBCV p. 29). Story: Lazy Jack (*Jackanory* B.B.C.).

Letters The importance of the written word. Types of written languages, forms of communication (notes, letters, postcards, air-letters). Calligraphy, hand-writing, varieties of print. Penfriends. The postal service. The Letters of St Paul. Poem: 'The Postman' J. Stallworthy *Town and Country* (Evans).

Local History What is of local historical interest? Where can local records be studied? How to study local history—archaeology, maps, remains, interviewing long term residents etc. Create a local guide book or historical display. Re-enact local life through the ages.

Loneliness 'I wandered lonely as a cloud' (William Wordsworth). Solitude. We're all alone at times. Those who are especially lonely—orphans, refugees, the old. The loneliness of those new to school, those without friends. What to do when you are alone. Song: 'Eleanor Rigby' (Beatles).

Love What is love? Real love is caring for people. We all need love. Those who love us. The difficulty of loving people all the time. The importance of forgiveness. People who show love today e.g. Mother Teresa, the Samaritans. 'Love thy neighbour' (*Matt.* 19.19). The Greek and Roman gods of love— Eros/Cupid. 'The King of Love my Shepherd Is' (MHB 30).

Luck Lucky charms—horseshoes, white heather, black cat etc. Lucky numbers, number 13. Lucky gestures—thumbs up, crossed fingers, touching wood. Astrology and lucky days, lucky jewels. Is there such a thing as luck? Superstition—ladders, mirrors, salt, clover, magpies, Friday the 13th.

Machines Machines in our lives—could we live without them? Large machines e.g. buses and small machines e.g. scissors. Energy to drive machines—wind, water, springs etc. Use of wheel, lever (e.g. see-saws), screw (e.g. car-jack). Machine made and handmade articles. What can man do that machines cannot? Song: 'Wheels keep turning' (*Apusskidu* p. 24).

Magic   From the Persian 'magus'—wise man viz the Magi. Charms and spells e.g. Open sesame, abracadabra. Black and white magic, witches and wizards. Conjuring and magic tricks. Magic squares in maths. Magic lanterns. See *Puffin Book of Magic Verse*.

Markets   Survey local markets. Market towns, market places, market days, market crosses and stalls. Special markets: Smithfield, Billingsgate, Petticoat Lane, market gardens, supermarkets, the Stock Market, the Common Market. Memory game 'One day I went to market and I bought . . .'

Martyrs   'Martyr' means witness (Greek). The martyrs in every age e.g. Socrates, St Stephen, Joan of Arc, Thomas à Becket, Martin Luther King. Would you be prepared to die for a good cause?

Measurement   The history of measurement—Egyptian, Roman, old English. Body measures: cubits (elbow to fingertip), fathom (arms outstretched), spans, paces, feet. Standard measures—the metric system. Size. Note: Goliath was 6 cubits and a span—how tall is that?

Messages   History—pigeon post, town criers, morse code, smoke signals. Messages at sea—the language of flags (Nelson). Postal services, telegrams, radio and TV. Messages in bottles, special messages—SOS. Messages in school. The message of Jesus.

Missionaries   Christian missionaries—Saints Peter, Paul, Boniface etc. Missions to Africa (Livingstone, Schweitzer); missions to India (Mother Teresa); UN peace missions. Having a mission in life.

Money   Currency, coins and notes. Decimal coins and coin collecting. History of money—use of shells, salt and gold. The Royal Mint. Foreign currency and rates of exchange. Bible: Widow's mite, the thirty pieces of silver. Is money the root of all evil?

Mountains   The stories of mountains—Mt Sinai, Mt Olympus, the conquest of Everest, volcanoes and Vesuvius. Mountain ranges and mountaineering. Song: 'Climb Every Mountain' (*Sound of Music*   Rogers & Hammerstein). Poem: 'Everest climbed' I. Seraillier (*Puffin Quartet* p. 185).

News   What's in the news today? The latest news, local news, school news. The news media, which newspapers are read. Gospel means 'good news'. What is good news?

Night Why do we have night? The need for sleep. People who work at night. Plants and animals. The night sky. The world of dreams and nightmares. Song: 'All through the Night' (Welsh trad.). Poem: 'In the Dark' J. Pridmore (FPB p. 21).

Numbers History of numbers—tallies, Roman numerals, the Arabic zero. Numbers around the world. Number rhymes, lucky numbers, number patterns, number facts. The numbers in your life. Who lives at No. 10?

Old Age The old people that we know, grandparents, neighbours. The old who are poor and lonely. How can we help? Invite a speaker from Help the Aged. Visit an old peoples' home—perhaps to sing songs, present Harvest offerings, Christmas cards or creative work. Poem: 'Alone in the Grange' (FPB p. 94). Resource Book: *Old Age* Lee Toomey (Wayland).

Parks A survey of local parks, nature trails. Famous parks, the royal parks, national parks. Design your own park. Poem: 'The Park' Olive Dehn *Town and Country* (Evans) p. 28.

Patience Patience is a virtue—do you have it? Being patient with other people, people who are patient with us, and the need to be patient with ourselves. The patience of Job.

Pattern Patterns in nature, patterns in art, crafts and movements, pattern in dressmaking. Geometry, Altair designs, spirograph, tessellations. Patterns in carpet, wallpaper, cloth. Patterns in life—whom do you pattern yourself on?

People Who Help Us People in our neighbourhood who help to make life easier—e.g. policemen, bus conductors, shopkeepers, school crossing patrol, firemen, ambulance drivers, postmen, milkmen. People who help in school—cook and dinner helpers, caretaker, secretary, welfare ladies, parents etc. Poem: ' The Dustbin Men' G. Harrison (FPB p. 38).

Pets A survey of pets in school. How to look after your pet, what it's like to be a pet (imaginative writing), the work of the RSPCA. Poems on dogs (FPB pp. 54–56). Poems on cats (FPB pp. 58–61).

Pilgrims Journeying to Holy places—Canterbury, Mecca, the Holy Land. The Pilgrim Fathers of 1620, *Pilgrim's Progress* (John Bunyan), Chaucer's Tales. Hymn: 'He Who Would Valiant Be' (CP 44).

Pioneers The first to lead the way, to try to discover something new. Pioneers in exploration, in medicine, in science. The pioneer you admire most. What would you like to be the first to discover?

Poetry Hold a poetry festival—recite favourite poems, make up poems, story poems. Illustrate poems in art, movement and drama. Try making sound effects and playing music to poetry.

Pollution Pollution of the air, of river and sea, and of the countryside. The effect on human, animal and plant life. Noise pollution. How you could improve your environment. *The Pollution Handbook* by R. Mabey (Penguin) is illustrated with childrens' project work.

Prophets What is a prophecy? Prophets of the Old Testament, the Prophet Muhammad. Astrology and reading the stars. Famous prophecies—oracles, the Ides of March, Old Moore's Almanack. What prophecies for the future do you have?

Protest In a democracy we have a right to protest about what we think is wrong. Protests at work: strikes, working to rule, marches, demonstrations, carrying banners, signing petitions, sit-ins. Protest songs, Speakers Corner. Local causes. Bible: Jesus and the Moneychangers (*Matt.* 21.12).

Rain The water cycle. Rain gauges, rainfall statistics. Great rains—monsoons, thunder and lightning. The effect of drought. St Swithin and rain-dances. When did it rain frogs? 'Raining cats and dogs'. Rainbows. Song: 'Singing in the Rain'.

The Red Cross The founding by Henri Dunant. Work of the Red Cross. Why the symbol was chosen (Swiss flag). Its equivalent in Muslim countries (The Red Crescent). The motto of the Red Cross 'Serve one another'. See *The Red Cross Story* B. Peachment (Religious Education Press).

Rescue The work of lifeboatmen, army, air, sea rescue, mountain rescue, lifeguards, mining rescue, flood rescue, underwater rescue, RSPCA rescue, St John's Ambulance Brigade etc. Bible: The Lost Sheep (*Luke* 15.4). Poem: 'The Rescue' I. Serailler (FPB pp. 52–53).

Rhythm The rhythms of nature, night and day, sun and moon, months, years, seasons. The rhythm of plants, opening and closing, growth and dormancy. The rhythm of life cycles, the rhythm of the body, pulse and heartbeat. The rhythm of the sea. Rhythmic sounds and music. The rhythm of words e.g. Longfellow's *Hiawatha*.

Rivers Survey local rivers, report on river life and pollution. The work of locks. River transport. Fords, river beds (and the treasures within) Design of bridges. The greatest rivers of the world. The pleasures and dangers of the river. Song: 'Michael Row the Boat Ashore' (*Ta-ra-ra boom-de-ay*, Black).

Roads   Local roads, traffic survey, roadbuilding. Roman roads. Road travel through the ages. Roads of the future. Road safety and the Green Cross Code. Bible: Road to Emmaus. Poem: 'Roads' Leonard Clark (COL).

Salt   Where salt comes from, rock and sea. The uses of salt in flavouring, preserving. The importance of salt for the body, perspiration. 'Salary' = salt allowance. Salt crystals, salt mines. Salt and superstition. Lot's wife. Salt solution. To 'rub salt into a wound', 'salt of the earth', an 'old salt', to be 'worth one's salt'.

School   What was it like when your parents were at school? What is the history of your school? How many people are involved in running your school? Why go to school? What would your dream school be like?

Scientists   Stories of great scientists, men and women—Archimedes, Leonardo, Galileo, Newton, Pasteur, Marie Curie etc. The use of theory, observation and experiment. Branches of science, and scientific apparatus. The wonders of modern science. Science fiction— the science of the future?

Shape   Shapes around us, regular and irregular. Geometry and the study of shapes. Making shapes with the body e.g. semaphore. Shape in design, tessellations, jigsaws. The streamlining of birds, fish, aeroplanes. Shape in nature. Are you symmetrical?

Ships and Boats   The history of boats from dug-out to QE II. Sea shanties. The life of sailors. Pirates. Parts of a ship. Caught in a storm (creative writing). The work of the RNLI lifeboat service. Poem: 'The Ships' J. J. Bell (BTP p. 393).

Shepherds   A man who tends his flock. Kinds of sheep and pasture. Sheep for meat, skin and wool. Sheepfarms and sheep dogs. Shepherd's crook and shepherd's pie. The Good Shepherd, Jesus Christ. The Lost Sheep (*Luke* 15.4). The 23rd Psalm. Shepherds at the Nativity. The Wolf in Sheep's Clothing (Aesop).

Skins   The functions of skin—pores, hair, oil and sweat, care of your skin, skin colour. Animal skins, camouflage, leather, fur. Animals that shed skin. Skin grafting, 'getting under one's skin', 'the skin of one's teeth', 'keep one's eyes skinned'. Have you a thick skin?

Small is Beautiful   The beauty of small things—babies, jewels, flowers, snowflakes. Use of the microscope. Bigger is not necessarily better. 'The prettiest things come in the smallest packages'. The virtue of smaller cars. Famous small people—David, Napoleon.

Sound Close your eyes, what can you hear? Sounds around us, sound waves, vibrations. Musical sounds. Pleasant and unpleasant sounds. Sound effects, which travels faster, sound or light? The effect of loud noises e.g. Joshua and the Walls of Jericho.

Speed The pace of life is getting faster and faster. What advantages and disadvantages has speed brought? The speed of travel, enjoyment of fast movement, speed records (see *Guinness Book of Records*). Speed limits (in 1865 it was 2 mph, in 1896 it was 12 mph, in 1903 it was 20 mph). Discuss the saying, 'More haste, less speed.' Story: The Hare and the Tortoise (Aesop).

Stories The pleasures of books and reading. Favourite stories, famous storytellers. Stories which teach a lesson–fables and parables. The difference between folktales, myths and legends. Tall stories, funny stories. Fact and fiction.

Strength The strength of a chain is its weakest link. Being strong in mind and body. The strong-willed 'mind over body', those who resist torture and repression, martyrs. Testing bodily strength, endurance, building strong muscles. The strong men of circuses and the Bible (Samson, Goliath).

Swimming Swimming as the best exercise, swimming for safety, the different strokes, diving, life saving, swimming galas and certificates. Water polo. Swimming gear—snorkel, flippers, hats, wings etc. Cross channel swimmers. Animals that swim—dolphins.

Symbols Pictures which tell us something. Symbols on roadsigns, weather charts. Religious symbols—the cross, crescent, the Star of David, the Buddhist Wheel, the Chinese yin/yang sign. Symbolism of colours, of metals and gems. Symbols of saints, in heraldry. Symbols for poison and danger. Symbols of companies e.g. British Rail. Symbols on badges—your school badge?

Talents What is a talent? Different talents—scholastic, artistic, sporting, domestic etc. Hidden talents. Making the most of talents (practice, concentration, the will to succeed). We are all good at something. Bible: Parable of the Talents (*Matt.* 25. 14–30).

Tea Where tea comes from. The tea plant (a camellia shrub). Processing tea. Kinds of tea, herb teas. Teahouses, kinds of teapots and teaspoons e.g. Apostle spoons. History of tea—in Pepys' Diary, the tea trade—clippers and smugglers, the Boston Teaparty. Story: 'The Mad Hatter's Tea Party'. Poem: 'On Making Tea' (J V III p. 36).

Television What are your favourite TV programmes? How much do you watch? The value of educational programmes e.g. wildlife, news. Are there better ways of spending your time? How does a television work? The production team. Your own programme e.g. 'This is your Life' (choose a well known character from history), or a quiz, or a news report of a Biblical story.

Temptation 'Lead us not into temptation'—what are temptations? When have you been tempted? The need to overcome temptation. Bible: Eve tempted by the serpent, Jesus tempted by the Devil (*Matt.* 4).

Theatre The history of the theatre (Greeks, medieval mystery plays, Shakespeare's Globe, modern theatres). Creating a production— author, director, actors, set designer, musicians, choreographer, stage crew, lighting, costume design, props, make-up, usherettes etc. Invite an actor or actress to talk of their work. See the anthology *Strolling Players*.

Time Are you always on time? Timekeeping—clocks, sundials, time-tables. GMT and summertime. Musical time, percussion rhythms, beating time. Music: *Clock Symphony* (slow movement) Haydn. Bible: 'To everything there is a season' (*Ecclesiastes* 3). Poetry anthology *Time's Delights*.

Toys How we learn through play. Favourite toys, discarded toys, toys through the ages. Mechanical toys, educational toys, home-made toys. Constructional toys. Toys—are they value for money? Design a toy. Collect toys for children in need. Music: *Toy Symphony* Mozart. Story: 'The Tin Soldier' Hans Andersen. Poem: 'Broken Toys' J. Kirkup (FPB p. 10).

Treasures Man's search for treasure, the idea of 'treasure islands'. Pyramids and archaeology. Exploration, metal detectors, treasure trove. The things we treasure e.g. shells, toys, momentoes. 'Treasures on earth' (*Matt.* 6. 19–21). Story: The Strange Treasure p. 241.

United Nations The organisation of almost all 'peace-loving states', the world family of nations. The headquarters in New York. The work of UNICEF and WHO. Its peace-keeping role. The UN flag and charter, UN Day (24th October). Can you do an A–Z of UN nations? Song: 'The Family of Man' (FFC p. 20). Bible: 'Swords into ploughshares' (*Isaiah* 2.4).

Voices How voices are used in speaking, singing, shouting, cheering, etc. Use of vocal chords, the voice box. Losing one's voice. Identifying voices, accents, foreign languages. Disguising one's voice (have a quiz). Recording voices. Echoes (see the Greek legend).

Washing The effect of germs and the need to keep clean. The washing of bodies, clothes, carpets, cars, pets etc. Washing-up (who does it?) Washing hands before meals, 'washing one's hands of something', viz Pontius Pilate. Baptism—the washing away of sins. Washing machines, dishwashers, detergents (whitest? cheapest?), launderettes. Song: 'Dashing away with the Smoothing Iron' (trad.)

Weather Types of weather. The importance of weather. Weather forecasting, instruments used: raingauges, windvanes, hydrometer, barometer, radar, satellite pictures. Old weather sayings. Weather around the world. Poems: *Weathers and Seasons* D. Saunders & T. Williams (Evans).

Weddings Wedding customs—church and registry weddings—bride, groom, trousseau, best man, bridesmaids, cake, guests, ring, vows, bells, honeymoon. Wedding anniversaries. Note: 'wed' is Anglo-Saxon and means a pledge. Bible: Marriage at Cana (*John* 2.1). The Ten Virgins (*Matt.* 25.1). Music: *Wedding March* by Mendelssohn.

Wheels Man's first invention? The need for hub or axis, spokes and frame. Wheels for transport. Mechanical wheels, wheels with cogs (clockwork). Wheels for pottery, grinding, pulleys, spinning, steering. Catherine wheels, roulette wheels, wheel-barrows, wheelchairs. The wheelwright. To put a spoke in someone's wheels. The Wheel of Life (Buddhist). The Wheel of Fortune.

Work There is work for each of us to do at home and at school. Doing our best—'if a job is worth doing . . .' Working together—'many hands make light work'. The work of fathers and mothers. The problem of the unemployed; what to do with increased leisure. History of children working in factories and mines. Children today who have no school and must work. The parable of the Workers in the Vineyard (*Matt.* 20)—what does it teach?

The Zodiac What are the signs of the zodiac, under which sign were you born? The sign, symbol and ruling planet of each zodiac sign. The earth, air, fire and water signs. Horoscopes. Music: *The Planets* Holst. Story: *Ludo and the Star House* by Mary Stewart (Hodder).

Stories

Anansi the Spider

Anansi the spider is well known to children in the West Indies. There are many funny stories about him because he is such a clever spider, full of tricks. They are called Anansi stories, and this is how they got their name.

Once upon a time, long, long ago, all things were named after the Tiger, for he was strongest of animals and king of the forest. The lily whose flower bore red stripes was called Tiger-lily, the moth with striped wings was called Tiger-moth, and the stories which animals told in the forest were called Tiger Stories.

Of all the animals in the forest Anansi was the weakest. Nothing was named after him. So one day Anansi said to the Tiger, 'Please, Tiger, just because I am weak everyone laughs at me. Your stories, would you let them be called Anansi Stories?'

'All right,' said Tiger. 'You can have my stories, but on one condition. You must bring me Mr Snake—alive.' The animals of the forest laughed. How could Anansi catch the great poisonous Snake?

The first thing that Anansi tried was to dig a large slippery hole, and put the Snake's favourite food, an avocado pear, in the bottom. Snake glided down the path and spied the hole. Carefully he wrapped his tail round a tree, lowered his body down the hole and ate the avocado pear. Then he pulled himself out by his tail and went on his way.

Next Anansi made a noose, covered it with leaves and placed two young bananas inside it. Soon Snake was gliding slowly towards it. Snake lay on the noose and began eating the bananas. Anansi pulled as hard as he could. The noose tightened but Snake slid through.

'If you do that again,' said Snake, 'I will bite you.'

'But I only want to measure you,' said Anansi. 'I bet with Tiger that you were the longest in all the jungle, even longer than that bamboo tree.'

'Of course I am,' said Snake. 'I am much longer than that!'

'I will cut it down for you,' said Anansi. 'You must lie down beside it and let me see.' Snake agreed to this, so Anansi cut down the longest bamboo, and Snake stretched out beside it.

'I will tie you at one end and that will help you stretch,' said the Spider. Anansi tied Snake's tail.

'Now stretch!' Anansi said. Snake did so, and as his head reached the end of the pole Anansi tied it as hard as he could.

'Got you!' laughed Anansi. And he had! Snake was tied fast at both ends to the bamboo.

'There you are, Tiger,' said Anansi. 'Can the stories be named after me now?'

'I always keep my promises,' said Tiger. 'You can have the stories. And this shall be called the first Anansi Story.'

(*West Indian folktale*)

Androcles and the Lion

Androcles was a slave who lived two thousand years ago in the city of Rome. He worked for a harsh master who treated him cruelly. One day Androcles could stand it no longer and he decided to run away.

Late one night when all the household had gone to bed, Androcles crept out of his dingy room, stole quietly across the courtyard, and slipped out through the back door. He knew he must hurry. By morning the soldiers would be out looking for him. So Androcles ran and ran, out of the city, away from his cruel master.

After many days travelling Androcles found himself in a wild, mountainous country. Here he thought he would be safe. He was tired of sleeping under trees so he found himself a large dry cave in which to make his home. Androcles ate a meal of berries which he had gathered in the forest, made himself a bed of leaves and lay down to sleep.

A little while later Androcles heard a noise. At first he took no notice. Then it came again, a sort of snuffling sound. Androcles sat up and rubbed his eyes. To his amazement he saw that it was a lion. Androcles froze in terror. There was no escape. The lion moved slowly towards him. Then Androcles noticed that the lion was limping. Instead of leaping at Androcles the lion held out its huge paw as if it had been hurt. Androcles looked carefully at the paw and noticed a great thorn sticking in it. Carefully Androcles took the thorn in his fingers and pulled it out. The lion seemed pleased to have the thorn out of his aching foot, and lay down quite peacefully to sleep by the side of Androcles. In fact the lion stayed with Androcles, guarding the cave, and bringing food to him.

As the days went by Androcles became less afraid of going out, knowing that his friend the lion was never far away. One day as Androcles was walking through the wood he felt a rough hand on his shoulder. Androcles turned round to see himself surrounded by animal hunters. They guessed that he was a runaway slave, and tied him up. In Rome they would get a rich reward for bringing back a runaway slave.

The penalty for a slave caught running away was death. Androcles was told that on the following day he would be thrown to the lions. The great stadium was packed with people come to see the show. The prison gate was opened and Androcles found himself in the middle of a circus ring. With a roar the animals' cage was opened and a great lion came bounding out. The lion headed straight for Androcles, its eyes flashing, its sharp teeth and claws bared. Androcles could do nothing but wait for the animal to pounce. The crowd cheered and then grew silent. For instead of leaping upon Androcles the great lion stopped and lay down at his feet. It was then that Androcles recognised his friend, the lion from the cave. He must have been captured by the animal hunters. The crowd was amazed. The Emperor sent for Androcles. The crowd roared for Androcles be set free. They gave the thumbs up sign which meant 'Let him go free'. The Emperor agreed. So Androcles and his lion were released, and no doubt as in all the best stories they lived happily ever after.

(Roman legend)

Anne Frank

In the Second World War the Jewish people who lived in Germany suffered greatly. The German leader was called Hitler and he hated the Jews. When things went wrong in Germany the Jews were blamed. Hitler decided to imprison or kill all Jews, not because they had done anything wrong, but just because they were Jews.

Many Jewish people fled from Germany. Among them was the Frank family. Anne, her elder sister Margot, and their mother and father moved to Amsterdam in Holland where they started a new life. Then in 1939 the war began. Germany invaded Holland. Then the cruelty towards the Jews began again. Every day thousands of Jewish people, old and young, were rounded up by Hitler's secret police. They were taken away and never seen again.

The Frank family knew they must hide, or they too would be captured and killed. But where to hide? Mr. Frank had an idea. Upstairs in the house where Mr Frank worked there were several spare rooms. The Frank family decided to hide in these rooms. A bookcase was pushed in front of the stairs, and the only window was blocked up. No one would know they were there—except for the kind Dutch friends who kept them supplied with food and books.

For two long years the family stayed in hiding, never able to go out, never able to make much noise and always fearful that they would be discovered. On Anne's thirteenth birthday she got a diary for a present. She called it Kitty and pretended it was an imaginary friend. From it we can learn what life was like during those years.

In Anne's diary she tells of narrow escapes when German soldiers came searching the house. She tells of quarrels that broke out, of her happiness and her boredom, and of the long hours she spent reading. Although it must have been a hard life, Anne is never bitter in her diary, even about the people who kept her from her freedom.

Then one day what they had been dreading all this time suddenly happened. Their secret hiding place was discovered. The bookcase was pulled away and they could hear the sound of feet pounding up the stairs. The police searched the rooms and threw all Anne's books on the floor. The family were all taken away and put into concentration camps. Anne never saw her parents again, and, just before the war ended, she died.

The only member of the Frank family to survive was Anne's father. When the war was over he went back to their house in Amsterdam. There he found Anne's books still lying on the floor, and among them was her diary. In it you can read what it was like to live in those dark times. So although Anne died, this brave girl will never be forgotten.

Atalanta's Race

There was once a king in Greece who had only one daughter, called Atalanta. When she was born her father was angry that the baby was not a boy. He ordered his servants to carry the young child into the forest and leave her there. He did not care whether she was eaten by wild animals, or killed by cold and hunger.

But Atalanta was lucky. She was found by a mother bear who nursed her. Later some hunters found her living in a bear's cave. One of the hunters took pity on the baby girl and brought her to his home. There she lived as his daughter. Every day they went out hunting together. Atalanta grew into a beautiful girl as well as the fastest runner in the kingdom. One day the king decided he would go and see the girl who could run so fast. When the king saw Atalanta he was amazed to recognise the birthmark on her arm. After learning of her strange history, he knew that he had found his daughter again. Overjoyed he took Atalanta back to his palace.

'Now you must find a handsome young man to marry,' he said to her.

But Atalanta did not want to marry anyone.

The king was growing old. He begged Atalanta to have a husband to help her rule the country when he died. At last Atalanta agreed.

'But I will only marry a man who can beat me in a race,' she said. 'If *I* win then his head shall be cut off.'

Many tried. But Atalanta who had run with the deer of the forest beat them all. And the unhappy losers were put to death just as she said.

A certain young man called Melampion saw Atalanta win one of her races, and was charmed by her beauty and grace. More than anything else he wanted Atalanta for his bride. How could he hope to win her?

'Perhaps the Goddess of Love will help me,' he thought.

So he went to the temple and prayed to the Goddess of Love to help him so that he could beat Atalanta. The Goddess drew near. She felt sorry for the young man who was so deeply in love. In a gentle voice she called him by name. He looked up and to his surprise saw three apples of pure gold lying before him. Carefully he picked them up, hid them in his tunic, and hurried from the temple.

On the day of the race a bright sun shone on those who came to watch. Atalanta and the young man stood ready on the starting line. The crowd cheered. The old king rose and gave a signal. They were off! Like the wind they flew, and the watchers held their breath. Gradually Atalanta moved into the lead. But what was that? A bright and glittering ball rolled in front of her. The young man had thrown the first of the golden apples. Hardly stopping, Atalanta bent down and picked it up. The young man raced ahead, but soon he was overtaken again by Atalanta's long, smooth strides. A second apple fell in Atalanta's path. Atalanta stooped to pick it up and again the young man went in front. In no time Atalanta had caught him up. The winning post came in sight with Atalanta well in the lead. The third apple came rolling beside her. Once again she stopped to pick it up, and the young man sped past her. As they crossed the finishing line he was just in front. Atalanta, the winner of so many races, had lost. The crowds cheered the winner. He had won not only the race but the hand of the princess—with the help, of course, of three golden apples.

(Greek legend)

The Story of Baden-Powell

Boy Scouts and Girl Guides started from the idea of one man—a man who loved life and the outdoors. His name was Robert Baden-Powell.

As a boy Baden-Powell loved to walk through the woods, searching for the tracks of animals. He did not know what all the marks meant but he was keen to learn. He often went camping with his friends. Once they went by canoe all the way across England. When they came to the end of one river they carried their canoe to the next. They caught fish and cooked their own meals. Baden-Powell realised you could learn a lot by camping and by living outdoors.

When he grew up Baden-Powell became a soldier. He had many exciting adventures, but his most dangerous moment came at a town called Mafeking in South Africa. Baden-Powell was sent to South Africa where the people called Boers, who were originally farmers from Holland, were fighting the British. The Dutch Boers wanted South Africa for themselves.

Baden-Powell was put in charge of defending Mafeking. He was not given many soldiers to help him. When war was declared thousands of Boer soldiers came to attack Mafeking. They surrounded the town and ordered Baden-Powell to surrender.

Baden-Powell refused. But how could he protect the town with so few soldiers? He had an idea. He would get the young boys of the town to help. He asked the young boys to run messages and become scouts for him. They were called cadets and they did much to help the soldiers defend the town. The boys were so busy running from one point of the town to another that the Boers thought there were many more soldiers than there really were. So rather than attack, the Boers were content to wait. One day Mafeking would run out of food and they would have to surrender. The seige lasted for months. When all the food was gone Baden-Powell ordered the horses to be killed one by one for food. Even their skin and bones were boiled to make soup. After 216 days the British army came to rescue the starving town of Mafeking. Baden-Powell became a hero and when he came back to England huge crowds were there to cheer him.

But Baden-Powell did not forget the boys of Mafeking. They did as much as the soldiers to save the town. So in 1907 Baden-Powell organised the first boy scout camp. He taught the boys how to put up a tent, how to light a fire, and how to cook. The boys followed Baden-Powell through the woods, and learnt to look carefully at small things, how to track animals and sail boats. These camping trips were so popular that Baden-Powell retired from the army and spent the whole of his life helping boys to form scout troops. He gave the scouts a uniform like the one he used at Mafeking, and he made the fleur de lys their special badge. All Scouts learned to 'Be Prepared,' and how to look after themselves and help others.

In those days girls were not supposed to run, or swim, or ride a bike. So Baden-Powell asked his sister to help him start scouting for girls, and these became what we call Girl Guides. Later the Cubs and Brownies were formed. Now there are Scouts and Guides all over the free world. Baden-Powell remained a Scout all his life. He died when he was 84. His last message to the Scouts contained these words: 'The real way to get happiness is by giving happiness to other people.'

The Bear That Spoke

One day in the cold lands of Canada two friends went out hunting. They were tracking a moose through the great pinewood forests. Snow carpeted the ground, and as their feet crunched through it they heard no sound. They did not suspect that as they followed the track of the moose there were two eyes watching them. The two hunters stopped, hoping to spot the flash of antlers through the trees. Behind them a dark shadow moved across the snow. Closer and closer it came. One of the hunters glanced round. 'It's a bear!' he shouted.

The huge bear, a mass of brown fur and claws, was almost upon them. Without a second's thought the two men ran. They knew that their only hope was to find a place of refuge. One of them pointed to a nearby pine tree, and as soon as he reached it began to climb faster than he had ever climbed before. His friend however tripped over a root in the snow. He fell with a crash.

'I think I've sprained my ankle!' he shouted.

The man in the tree looked round. The bear was still some way off. But he decided to carry on climbing.

The man on the ground lay quite still. The nerves in his body tingled with fear as he listened to the 'scrunch, scrunch' of paws on snow. The bear ambled up to him, and began to snuffle round his head. The man could feel the hot breath of the bear on his face. He didn't move a muscle. There was a scuffling of snow as the bear moved away.

'He's left me alone,' thought the man. 'He must have thought I was dead.' At once he felt the pain surge back into his sprained ankle.

High in the tree his friend saw the bear disappear into the bushes. He waited a few more minutes until he was sure it was quite safe, then slowly climbed down. He ran quickly to his companion who was still lying flat on the ground. The man's sprained ankle was soon bandaged up. Seeing his comrade was none the worse for his meeting with the bear, the hunter who had climbed the tree said, 'Oh, I knew you'd be all right. I guess you were safer down here than I was up that tree.' Trying to cheer his friend up he added, 'Hey, that bear was so close he seemed to be whispering something in your ear. Come on, tell me, what did he say?'

The other hunter, feeling rather hard done by, decided to say just what he thought.

'Well,' he replied, 'the bear did say that I shouldn't trust a friend who deserts you when things get difficult.'

(Canadian folktale)

Beethoven

Beethoven was born in Germany in 1770.

When Beethoven was a boy he would practise day and night at the piano and violin. He gave his first concert when he was eight years old and by the time he was thirteen he had become a church organist.

Life for Beethoven was never easy. His home was burnt down when he was a boy and his family moved to a town on the great river Rhine. One day the river overflowed its banks and flooded Beethoven's house. The whole family had to rush upstairs and escape through a window.

The more that Beethoven practised the piano the better he became. When he was seventeen the great composer Mozart heard him play the piano and said, 'Keep a watch on this boy, one day he will give the world something to talk about.' Beethoven began to write his own music and soon became a famous composer.

One evening as the moon shone down on the narrow streets of a town in Germany, Beethoven heard the sound of music coming from a small cottage.

As he drew closer he could see a little girl playing the piano. She was in fact playing a piece of music that Beethoven himself had written, but suddenly she stopped and burst out crying. Beethoven went into the cottage, and he discovered that the girl was blind. She had no music that she could read in order to play more tunes. So Beethoven sat down and made up a piece of music for her to play. As he played the candle in the room spluttered out, so Beethoven opened a window and the moonlight flooded into the room. Then Beethoven began to play his new piece of music in the moonlight. It was a simple tune with beautiful notes that the blind girl could copy. Later, when he got home, Beethoven wrote out the piece of music that he had been playing, and he called it the 'Moonlight' Sonata.

As Beethoven grew older something terrible happened to him—he began to go deaf. He could no longer hear the lovely music that he played on the piano. Sometimes he conducted an orchestra but he could not hear what they were playing, and the music went wrong. Beethoven had to use an ear trumpet if he wanted to hear anything, and visitors had to write messages to him on a board. Soon he was stone deaf, and he realised that he would never hear music again. Beethoven grew so sad and desperate that he wanted to kill himself. But with help and encouragement from friends he carried on composing. Some of his music was sad, but most was full of joy and hope.

During the Second World War coded messages were sent out from Britain. The signal was given by the opening of Beethoven's Fifth Symphony, the Morse Code signal of V for Victory—dot dot dot dash. In today's united Europe the theme music for the Common Market is taken from Beethoven's Ninth Symphony and is called the 'Song of Joy'.

The Beggar and the Fox

A holy man was once crossing a rocky desert, on foot, when he came upon a sight which made him sad.

'Bless me,' he said. 'Look at that poor fox lying there. It hasn't got any paws. It must have been caught in a trap. Well I hope the good God has pity on him and puts him out of his misery soon. He certainly won't live long in that state.'

And as the holy man could do nothing for the fox, he went on his way shaking his head sadly.

A month later the holy man came the same way and saw the fox still lying there.

'Goodness, gracious me,' he said. 'There is the same fox. I wonder how it has survived for so long. It looks so healthy, see how bright its eyes are!'

The old man continued on his way still wondering about the fox.

That night he lay in bed thinking about the fox, still puzzling how it kept alive although it could not move. So the next morning he decided to go back to the desert to find out more about this mysterious animal. Soon he was back on the same stony path looking at the fox. Just as he was moving towards the fox he jumped back in terror for suddenly he saw a terrible shadow between the rocks.

'God in heaven have mercy on me!' he cried. 'It's a lion! I am done for, it must have seen me.'

Trembling with fear he shut his eyes tight and waited for his end to come. Nothing happened. Time went by . . . still nothing. So very carefully he opened his eyes to see what had happened. The lion was still there but it was lying down next to the fox, munching contentedly on some meat it had brought. To the holy man's surprise the lion left his last chunk of meat for the fox to eat, and then disappeared between the rocks.

'Now I understand,' said the holy man. 'The lion is providing for the fox. How marvellous! If I hadn't seen it with my own eyes I wouldn't have believed it. Well, there's a *lesson* to be learned there. From now on I will be like the fox, and live on what others give to me.'

So he went back to the city and sat down with his few possessions by the city gate.

'Like the poor fox,' he said to himself, 'I will sit here and wait for the generosity of others.'

He sat there for several days, but everyone walked by him. Neither a friend, nor a stranger stopped to give him anything. He grew thinner and thinner, and weaker and weaker. He could feel his bones sticking out, and his stomach rumbled with hunger. Still he sat there.

After a few more days he was too weak to move, and at last someone stopped to speak to him.

'So there you are,' said the voice of one of his old friends. 'What on earth are you doing out here?'

The holy man tried to speak but his voice was barely a whisper. Slowly he told the story of the poor fox and the lion. 'Surely,' he said, 'there's a lesson to be learned from that!'

'Of course there is,' said his friend. 'But how could you have been such a fool? Couldn't you see that you were supposed to imitate not the needy fox, but the generous lion!'

(*Adapted from Sadi*)

The Bell of Atri

There was once in the city of Atri a good and wise king. He wished for nothing more than that his people should be happy and live in peace. So that there might be justice throughout the city he ordered a great bell to be hung in a tower. Tied to the bell was a long rope which nearly reached to the ground.

The bell of justice hung in the centre of the city. Its rope was so long that even a small child could reach it. The call of the town crier went down every street: 'Oyez! oyez! Hear ye the order of the king! If there be any among you who has not been justly treated let him ring this bell. Young or old, rich or poor, the king will hear your story, and justice will be done.'

The great bell of Atri hung in its place for many years. Many times it was rung by the poor and needy, and all who had been treated unfairly received justice from the king. As time went by the rope become old and frayed. A new one was needed, but none could be found which was long and strong enough. So the king had to go to another city for one, but it would be some time before the new rope arrived.

'What can we use to ring the bell with while we are waiting for a new rope?' asked the people. Someone had a bright idea. He cut down a long grapevine, and tied it to the great bell. It was spring time and the long vine rope was green with fresh leaves and shoots. The vine would do until the proper rope arrived.

Somewhere in the city lived a rich old soldier. He owned a horse which had carried him through many battles. By now the horse was too old and lame to do any work. So his cruel master turned him out of his stable, into the streets.

'Go and find your own food,' he said. 'You are no use to me.'

The old horse went limping off, and as the days went by he grew thinner and thinner. Just as he was about to collapse the old horse saw some fresh leaves hanging down in front of him. Tired and hungry as he was, the horse stumbled up to the leafy branch and gave a pull.

'Bong! Bong!' went the great bell.

From all sides people came to see who was pulling the great bell. There before them stood the old horse chewing on the grapevine.

'Bong! Bong!' went the great bell.

The king asked who it was ringing the bell of justice. To his surprise the old horse was brought in. The horse could hardly stand, its ribs stuck out and its legs were thin.

'Whose horse is this?' demanded the king.

Nobody knew, but it was not long before he found out the sad story of the old horse.

The king sent for the horse's cruel master, and ordered him to build a brand new barn for the horse and to feed him on the best of hay for the rest of his life. The old soldier realised how mean he had been to his faithful old horse, and felt truly sorry. Once more justice was done, and soon a new rope was found for the bell of Atri.

(A legend from Italy)

The Birds of Capri

In many countries birds are still hunted. Sometimes they are hunted so that they can be killed and eaten, sometimes so that they can be put in cages and sold as pets. If birds have bright coloured feathers and beautiful singing voices they are often in danger. In Europe these birds are very rare since so many have been caught and have died. Italy is one country where men still trap birds. This is a true story of one man who tried to stop the trapping of birds. His name was Dr Axel Munthe.

Dr Munthe loved to spend his holidays on the island of Capri in Italy. The sun always shines there and the sea around the island is sparkling blue. He liked Capri so much that he decided to buy a house and live on the island. But there was one thing about living on Capri that Dr Munthe did not like, and that was the way that the people of Capri treated their spring visitors— the birds.

Every spring flocks of birds go to Capri. They are migrating—flying north from Africa where they have spent the winter. It is a long way from the hot lands of the south to their colder northern homes and so the birds liked to stop for a rest on the way. One of these resting places is Capri.

When spring came the birds came too. Dr Munthe was glad to see them, and so were the people of Capri. They liked to catch the birds and sell them. To do this they made nets of very thin cotton which they hung across the bushes and trees. The nets were so thin that they could not be seen in the dark. The birds that flew to Capri were tired after their long journey. They arrived in the evening, and as they came in to land on the bushes and trees they became tangled up in the nets. They were then easily caught, put into small boxes, and sold in the town market. The birds stayed for the rest of their lives in tiny cages.

Dr Munthe did his best to stop the suffering of these wild birds, but the people of Capri got money from selling their birds and they would not listen to Dr Munthe. Dr Munthe asked the queen of Italy to help stop this trade but she could do nothing. So Dr Munthe decided to do something about it himself.

When next spring came he went out into the fields where the nets were, carrying with him a gun. He fired a shot into the air. The birds were frightened off and escaped the nets. The next morning the people were angry that they had trapped none of the birds. Dr Munthe was arrested, brought before a judge and ordered to pay a fine of £100. Dr Munthe said he would stop firing his gun, but would not stop helping the birds.

So next he trained his dogs to bark whenever they saw a bird. He took the dogs with him to the fields where the traps were waiting. When the birds came the dogs barked, and again they were saved from the nets. The bird trappers were angry once more. They killed one of Dr Munthe's dogs, and he realised that this plan would not work either. What could he do? He had another idea.

He decided that he would buy the fields where the traps were laid. But the man who owned the fields would not sell them. Dr Munthe thought he had failed again. Then the owner of the fields became ill. He sent for Dr Munthe. 'Sell me the fields and I will cure you,' said the doctor. The man felt so ill that he agreed. Fortunately the medicine that Dr Munthe gave him worked. So he bought the fields and the birds of Capri were safe. All because one man was determined to save them from the bird traps.

(From *The Story of San Michele*—the autobiography of Axel Munthe, 1929)

The Bishop's Candlesticks

Many years ago there lived in the town of Dijon in France a kindly old bishop. He was generous to all in need, no beggar was ever turned away from his door and no one who needed help was ever refused.

One day a poor traveller arrived in town. He was a large, rough-looking man in dirty ragged clothes. His face was sullen and he had a wild look in his eyes. People in the town were at once suspicious of this strange man and no innkeeper would give him a bed for the night. At last a woman took pity on the weary man and directed him to the Bishop's house.

The Bishop sat before a fire waiting for his evening meal. Suddenly the door burst open. It was the wild-looking stranger.

'I am looking for lodgings,' he said, 'and I was sent to your door. My name is Jean Valjean and I am a convict. I have been in prison for nineteen years. No one will give me a room for the night, not even a kennel to sleep in. I have walked all day and can't go any further.'

'Come in,' said the Bishop. 'Warm yourself by the fire, have supper with me and stay the night.'

So the convict stayed, ate a meal with the Bishop by candlelight and was given a clean bed to sleep in. But that night, as he lay in bed, Jean Valjean did not think of the food that he had eaten; he was remembering the gleaming silver plates on the Bishop's table. Then, when all was quiet, he crept downstairs, took the silver plates from the cupboard, put them into his bag and escaped into the night.

When the Bishop rose next morning he was surprised to see his guest and the silver had gone. But soon there came a knock at the door and there between two policemen stood Jean Valjean.

'We caught him running away with a bag full of silver,' said the policeman.

'Oh there you are,' said the Bishop to Jean Valjean. 'I'm glad you came back. You forgot the candlesticks, I meant to give you those as well.' And he handed his silver candlesticks to Jean.

'So you gave him the silver?' said the policeman in surprise. 'We thought he was a thief.'

'I have given him the silver so that he can make a new start in his life,' said the Bishop. 'Please let him go.'

The convict could hardly believe his ears, and tried to thank the Bishop.

'Do not thank me,' said the Bishop. 'Just remember to use the money to become an honest man.'

Jean Valjean the convict went on his way a different man. He remembered the Bishop who had forgiven him, and he kept the silver candlesticks to remind him for the rest of his life.

(*Adapted from Victor Hugo*)

The Boy Who Always Asked Questions

There was once a boy who always asked questions. 'Why is the grass green?' 'What holds up the sky?' 'Why have I got hair on my head?' He asked so many questions that his mother and father felt quite dizzy. They were always too busy to give him proper answers, but he kept on asking. 'Why have we got two eyes and only one nose?' 'Why does rain come down and never go up?' 'Why is there salt in the sea?' At last his parents grew so tired of all his questions that they told the boy he must leave home and seek his fortune.

So the boy set off. On the way he saw a beautiful girl sitting at a spinning wheel outside a little thatched cottage. She had long blonde hair and the boy at once fell in love with her. She was still spinning when the boy walked up to her.

'Excuse me, miss,' he said. 'Why does your spinning wheel always go round the same way?' The girl carried on spinning. So the boy tried again.

'Pardon me, miss. Can you tell me where this road leads to?' The girl did not look up, indeed she did not seem to know that he was there at all. He tried a few more questions, but still no answer. Then an old man came out of the cottage door.

'I'm afraid my daughter won't speak to you. She won't speak to anyone, not even to me her father.'

'Why won't she speak?' asked the boy.

'I don't know, ask her yourself.' So the boy did, but he got no answer.

'Any man who can make her speak,' said the father, 'can have her for a wife.'

The boy tried—'Why do bees buzz?' 'What are toenails for?' and so on, but not one word came in reply. Sadly the boy went on his way. He waved to the girl but she just kept on spinning.

Soon the boy reached a big city. Here he hoped to find his fortune. Having asked many people the way, he came to a big castle. A great crowd had gathered in the courtyard of the castle, for the king was seeking the cleverest man in the kingdom to marry his daughter the princess. 'Whoever can answer all the king's questions can marry the princess,' announced the royal herald.

The suitors had done very well and a few had answered every single question. They waited for the next one. But the king was looking round anxiously, and whispering to his counsellors. He had run out of questions! The herald was called, and forth came the announcement: 'His Majesty asks if there is anyone who would like to come forward and give him some questions.' There was silence. No one came forward. The king looked even more worried. Suddenly someone came forward from the crowd. It was the boy. He began whispering to the king. The king smiled. The boy kept on whispering. The king looked as if his head were spinning. So many questions!

In no time the king had found the cleverest suitor. He turned to the boy.

'Thank you for your questions. Now you may have anything that you wish—for one good turn deserves another. Now what in all the world would you most like?'

'A flying cow please,' said the boy.

The king looked a little puzzled, but as this is a fairy story, in a few minutes the boy left the palace holding a lead, and on the end of the lead, about five metres up in the air, was a flying cow.

It was not much of a fortune but the boy seemed pleased as he made his way back home. The first place he stopped at was the little thatched cottage. Outside, the girl still sat spinning. She looked up when the boy came near and her mouth dropped open.

'What's that?' she exclaimed.

'It's a cow,' said the boy.

'I often wondered why cows didn't have wings,'—for the first time the girl laughed—'it's a bit difficult to milk isn't it?'

She was speaking again! Her father was overjoyed. The boy asked her to marry him, and she agreed. Now he would have a wife to answer all his questions. He had found his fortune at last.

(European folktale)

The Story of Braille

Louis Braille was born in a little village near Paris in the year 1809. If you visit the village where he lived, called Coupvray, you will see outside his home a message written in both French and English. It reads, 'He opened the doors of knowledge to all those who cannot see.' The farmhouse is now the Louis Braille Museum.

Louis Braille's father was a saddler, making saddles for horses by cutting up thick leather skins. When Louis was a little boy, only three years old, he wandered into his father's workshop. The smell of the leather was good, and there were many shining tools to play with. Nobody was looking, so Louis picked up a sharp saddler's knife. A piece of leather was lying nearby. Louis took it and tried to cut it. But the leather was tough, the knife slipped, and its sharp curved point went straight into Louis' eye.

Louis screamed and his parents came running to see what had happened. They put a pad over his eye and the bleeding began to stop. But it was too late, for already dangerous germs had got in. Louis' eye became very sore. Little Louis rubbed his eyes and soon both of them became red and sore. For Louis the world grew darker and darker. Soon he could only see the outline of things, and in a while everything went black. His eyes were open but he could not see. Louis had gone blind.

Although he was blind Louis was able to do odd jobs around the house and help his father clean his workshop. Louis was a bright boy so his father arranged for him to go to a school for blind children in Paris. Being blind Louis could not read or write, but had to *remember* everything that he was taught. When he left school Louis was determined to spend his life helping other blind people. 'We who are blind are the loneliest people on earth,' he told his father. 'We can tell different birds by their songs, and find our way with our sticks, but without books we can never really learn.' But how could people read if they could not see?

Blind people find out about the world by touching things. Someone had devised books for the blind with raised letters, but the letters had to be very big for blind people to recognise them. Braille invented an alphabet out of small dots which blind people could read by touching. His system has been improved since then, but it is still named after him. Today the National Library of the Blind publishes many thousands of books in Braille, as well as Braille newspapers and magazines. Blind people can also play music by 'reading' Braille music.

Of all those good men and women who have helped the blind, none has done as much as Braille did when he showed how blind people could read with their fingers.

The Story of Buddha

Introduction The Buddha was born in 623 B.C., in northern India. He was a prince, the son of a wealthy king, and his name was Siddhartha. When he was born, his father sent for fortune-tellers. They said that he would one day leave his home and family. This prophecy would come true, they said, when the prince found out about old age, sickness and death.

This made the king very unhappy for the prince was the heir to the throne. So he gave orders that the prince should never know about old age, sickness and death. Siddhartha was to live in a special palace and have everything that he wanted. That way the king hoped that his son would never know of the outside world and so the prophecy would never come true.

How the Prince Saved a Swan

When Siddhartha was a boy, he was not allowed out of the royal palace, and he never saw people who were old, ill or unhappy. All he knew about were his rich family, their servants in the palace and the animals that lived in the palace grounds. The young prince Siddhartha learned how to read and write, how to ride a horse and how to shoot a bow and arrow. He became very good at all these things, so much so that his cousin, named Devadatta, became jealous of him.

But even when he was young, Siddhartha was of a compassionate nature. Here is what happened when he first found an animal that was suffering.

One day, Devadatta shot a beautiful swan with his arrow. The young prince was with him.

'Look at that,' said Devadatta. 'Shot him first time!'

The great white bird fell bleeding to the ground. As soon as he saw the swan fall, Siddhartha ran over to it and carefully pulled out the arrow. Then he took some leaves and began to wipe the blood away. He nursed the bird in his arms, stroking its white feathers.

Devadatta came up and said in an angry voice, 'Take your hands off my swan! You've no right to touch it. It's my swan. I shot it!'

'Yes,' replied Siddhartha. 'But I am trying to save it.'

'That's not fair,' said Devadatta. 'It's mine. I shot it. If you don't give it back, I'll take you to court.'

'All right,' said the prince. 'We'll let the court decide.'

Devadatta and Siddhartha went before the Judge in the royal courtyard of the palace. Whilst they had been waiting, Siddhartha had not parted with the swan. He kept it and nursed it. Who should the swan be given to? To Devadatta who had shot it or to the prince who had tried to save it? The Judge had to decide. He saw that the swan was recovering from its wound and said that the prince should be allowed to keep it because, due to his care of it, it was alive. Otherwise, it would have died. After some time, the swan

153

recovered completely and the prince set it free again.

All his life the prince cared for animals. He would never kill living beings and he told his followers that they should *kill no living things*. This was the Buddha's first teaching.

Siddhartha Discovers Suffering

The years passed. Then one day Siddhartha saw some dancing girls in the palace talking of how beautiful the trees were in the royal park just outside the palace. So he asked the king for permission to visit the park. The king reluctantly agreed, but only after he had sent his soldiers to make sure that Siddhartha would see nothing sad or unpleasant there.

Then the prince, in his magnificent chariot, rode out into the royal park. The trees and the flowers were beautiful. But by chance, he happened to see an old man. He was amazed, for he had never seen an old person before, and asked who he was.

'Just an old man,' replied his charioteer.

'No one has told me about becoming old,' said Siddhartha. 'Will I become old and wrinkled like that?' Reluctantly, the charioteer said that he would.

'I don't want to be old like that,' said the prince. 'Please drive me back to the palace. I must think about this.'

Later on he took another trip. This time he saw a sick man.

'Can anyone become sick?' he asked the charioteer.

'Yes, Sir,' came the sad reply.

'Turn back,' said the prince. 'I did not know that health could turn to sickness.'

On his next trip, he saw a funeral pass by. Startled, he asked, 'Why is that man lying under a white sheet? He does not move and the people are crying.'

'Sir, he is dead,' replied the charioteer.

'Will we all die?' asked the prince.

'Alas, my Lord, yes,' came the reply. 'No one escapes death.'

Siddhartha thought about this for many days, then took one more trip into the park. This time, he saw a holy man who was under a tree. Although he was poor, this man looked happy and contented. Siddhartha said to his charioteer, 'How can he be happy? Doesn't he know that old age, sickness and death come to everyone in this life?'

'He knows,' said the charioteer. 'But there is a way to happiness and it is up to each man to find it.'

That night Siddhartha decided to leave his home and family and search for a way that would end man's suffering. Leaving his riches behind, he put on a simple yellow robe, picked up a begging-bowl and went out into the world. He was 29 years old.

For six years, he went from teacher to teacher trying to find out why there is suffering and unhappiness in the world. At last, he realised that he must find out the answer for himself. He thought long and hard, sitting under a fig tree called the Bodhi tree.

Finally, the answer came to him that people suffer in life because they are selfish. He discovered that the secret of a happy life lay in helping others and loving all living things. From that day forward, he became known as the Buddha (the Awakened One) which means the person who discovered the secret of real happiness.

Even though he died 2500 years ago, people still remember the Buddha and try to be like him.

The Cargo of Wheat

Seven hundred years ago Stavoren was the richest and most beautiful city in Holland. The people of that town had many ships sailing to different parts of the world bringing back rich cargoes from the strange countries they visited.

The people of Stavoren were proud and hard. The richest, the proudest and the hardest of all was a lady. One day she sent for the captain of her grandest ship and said to him, 'Sail at once, my man, and bring me back a large cargo of the most precious thing in the world.'

'What is it that you want?' asked the captain.

'You must find out what the most precious thing in the world is,' said the woman, 'and bring me a large cargo of it. I am the richest person in Stavoren, and I want to amaze all my neighbours.'

As soon as the ship was ready the captain set sail. On reaching the open sea he called all his crew together and told them the orders that his mistress had given him. 'Now what in your opinion,' he asked, 'is the most precious thing in the world?'

'Gold,' said the first mate.

'Oh, no,' said another, 'fine silks are worth more.'

'The most precious cargo,' said a third, 'would be diamonds.'

The captain did not know which advice to take. Then the cabin boy spoke up. 'If you've ever been hungry you know what the most precious thing in the world is. It is what makes our daily bread—wheat.'

The captain and the sailors laughed at the cabin boy, but after talking it over they had to agree. They set full sail, and steered into the Baltic Sea to the port of Danzig. There they filled the ship with sacks of wheat and set out on the return voyage.

While they were gone their proud mistress had told all her rich friends in Stavoren that her captain was bringing back to her the most precious thing in the world. Everybody became curious and could not wait for the ship to return. In a few days the great ship sailed back into port.

'What have you brought me?' asked the lady impatiently.

'A large cargo of the finest wheat in the world,' said the captain.

'What!' screamed the woman. 'That common stuff! You wretch! You've made me the laughing stock of Stavoren. Now throw it all into the sea.'

In spite of the cries of the poor and hungry, the bags of wheat were emptied into the sea.

'One day,' said the captain, 'I hope you will find out what it is like to be hungry.'

The woman just laughed. After all she was the richest person in Stavoren. Soon after that a great storm began to rage. It lasted for many days and when it was over news came that all her ships had been wrecked. The storm filled the harbour of Stavoren with mud and sand, no ships could sail and all trading had to end.

The proud lady lived for some time by selling off her jewels. When these were gone she had nothing. Her rich friends did not want to know her. It was April and as she passed the deserted seaport she noticed that the sandbank was covered with green. The wheat she had thrown into the sea had been washed up by the storm and was sprouting in the mud. For the first time in her life the woman knew what hunger was. She waited patiently until autumn when the wheat was ripe, then led the poor people to the sandbank where they could gather the corn. When later the wheat was made into bread she realised that the captain *had* brought her the most precious of things.

(*Dutch legend*)

Columbus and the Egg

Five hundred years ago most people believed that the Earth was flat. Only a few thought that the Earth was round. One of those was Christopher Columbus. He said that he could sail around the world, and bring back with him the riches of China and India. Those who thought the Earth was flat said he would fall off the edge. Even those who believed the Earth was round thought that Columbus would have trouble sailing uphill on the way back!

At last on 3rd August 1492 Columbus set sail from Spain, and headed westward into an unknown sea. He carried with him a letter from the King and Queen of Spain which he said he would hand to the Emperor of China. He had three small ships, the *Nina*, the *Pinta* and the *Santa Maria*. No one had heard of sailing across the Atlantic before. No one knew that America lay undiscovered across the ocean.

The ships sailed for thirty days. No land was sighted. The sailors grew afraid. The sea seemed to go on for ever. They complained to Columbus and told him to turn back.

'Give me three more days,' said Columbus. 'I know that we will find land.'

Three days later they saw some birds, and some branches floating in the water.

'Look,' said Columbus, 'we must be near land now.'

On and on the ships sailed. Still no sight of land. The crew was getting angry and restless. Then one day from high up in the crow's nest came the cry, 'Land ho!' The lookout could see an island ahead.

'Hooray!' cheered the sailors. 'We have reached China!'

On 12th October 1492 Christopher Columbus carried the Spanish flag onto the new island. He knelt and thanked God for giving him a safe journey. He named the island San Salvador. Suddenly he noticed that strange people were watching him. Natives! They didn't look like Chinese. 'Perhaps this is India,' thought Columbus. So he called the natives Indians. He was rather surprised to see an Indian put a roll of brown leaves into his mouth and light it. The Spanish sailors had never seen tobacco before.

Columbus found many islands, but he never reached China, with its mountains of gold. At last it was time to return. Columbus took back with him six Indians, and some strange birds he had found. After an exciting journey they arrived back in Spain. Columbus was a hero.

Later the King gave a great feast for Columbus. This made some of his nobles jealous. Columbus was only a sailor, even though he called himself an admiral.

'Anyone can sail across the sea,' they grumbled. 'What makes him so special?'

When Columbus heard these moans he sent for some hard-boiled eggs. 'Can you make them stand up on end?' he asked. Each one of the nobles tried, but the eggs kept rolling over.

The King turned to Columbus. 'You show us how,' he said.

Columbus took an egg and slammed it down on the table. The egg stood up on its broken end.

'Anyone could do that,' grumbled one of the nobles.

'Yes,' said Columbus, 'but I thought of it first!'

The Courtesy of Saladin

During the Crusades the knights who went out to fight the Muslims for the holy places of Palestine came back with many new things they had seen and learned from their enemies. They brought back with them perfumes and medicines, carpets, Arabic numbers, strange fruits like cherries and apricots, and stories of the courtesy of the Arabs. Here is one of those stories.

The Crusading knights of King Richard had driven the Muslim army back into the great walled city of Acre. Inside this great city was Saladin, the chief of all the Saracens, and the remains of his once proud army. King Richard and his knights felt very pleased with themselves. They were driving their enemies out of the Holy Land, and now they had their greatest enemy Saladin himself trapped inside the city. But the question was, how were they to get him out? The walls of the city were very thick. Whenever the Crusaders came close to the great wooden gates they were driven back by a hail of stones and arrows. There was no way into the city. What could they do? They decided that the only way to win was to starve Saladin into surrender.

So the great army of King Richard camped all round the city and waited. No one was allowed in or out of the city gates.

'They will soon give in,' thought Richard, 'when their food runs out, and they have nothing to eat.'

The trouble was that King Richard's own men were rather short of food, but what was worse, as time went on they began to run out of water. The country around was a desert, the sun scorched down and the rivers were running dry. Day after day the knights sat in their tents sweating under their heavy armour and chainmail, waiting for Saladin to surrender. But nothing happened. They grew hotter and hotter, and thirstier and more bad tempered.

What the Crusaders did not realise was that inside the city there was a great store of food. Fresh fruit and vegetables were growing in their gardens, the people stayed cool in their houses, and inside the city was a spring of fresh water. Saladin gazed down from the city walls and saw how the Crusaders were suffering in the heat. Weeks had gone by, and still nothing happened. Then one day the great wooden gates of the city creaked open. Were they surrendering at last? King Richard was called from his tent to look. Through the gates of the city came a cart pulled by two huge oxen. Piled high on the cart were great, round things, coloured green. The wooden gates shut again, and the cart rumbled towards King Richard's camp.

'Look out!' shouted one of his knights. 'It might be a trap.'

The Crusaders stepped back as the cart moved closer and closer to the tents. Tied to the top of the carts was a message. King Richard called for it to be read to him. It read: 'A gift to King Richard, my honoured guest, by courtesy of Saladin.' The King looked suspiciously at the pile of round green balls.

'Which of my knights will test for me this gift from my enemy?' asked the King.

The knights eyed each other and shifted uneasily in their chainmail. At last one of them stepped forward. 'I will, Your Majesty,' he said, and very carefully he lifted one of the great balls from the cart. The other knights stepped back. The brave knight took his sword and cut into the skin of the ball. Inside it looked sweet and juicy. Slowly the knight raised it to his lips and sucked. A smile spread across his face and he sucked again. It was cool, sweet water tasting of honey. Saladin had sent them a precious gift—a gift of melons!

(*A legend from the Crusades*)

The Crowded House

There once lived a poor Jewish farmer named Yitzak who had a very large family, and lived in a very small hut. Yitzak's house was so crowded that his children had to take it in turns to sleep in the one tiny bed, and when everybody was in the house, hardly anyone could move.

At last Yitzak could stand it no longer. So he went to see the Rabbi to ask him what to do about this impossible situation.

The wise Rabbi thought hard and long, and at last he had an idea. 'I will tell you what to do,' he said. 'Bring your chicken to live with you inside the house.'

Yitzak couldn't understand how the chicken would help, but he trusted the Rabbi's wisdom and did as he was told. But as soon as the chicken was inside the house it grew frightened and flapped around the room, knocking Yitzak over and scattering its feathers everywhere.

So Yitzak went back to the Rabbi and complained. 'It only makes things worse,' he said.

'In that case,' said the Rabbi, 'bring in the goat to join your family and the chicken.'

Yitzak was even more confused, but he did as he was told. Soon the goat was running around eating everything he could see. First he ate Yitzak's bedspread, and then he started on the children's clothes. Yitzak hurried back to the Rabbi. 'My house is more crowded than ever!' he cried.

'In that case,' said the Rabbi, 'bring in your cow to live with your family, the chicken and the goat.'

Yitzak couldn't understand what was going on at all, but he trusted the Rabbi's wisdom. So he went home and brought in the cow. But the huge cow immediately knocked over all the pots and pans and plates, and then stepped in the baby's cot. By now the house was so crowded that no one was able to move. They all had to press themselves against the wall so that Yitzak could squeeze past. Then he rushed off once more to see the Rabbi.

'Rabbi,' he cried, 'there is no room to breathe in my house. If it stays like this we will all go mad!'

'Don't worry,' said the Rabbi. 'I have another idea. Go home and take the chicken, the goat and the cow out of the house.'

Yitzak was completely and utterly bewildered, but he did as the Rabbi had said. He put all the animals back in the yard, and then an amazing thing happened. Without the animals the house seemed as big as a mansion. There was room now to breathe, to walk around, to play games, enough room for all his children, his wife and himself. So Yitzak and his family learnt how to appreciate what they had, and they lived happily ever after in their huge little house.

(*Traditional Jewish story*)

Daedelus and Icarus

King Minos was one of the greatest kings the world had seen. He ruled the island of Crete and lived in a beautiful palace decorated with wonderful paintings and red pillars. His ships roamed the seas to bring him the treasures of the world. But the most prized of the King's possessions was not made of gold or silver—it was a fearful monster called the Minotaur.

The Minotaur had the head and shoulders of a bull, and the body of a man. The Minotaur was very savage so the King wanted to keep it in the safest place possible. He asked Daedelus, who was the greatest inventor in all of Greece, to build a home for the Minotaur—a home from which the monster could never escape. At the King's command Daedelus designed the Labyrinth, which was a maze of many walls and passages. Once inside it was almost impossible to find your way out.

The King was very pleased with Daedelus, but Daedelus was not happy. Although he was richly rewarded for his maze he felt that he was a prisoner in Crete. King Minos was so afraid that Daedelus might reveal the secret of the maze that he would not allow him to leave the island. Daedelus longed to return to his home in Greece, but how could he go when every ship which left the island was guarded by the King's men?

One day as he stared out to sea, Daedelus saw the graceful seabirds skimming high in the air, and he had an idea. If he could not escape by sea perhaps like the birds he could fly! Daedelus began to study the flight of birds, and to observe how their wings were made. He saw how the feathers of a bird overlapped, where some were small and others large. He measured the length of the wings compared to the size of the bird's body. He noticed how birds could glide along currents of air.

When he had found out all he could about the flight of birds, Daedelus with his son Icarus, began to collect as many feathers as they could. Then in secret he began to build two huge wings. He stuck the feathers together with beeswax and bent them into a curve like a bird's wing. He made a second pair, smaller this time, for his son Icarus. At last they were ready.

So very early one morning, before the sun was up, Daedelus took Icarus and their golden wings to the highest cliff by the sea shore. As Daedelus fixed the wings onto his son's shoulders he said, 'Now listen Icarus, follow me, and remember on no account must you fly too near the sun. Stay close behind me.'

Then having fixed his own wings, Daedelus took a great breath and jumped from the cliff. He was flying! Icarus followed his father, and soon two figures like great birds were flying over the shiny sea. It was a wonderful feeling. The ships on the sea looked like toy boats. Daedelus kept a watchful eye on his son, but the further they flew the less he looked back to Icarus. Icarus began to soar and swoop like a bird. He forgot his father's warning and flew higher and higher. By now the sun was shining brightly in the cloudless sky. As Icarus flew nearer to it, the wax on his wings began to melt. Icarus did not notice the first few feathers flying off his wings. He waved them faster and faster, but it was too late. With a shock of terror he realised that he was falling. His wings broke and fell from his arms. His body crashed into the sea.

In a while Daedelus looked round.

'Icarus! Icarus! Where are you?' he cried.

Nothing could be seen of his son, except far below a few feathers floating on the water.

(*Greek legend*)

The Day I Caught a Bus

Here is a story by a schoolboy, written about his favourite hobby—fishing.

My name is Graham. I like to go fishing whenever I can. Near us there's a shop which sells fishing things. It's called Bert's Tackle Shop. One day I asked Bert if I could help him out in his shop on Saturday mornings.

'All right,' he said, 'but remember to ask your Mum and Dad first.'

So I did. They said it was O.K., once I'd finished my homework. That's how I got my job at Bert's Tackle Shop.

It was great fun in the shop, looking after the rods and helping people choose their bait. The shop closed at lunchtime as it was a Saturday.

'Thanks Graham—here's a pound for you,' said Bert. 'Are you fishing tomorrow?'

'Yes,' I said.

So Bert said, 'Here take some maggots with you.' He put a big handful of maggots in a plastic bag. I put the bag in my pocket and off I went.

I had to catch a bus. There was a long queue. By the time I got the bus it was nearly full. So I had to stand. As I was standing there I thought of the lovely rods Bert had in his shop. You could have caught a shark with some of them. All of a sudden there was a scream. I'd forgotten all about the maggots in my pocket. Some of them had fallen out of the bag into the shopping of a lady standing next to me. That's when she screamed. I picked out the plastic bag to have a look, and more of the maggots fell out. Then someone jogged me and I dropped the whole lot. What a mess. There were maggots everywhere—down the backs of seats, on the floor, in shopping bags, in people's hair. One little girl even got a maggot in her ice cream. People were brushing maggots off their clothes, out of their shoes. Everyone was looking to see if they were sitting on a maggot. I thought I'd better get off quick, so I rang the bell and ducked for the door.

Bert asked me the next week whether I'd caught anything with the maggots.

'Only the bus,' I said.

The Death of Becket

Over 800 years ago England had a king called Henry II. He was not only King of England, but he was Duke of Normandy in France as well. When Henry was young his best friend was Thomas à Becket, who was also a Norman. The King and Thomas were both fine, strong young men. They loved to ride, hunt and drink together. They were the very best of friends. So when the King was asked to appoint a new Chancellor, he chose his best friend Thomas.

Thomas was good at being Chancellor, and advising the King what to do. Henry was a lively King, full of ideas and always wanting to be doing something. Unfortunately he had one big weakness—he had a very bad temper. When the slightest thing upset him he would fly into a terrible rage, and say things which he was sorry for when he cooled down. Thomas knew how to deal with the King's outbursts, he could put things right and smooth things over. No matter how angry the King got, Thomas would always remain patient and helpful.

One day the Archbishop of Canterbury died, so the King decided that Thomas was just the man to take his place. Thomas would be sure to settle any quarrel between the King and the Church. The King did not realise that now Thomas was Archbishop of Canterbury, he was the head of the Church. Thomas felt that he had a new master—he no longer worked for the King, but for God. King Henry did not understand that.

Just as Thomas had been a good servant of the King, he now became a good servant of the Church. Soon Thomas and Henry began to quarrel. They could not agree about certain laws and customs. The King said he was right. Thomas said that what the Church said was right. Things became so bad that Thomas was banished to another country. After six years he returned to England, hoping that everything now would be all right. But it was not to be.

A quarrel broke out about who owned some land near Canterbury. Thomas said it belonged to the Church, but some of Henry's barons said it belonged to them. When news of this was brought to the King, he flew into one of his rages. 'Will no one rid me of this troublesome priest?' he cried.

Four knights who were with the King looked at each other. Here was a chance to win the King's favour they thought. So off they rode together to the town of Canterbury where Thomas lived.

It was a Tuesday night, four days after Christmas. There in the middle of the town stood Canterbury Cathedral. Candles shone through the coloured windows. From inside came the sound of prayers. Out of the shadows came the knights, beating upon the great doors with their swords. Thomas ordered his monks to open the door. The knights walked up to Thomas Becket and stabbed him to death.

The news of this terrible murder spread quickly through the land. Everyone blamed King Henry. They thought that he had ordered the knights to kill Thomas. The King was full of sorrow that his few angry words had killed his old friend. To show how sorry he was he walked barefoot through the streets of Canterbury and prayed for forgiveness in the Cathedral, and told the monks to whip him as a punishment. But nothing he did could bring back the man we now call Saint Thomas Becket.

If you go to Canterbury you will see these words cut in the wall over the spot where Thomas was killed: 'Thomas Becket Archbishop—Saint—Martyr—died here Tuesday, 29th December 1170.'

All because of a few angry words.

The Story of Divali

Long ago, the story says, there was a king in India who was growing old. 'One of my sons must rule in my place,' he said, and he chose Prince Rama whom all the people loved because of his courage.

But one of the king's wives, Kaikeyi, the mother of Prince Bharata, was angry that her son was not chosen. More than anything else Kaikeyi wanted her son to be the next king, and now Rama had been chosen. How could she persuade the king to change his mind? Then she remembered.

Years before the king had taken Queen Kaikeyi out hunting in his chariot. Suddenly a tiger had attacked the king, and Kaikeyi had killed it with her bow and arrow. While she nursed the badly mauled king back to life, he said to her, 'Good wife, you saved my life, and you have nursed me back to health. For these two good deeds I will grant you two wishes.'

Kaikeyi had laughed and said, 'Your love is all I need, I don't want any other wish.' Now she remembered the two wishes, so she went back to the king.

'My lord,' said Kaikeyi, 'do you remember long ago when I saved you from that tiger in the forest, and nursed you back to life, that you promised me any two things that I wished?'

The king thought and after a while said, 'Yes Kaikeyi, I do.'

'Will you grant me those two wishes now, my precious lord?'

'Why certainly,' said the king, 'I swear that I shall do whatever you wish.'

'First,' said Kaikeyi, 'make Bharata, my son, king instead of Rama. Second, banish Rama for fourteen years.'

The king could not break his promise, so Rama was sent into the forest, and Bharata was made the crown prince.

The king was broken hearted and soon he died. Prince Bharata was upset by his mother's trick, and went in search of Rama.

'Our father is dead,' he said. 'Come back and be our king.'

Rama refused. 'I was banished for fourteen years,' he said. 'I will not return until that time is over.'

'Give me your golden sandals,' replied Bharata, 'I will put them on the throne in your place. They will remain there until you return to claim your throne.'

So it was when fourteen years were over, Rama's brother went to fetch him.

'Let us go to greet Rama!' cried the people. They hurried from their houses with lamps in their hands to light their way through the dark forest. It was a day of rejoicing when King Rama claimed his sandals and his throne. It was a day of light after a time of darkness.

The Dolphin and the Lyre

Long ago men looked into the night sky and saw pictures in the stars. Each group of stars made a pattern which stayed the same as it moved across the sky from west to east. They made interesting shapes like animals or giant people. Sometimes stories were made up about these stars. One is called the Dolphin, the other has two curving arms and is called the Lyre. The Lyre is a kind of harp. What could connect a harp with a dolphin?

There once lived a famous musician called Arion. There was no one in the whole kingdom of Corinth who could play sweeter music. Whenever Arion picked up the harp everyone stopped to listen. Not only was he a musician but he was a poet also. He liked to enter competitions, where his songs always won first prize.

One of these competitions was held on the island of Sicily. Here again he was the winner of many rich prizes with his lovely singing and playing. These he carried back to his ship, ready to return to Corinth. The sailors could see the precious objects of gold and silver that Arion was bringing back with him. How they wanted to get their greedy hands on the prizes! So they plotted together to kill Arion and share among themselves what he had won.

That night Arion had a dream. In it the god Apollo appeared before him, golden and shining. Apollo was the god of music. In his dream Apollo told Arion of the sailors' plot to kill him. He also told Arion of a way to escape.

When morning came the sailors gathered around Arion and told him he was about to die. Arion begged that he might for one last time sing to the music of his lyre. The sailors agreed to let him sing one song. As Arion sang, fins began to appear in the waters around the ship. Just as he ended the song Arion leapt into the sea. The ship sailed on, leaving Arion sinking under the waves.

Fish with great shining bodies swam towards Arion. It was a school of dolphins. They had heard the beautiful sound of Arion's song as it drifted over the sea and had swum closer to hear him. One of the dolphins rose to the surface with Arion riding on its back. On they swam with Arion astride the dolphin, one hand clutching the fin on its back, the other still holding his precious lyre. Arion was carried like this right back to land.

Eventually Arion returned to Corinth to find that the sailors were busy telling the king how Arion had drowned in a storm. Just as they had finished their story, in walked Arion. The king ordered that the sailors be put to death for trying to kill his favourite musician. So Arion recovered his prizes, though to him no prize was as precious as his lyre. That night the god Apollo made a lyre and a dolphin out of the stars, so that all would remember how Arion was saved by a dolphin who loved music.

(*Greek legend*)

The Dragon's Teeth

There was once a prince called Cadmus who grew tired of his life in the royal palace. He wanted to create a city of his own and be its first King. For many years he searched, travelling over land and sea, looking for the right place to build his city, but he could not decide which would be the best site.

One day he was resting at a town called Delphi when he heard a voice which said, 'Follow the cow. Where the cow lies down, there is your home.' The words seemed to come from a hole in the rocks, or had he been dreaming? The words echoed in his mind. Later that day Cadmus saw a cow standing by the roadside chewing the grass. As Cadmus came closer the cow walked leisurely away. Was this the cow that the voice had spoken of? The cow walked on and Cadmus followed. For miles they walked until at last the cow lay down. 'This then,' said Cadmus, 'will be my home.'

His city would be here, but first they would need to find water. He sent one of his friends to see if there was a river nearby. His friend had not been gone long when he was suddenly startled by cries, shouts and screams coming from the river. Cadmus ran to see, and there appearing from the waters of the river was the giant head of a dragon. As its great jaws opened Cadmus could see many rows of sharp shining teeth. With a crunch the jaws closed on the body of Cadmus' friend.

Cadmus was so angry to see his friend killed that he drew his sword and rushed at the monster. The dragon hissed in rage and his rows of teeth flashed in the sunlight, then he snapped his mighty jaws at Cadmus. Cadmus ducked just in time and stabbed the monster with his sword. The dragon lashed its tail, writhed in the water, and then lay still. It was dead. Cadmus sat down exhausted. A strange voice seemed to be whispering to him, 'Cadmus, take out the dragon's teeth and plant them in the earth.' Was it a god speaking to him? It was a strange request, but Cadmus obeyed. He cut out the dragon's sharp fangs and sowed them in the ground.

When he had finished Cadmus leant on his sword, quite out of breath, and wondered what would happen next. Suddenly helmets and spears began sprouting from the ground. Armed soldiers were growing from the earth, a vast army was growing from the dragon's teeth. Fear struck at Cadmus' heart. If the soldiers attacked he would be killed at once. So he picked up a large stone and flung it into the middle of the army. The soldier who was hit thought that he was being attacked so he started to fight the soldiers around him. Confusion spread and soon all the soldiers were involved in a fierce battle with each other. At last when only five soldiers remained standing Cadmus shouted at them, 'Stop!' They obeyed, then looked at Cadmus waiting for his next order. 'Come,' said Cadmus, 'instead of fighting use your strength to help me build my new city.'

And that, according to the legend, is what happened. The soldiers who had been the dragon's teeth helped Cadmus build a new kingdom.

(Greek legend)

The Emperor's New Clothes

Many years ago there was an Emperor, who was so fond of new clothes that he spent all his money on getting the latest fashions. He had a different suit for each hour of the day. People would say of other kings, 'He is sitting in counsel,' but it was always said of him, 'The Emperor is sitting in his wardrobe.'

One day two rogues, calling themselves weavers, arrived at court. They declared that they could weave material of the most beautiful colours and patterns. The clothes made from this would remain invisible to anyone who was unfit for office, or who was too stupid to see.

'These must indeed be splendid clothes!' thought the Emperor. 'If I had such a suit I could find out who in my realm was unfit for office, and who was a fool.' So he gave the weavers a large sum of money and ordered them to begin work at once. The two pretend weavers set up a loom and called for the finest silk and thread of gold which they quickly hid away.

'I should like to know how the weavers are getting on,' thought the Emperor. But rather than go himself, he sent his faithful old Minister.

The honest old Minister went into the hall where he saw the rogues working with all their might at the empty loom. They asked him how he liked the design and whether the colours were not very beautiful. The poor old Minister looked and looked but he could see nothing. He did not want to be thought a fool, so he said, 'Oh it is admirable! I will tell the Emperor how beautiful it is.' The Minister listened carefully as the rogues described the patterns of the material, and went back to tell the Emperor.

The Emperor next sent another officer of his court to see when the cloth would be ready. He too could see nothing but empty frames.

'Isn't the cloth beautiful?' asked the rogues.

The messenger did not want to be thought unfit for office, so he too said to the Emperor when he returned, 'The cloth is beautiful, magnificent.'

So the Emperor himself decided to see the cloth. But when he arrived the two imposters were still busy at an empty loom. The Emperor could see nothing. Not wanting to seem a fool or unfit for office he said, 'Oh how beautiful.'

All his courtiers strained their eyes before saying, 'Magnificent! Charming! Excellent!'

The following day a great procession was to take place. The rogues sat up the whole of the night before, pretending to be hard at work finishing the Emperor's new suit. They rolled up the invisible cloth, cut the air with their scissors and sewed with needles without any thread.

'See!' they cried at last, 'the Emperor's new clothes are ready!'

So the Emperor came to be dressed. He took his old clothes off and the rogues pretended to dress him in his new suit.

'Do my clothes fit well?' he asked.

'Perfectly,' said the imposters.

Out walked the Emperor under a high canopy. The whole city had come out to see the Emperor's splendid clothes. They knew how special the clothes were supposed to be so all cried out, 'How beautiful, how elegant, how graceful are the Emperor's new clothes.'

'But the Emperor has got nothing on!' said a little child. And soon what the child had said was whispered through the crowd.

'The Emperor has got nothing on,' cried all the people.

The Emperor walked on trying not to notice, but he too realised what a fool he had been.

(adapted from Hans Andersen)

Ewongelema

Once long ago there was a terrible famine in Africa. All the animals were starving and there was no food to be found anywhere. After a long search they came to a huge tree which was covered in delicious fruit. None of the animals knew the name of the tree. Just as they were about to eat the fruit of the tree the Lion said: 'Wait! It is never safe to eat the fruit of a tree unless you known its name.' The animals agreed.

The trouble was that nobody knew the name of the tree. One or two animals said that they had known the name of the tree once, but now they had forgotten it.

'Well,' said the Lion, 'we must ask the Spirit of the Mountain. He knows everything. He will know the name of the tree, let us send our fastest runner to ask him.'

So they sent the Hare. It was a long way from the forest to the mountain but the Hare ran fast. Sure enough high above the forest sat the Spirit of the Mountain.

'O Spirit of the Mountain. What is the name of the tree that stands in the bush? We animals are dying of hunger. If only we knew the name we could eat the fruit and not starve.'

'Yes,' said the Spirit, 'I will tell you the name of that tree. It is Ewongelema.'

'Ewongelema,' said the Hare. 'Ewongelema. Thank you, Spirit, I will not forget it.'

The Hare kept repeating the name on his run back when ... bang! He ran straight into an anthill. When he got up he was quite dazed. What was the name? 'Ooh, woo ... oh dear.' The hare had forgotten. When he got back to the animals all he could say was 'Ooh, woo ... something like that.' So the animals sent the Water Buffalo.

When the Buffalo reached the mountain the Spirit gave him the same answer—'Ewongelema.' The Buffalo carefully repeated the name 'Ewongelema.' He thanked the Mountain Spirit and galloped back towards the animals. Faster and faster he went until ... bang! He ran straight into the anthill. When he got back to the animals he too had forgotten the name.

'I shall go!' roared the Lion. 'I shall not forget.' So off he went. The Spirit of the Mountain told the Lion the name, and he repeated it again and again all the way back. 'Ewongelema! Ewongelema! Ewongelema!' When ... bang! He landed head first in the anthill. 'Yoo, wong ...' The Lion growled. He too had forgotten the name.

Who would go now? 'Let me go!' said the Tortoise. All the animals looked at him, the slowest of all animals. They let him go but they did not think he would be of any use. Off the Tortoise went, plodding along on his little legs. Eventually he arrived at the Mountain, and once again the Spirit said, 'Ewongelema.' Slowly the Tortoise turned round and started on his long journey back. He was the last chance the animals had. Slowly and carefully he went, repeating the name over and over to himself. Oops, what was that in the middle of the path? Better plod round it. So the Tortoise missed the anthill.

When the Tortoise arrived he was so tired he could only whisper. 'Ewongelema!' But the animals heard. They knew the name. The fruit was safe to eat, and the hungry animals had a fine feast. The Tortoise had remembered, and the animals were saved.

(Zambian folktale)

Famous Footsteps

Robinson Crusoe

Robinson Crusoe is the story of a man shipwrecked on a desert island. It was written by Daniel Defoe and has become one of the most famous stories in the world. It is written as if Robinson Crusoe himself is telling the story.

We hear how his ship was caught in a storm, and wrecked on the rocks off an island in the South Seas. Robinson Crusoe was the only survivor. He managed to swim to shore. There he had to make his own shelter and find his own food. He lived all alone for the island was deserted, at least that is what he thought. But after many years of being quite alone a remarkable thing happened. This is how he described it:

'It happened one day about noon, going towards my boat I was exceedingly surprised to find the footprint of a man in the sand. I stood like one thunderstruck, or as if I had seen a ghost. I listened, I looked around me, but I could hear nothing, nor see anything. I went up a hill to see further, but I was all alone. I went up the shore to see if there were any more prints, but there was only one. How it came here I knew not, nor could I in the least imagine. Like a confused wretch I returned to my home, and terrified to the last degree; looking behind me every two or three steps, mistaking every bush and tree, and fancying every stump at a distance to be a man.'

Who made that footprint in the sand? Perhaps you would like to read on and find out for yourselves.

Quo Vadis

St Peter was the first Bishop of Rome. The Roman Emperor at the time was a cruel and ruthless man named Nero. Nero hated Christians and he ordered his men to hunt them down. When Christians were captured they were crucified or thrown to the lions. The man that Nero most wanted to capture was Peter, who was the leader of the Christians in Rome. Peter's friends urged him to flee from Rome, and at last Peter agreed.

Peter left Rome early one morning, and made his escape along a great Roman road called the Appian Way. Peter had travelled some distance when a very strange thing happened. In front of him he saw the figure of a man. Peter stopped in amazement. The man was Jesus. It was then that Peter spoke three famous words—'Quo Vadis Domine?' which means 'Where are you going, Lord?' Jesus replied, 'I am going to Rome to take your place as leader of my flock.'

At that moment Peter knew he must return to Rome. So Peter turned back, and as he turned he left his footprint on the cobbled stones. Once back in Rome Peter's friends were overjoyed to see him, but this joy did not last long for he was captured by soldiers, and Nero ordered him to be crucified. Peter said he was not worthy to be crucified in the same way that Jesus had been, so Peter chose to die on the cross upside down.

If you visit Rome you can still see Peter's footprint, for where the footprint was found a Church was built. It is called the Quo Vadis Church and it is on the Appian Way. There you can see preserved that same footprint, made in the cobbled stone when Peter turned back to Rome.

Feeling the Elephant

One day an Indian merchant was about to set out on a trip to Arabia when he had an idea.

'I will take with me an elephant,' he thought. 'The Arabs have never seen an elephant. They are a curious people. I am sure they will pay me well for the chance of seeing one real live elephant.'

So the merchant bought himself an elephant and took it with him on his long journey to the Arab lands.

After much travel the merchant came near to an Arab city. He camped outside the city walls until the sun set. When it was quite dark and he was sure that no one could see, he led the elephant into the city. Once there he shut the elephant in a large, dark house, and waited until the next morning.

When the sun rose the Arabs were surprised to see this notice pinned up outside the house: 'Hurry, hurry, come and see a real live elephant. On exhibition for one day only. Queue here.' Already one or two people were waiting outside the closed door, and soon a crowd began to gather. No one had ever seen an elephant before, and there was much excited whispering.

'What did an elephant look like? Was it that animal with a horn on its head? Would it bite?'

At the appointed hour the door opened and there was the Indian merchant. 'One at a time,' he announced. 'There is only room for one at a time.'

The elephant stood in a dark room. The windows had been blocked up to stop anyone peeping in. The first man paid his money and was told to go in.

Inside, it was pitch dark. The Arab could not see a thing. He reached out one hand, and yes he could feel the elephant! He moved his hand up the elephant's trunk and then down again. When at last he came out his friends crowded round him.

'What was it like?' they eagerly asked.

'It was just like a long fat snake,' said the man.

By now the second person was inside the dark room feeling the elephant. When this man reached out his hand he felt the rough skin of the elephant's ear. He walked carefully round the outside of the room, reached out, and felt the other ear. Again the crowd gathered excitedly round when he came out.

'Well?' they asked. 'What was the elephant like?'

'It had wings,' said the man.

'Nonsense,' said the first man. 'Snakes don't have wings!'

'Huh, you'll see if I'm not right. We'll ask the next one who comes out.'

The third man groped his way into the dark room. His hand touched the leg of the elephant, he felt carefully up and down, then came out to tell the others, 'It's a tall, straight thing just like a pillar.'

'No, it's long and floppy like a snake,' said the first man.

'It's a kind of bird!' said the second man, and soon they were involved in a great argument. Things got no better when a fourth man came out. He had felt all along the elephant's back.

'You can sit on it,' he said. 'It's just like a great big throne.' So the arguments raged on. Each one had felt the elephant, and each one had a *part* of the truth.

Only the merchant knew the whole truth, and he wasn't telling anybody.

(*Adapted from Rumi*)

The First Christmas Tree

An old German legend tells us how a spruce fir became the first Christmas tree.

Many of the customs of Christmas time belong to religions which are much older than Christianity. In Northern countries like ours, Midwinter's Day fell in the same week as our Christmas and it was always a time of strange customs and festivities. Houses were decorated with evergreens, candles were lit and a yule log was burnt as a sign that spring was returning. Not all the pagan customs were happy ones. One of the ways the pagan worshippers had of pleasing their gods was to offer sacrifices. The most terrible of these was to put to death a living person.

Germany in those days was a wild country, and not the place people wanted to go to preach the Christian message of peace and love. But there was one very holy man who said he would take to the dark German forests the message of God. He was an Englishman and his name was Boniface.

One frosty night in December he was walking in a wood when he came upon a group of people worshipping their pagan god. They had gathered under a huge oak tree to make a sacrifice to Thor, the thunder god. Their victim was to be a little boy. Boniface had arrived just as the boy was being led forward under the sacred tree to be killed. But what could Boniface do to save the boy from these fierce tribesmen?

Boniface seized a huge axe, and swung it with all his strength against the trunk of the greak oak. The crowd was amazed. The people expected Thor to strike him down with a thunderbolt. Instead the only sound they heard was that of the axe biting into the tree. A last great blow fell, there was a tremendous cracking sound, the greak oak slowly leaned over and came crashing to the ground. As the tree fell Boniface noticed something strange growing between its roots. It was a little fir tree, an evergreen spruce, with its tiny green spikes glistening in the light of the torches. Seeing it growing there gave Boniface an idea.

He turned to the people and said, 'From this night I bring you a new religion. Let the young fir tree be your new emblem. It is the wood of peace, since your houses are built of it. It is the sign of eternal life, for its leaves are evergreen. It points to Heaven and is from this day the tree of the Christ-Child.'

Many years later it was a German who brought the first Christmas tree to England. More than a century ago Prince Albert, the husband of Queen Victoria, set up the first decorated Christmas tree in Windsor Castle for the Royal Family to enjoy. And we have been enjoying them ever since.

The Five Pound Note

Mrs Brown was on her way to London. It was her birthday and she was going to spend the five pound note which her husband and children had given her as a present. As she climbed aboard the London train she was wondering what she would buy with her money. There was only one other person in the carriage—a shabby old lady who sat opposite her clutching her handbag.

Mrs Brown put her own bag down beside her and soon drifted off to sleep dreaming of the bright lights and big shops of London. After a while Mrs Brown woke up with a start. She had a feeling that something was wrong. She glanced at her watch and realised the train would be arriving soon, so she opened her handbag to take out a comb. When she looked inside she could not see her five pound note. Had she lost it? Hurriedly she searched her bag and her pockets. There was no sign of the money. Where could it have got to?

Mrs Brown did not know what to do. She looked across to her travelling companion. The old lady seemed to be fast asleep, could she have taken it? When Mrs Brown was asleep the old lady could have leant across and taken the money then. How else could it have gone?

The old lady herself was asleep so Mrs Brown realised she could find out whether her suspicions were right. Carefully she reached across towards the old lady's handbag. Mrs Brown's heart was pounding and the palms of her hands felt moist. With shaking fingers she opened the handbag and looked inside. To her surprise she saw a five pound note.

Mrs Brown wondered what to do. Should she wake the old lady and accuse her of stealing? Should she call a guard on the train, or wait till she found a policeman at the station? No, she had a better idea. Mrs Brown carefully took the five pound note from the old lady's bag and tucked it into her own handbag. Perhaps she would forgive the old lady, after all she was poor and Mrs Brown had got her money back. So she did not say a word about it.

As the train pulled in Mrs Brown put her bag securely under her arm, took one last look at the sleeping old lady, and went off to the shops.

Later that evening, when she got home with her present, Mrs Brown began to tell her husband what happened. 'You'll never guess what happened to me today,' she said.

'I know,' said her husband, 'you forgot your five pound note. I found it on the table after you'd gone,' and he took the note from his pocket and handed it to her.

Mrs Brown could not say a word. At once she realised her terrible mistake. The old lady had not stolen her five pound note after all. Mrs Brown was heartbroken. 'This has certainly taught me a lesson,' she said. 'In future I shall always check my facts before I accuse others of doing wrong.'

Food for Thought

Aesop was one of the most famous story tellers in Greece. He was a slave but everyone loved to hear his wise and clever stories. Aesop knew the importance of tongues to speak, and as a cook he knew the importance of tongue as a food to eat. Here is a story about Aesop's tongue.

One day Aesop's master asked him to prepare a meal out of all the best things he could find. Aesop said he would. When the time came Aesop's master could hardly wait for this beautiful meal to be served. He knew that Aesop was a good cook, and always did just as his master asked.

Aesop's master sat down and licked his lips. Aesop set the table and brought in a big dish. On the dish lay one piece of tongue.

'What is this?' asked his master. 'Is this the most precious food you could find?'

'Yes, master,' said Aesop. 'If there were no tongues there would be nothing to taste with, and no kind or pleasing words to speak. A tongue is the most valuable of things.'

'This tongue,' said his master, 'is food to eat and food for thought.'

When he had finished his meal, Aesop's master said, 'For my next meal I want you to make a dish out of all the worst things you can find, but make sure the result is tasty.' And of course Aesop said he would.

The time came for the next meal, and Aesop's master sat at the table, wondering what Aesop would bring him. Once again the master found on his plate a large tongue. 'Aesop, why have you given me tongue again?' he asked.

'Tongues are the best and worst of things,' said Aesop. 'Just as they bring happiness so they can bring unhappiness. Bad words, lies and unkind thoughts are all spoken by tongues. A tongue can be the worst of things.' Again his master had food for thought.

(*Traditional Greek story*)

The Forgotten Treasure

Once upon a time there lived a poor shepherd who spent all his days tending a small flock of sheep. He lived in a small cottage in a valley with his wife and two young sons. Every day he would walk with his sheep over the hills helping them to look for fresh grass to eat. One day as they were crossing a hill the shepherd saw a tiny blue flower. He had never seen one quite like it before. Carefully he picked it up and smelt it. Then he tied it to his shepherd's crook and called his sheep to him. He had decided to take this pretty blue flower back with him to give his wife. She was sure to be pleased. Then suddenly a small figure sprang out from behind a tree.

'You're a lucky man,' he said. 'What a treasure you have found to be sure. Take that flower and touch that rock on yonder hillside. The rock will open up and inside all the hidden treasure—gold, silver and diamonds, will be yours. But don't forget the best treasure of all!' And with that the little green man disappeared.

The shepherd stood there for a moment wondering what to do. Had he been dreaming? Well there was only one way to find out. He took the blue flower from his wooden staff, walked up to the rock and gently knocked on it. At once there was a great rumbling noise and the rock slowly cracked open. The shepherd peered inside. There were some steps in front of him which led down into the·darkness. Taking a deep breath the shepherd walked in and went carefully down. At first he could not see anything. Then slowly his eyes got used to the dark. There seemed to be heaps of things on the floor sparkling and winking at him. Gold! Silver! Diamonds!

Quickly the shepherd put the tiny blue flower down and, taking the old bag that was on his shoulder, began to scoop up as much treasure as he could. As he poured it into his bag a tiny voice seemed to be whispering in his ear, 'Don't forget the best! Don't forget the best!'

But the shepherd could only think of the gold, the silver and the diamonds. When he had picked up as much as he could carry he hurried away back up the stairs leaving the little blue flower behind. As soon as he was out into the open air ... Crash! The rock closed up again.

The shepherd ran home as fast as his legs would carry him, clutching his bag of treasures. 'Look what I've found!' he shouted as he came in the door. Quickly his family gathered round. 'I bet you've never seen treasure like this,' he panted as he opened the bag. And inside the bag there was nothing—nothing but dust and ashes. What had gone wrong? Then the shepherd remembered. He had forgotten the little blue flower, the flower that he had found for the first time.

As fast as his legs would carry him the shepherd ran back to the rock. But it was closed and try as he might he could find no way in.

Then faintly he heard these words: 'Forget-me-not! Forget-me-not!'

In his greed for riches the shepherd had forgotten the greatest treasure of all.

(European folktale)

The Story of Galileo

Galileo was one of the greatest scientists who ever lived. He was born in 1564, in the little town of Pisa in Italy. When he was young he studied to be a doctor. But he was always questioning things. He liked to experiment to find out if what people said was true really did work. One day he discovered that something which everyone believed, was not really true. And he could prove it.

Everyone thought that a heavy object fell to earth faster than a light one. Galileo found out by experiments that this was wrong. Nobody believed him. So he invited them all to see for themselves. The day came and the crowds gathered around the famous building in Pisa called the Leaning Tower. Galileo climbed right to the top of the tower with two cannon balls. One of the balls weighed half a kilo, the other weighed five kilos. While the crowd gazed from below Galileo dropped both balls from the top of the tower at exactly the same time. The crowd gasped—to their amazement the balls fell together and hit the ground at the same moment. Galileo had proved that the pull of gravity is the same for heavy and light objects.

The old professors were so amazed and angry at being proved wrong that they said it was all a trick. 'Galileo has played a trick on us,' they said. 'It must be magic.' But when they saw that anyone could do the same experiment they had to admit that Galileo had shown the truth.

Galileo loved to study the stars. He built a wonderful new telescope so that he could see further into the sky than any man before him. He was able to show that the moon was not just a smooth ball of metal, but that it had many mountains on its surface. He saw for the first time that Jupiter had many moons of its own. He was also able to study the sun.

One of the great ideas that Galileo studied was whether the sun really went round the earth, as his teachers had told him, or whether the earth went round the sun. Galileo now spent all his time studying the planets through his telescope, until he was sure that the earth, and all the planets, circled the sun. The professors and church leaders were angry when they heard this. 'The earth,' they said, 'is the centre of the Universe. Galileo is wrong. He should be punished for not telling the truth.' So Galileo was arrested and brought before the court.

It took great courage for Galileo to stand up and say, 'All of you are wrong. I am right, the earth goes round the sun and I can prove it.'

They would not listen. They said to Galileo, 'We will torture you, and then kill you, if you do not say you are sorry and tell everyone that you are wrong.'

Galileo knew he was right. But what should he do, stick to the truth and be tortured, or say he was wrong and escape? Galileo said he was sorry, and that he was wrong.

So they let him go saying, 'We don't trust you, Galileo. We will keep you from now on under house arrest. You will not be allowed to leave your house for the rest of your life.'

Galileo died a poor and unhappy man, but he knew that one day there would be others who would discover the truth for themselves.

The Story of Gelert

Many years ago there was a prince of Wales called Llewelyn. He loved hunting and had a fine pack of hounds. But there was one dog he loved more than all the others, and the name of this dog was Gelert.

Not only was Gelert a fine hunting dog, he was also a good-natured animal, and he was loved by Llewelyn and his family. One day the prince decided he would like a day's sport so he set out with his men for the hunt.

His faithful dog Gelert was left in the castle to guard Llewelyn's baby son who was lying asleep in his cradle. Soon the sound of the hunting-horn disappeared into the distance. Gelert was left alone.

After a while Gelert heard a strange sound. He pricked up his ears and sniffed the air. Something or someone was shuffling up the deserted corridor. Gelert stood in front of the cradle. What was that strange scent? The half-shut door slowly opened and a wolf stared hungrily in. Gelert growled.

For a moment the two animals stood facing each other. The wolf, his fangs bared, looked beyond Gelert and saw the baby. Here indeed was a tasty meal. The wolf leapt towards the cradle. Gelert leapt too, at the wolf's throat. The two animals were locked together, snarling and biting. The battle was long and savage. There was flesh and blood everywhere. The cradle was overturned but the baby lay safe under the blanket.

At last Gelert made one final effort and sank his teeth deep in the throat of the wolf. The wolf writhed, then lay still. Gelert fell to the floor, weak from loss of blood, and began to lick his wounds.

At that moment Prince Llewelyn returned from the hunt. A terrible sight met his eyes. His baby's cradle was overturned on the floor in a pool of blood. Gelert himself had blood on his mouth. Seeing the look of horror and amazement on his master's face Gelert came forward to lick his feet.

'Wicked animal, where is my son?' shouted Llewelyn. 'You have killed and eaten my only child.'

Gelert could only look up with innocent eyes. Llewelyn drew his sword and plunged it into his dog's heart. Gelert's dying howl did something that the noise of the fight had not done. It woke Llewelyn's child. Quickly Llewelyn pulled the cradle aside. There lay his baby boy, and beside him lay the body of the biggest wolf he had ever seen. The noble Gelert's only reward for saving the prince's son was death.

Today, south of Mt Snowdon in Wales, you will find the little village of Beddgelert. In Welsh Beddgelert means 'the grave of Gelert', and the faithful Gelert will never be forgotten while Beddgelert stands.

(*Welsh Legend*)

The Gift of Camels

The Arabs have always been great mathematicians. The numbers that we use were originally Arabic numbers. Here is a story in which we see some Arab mathematics. But what is important is not the mathematics but the message it gives. Here is the story.

One day an old Arab sheikh died. Although he was chief of his tribe he was not a rich man. All his wealth lay in his 'ships of the desert', the camels that he owned. His camels had provided him with food and milk, with transport across the sandy wastes, and with skins to make his tents. He had three sons, and now that he had died they would own the camels. But first they would have to listen to the reading of the old man's will, to see how his camels would be shared out between them.

The whole family gathered together in the old man's tent. His three sons were there ready to hear their uncle read the old man's will. The uncle read out how the herd of camels were to be divided between the three sons. The eldest would receive half of the camels, the second would receive one third of them, and the youngest would receive one ninth. The will ended with these words: 'Whatever you give in love, it shall come back to you.'

The sons now knew how the camels were to be divided, but how many camels did the old man have? They quickly rounded up the whole herd, and counted them. There were seventeen camels. How were they to be divided? The eldest was to receive half of them, but what was half of seventeen? The next was to receive a third, but what was a third of seventeen? The youngest was to receive one ninth, but what was one ninth of seventeen? They couldn't work it out, so they asked the best mathematicians of the tribe. But none could solve the problem.

So they went to see their uncle, perhaps he could help. The uncle took out the will and read it again: 'Whatever you give in love, it shall come back to you.'

'Now I understand,' he said, 'what I must do. I will give you one of *my* camels to add to the others, that will solve the problem.' The brothers scratched their heads. How would this help? Of course! Now there would be eighteen camels. The oldest son quickly thought of his share, a half of eighteen is . . .? The next son thought of his share, one third of eighteen is . . .? The youngest thought of his share, one ninth of eighteen is . . .? The camels could now be divided according to their father's will. Of eighteen camels the eldest would have nine, the next one six and the youngest two. How many camels is that? Seventeen! There was one camel over. What on earth would they do with the extra camel?

The three sons knew what they should do. They thought it would be a nice surprise for their uncle to give him his camel back. But the old uncle was not at all surprised.

'I knew something would come back to me,' he said. 'Always remember— whatever you give in love, it will come back to you.'

(Arab story)

The Goddess of the Sun

When the world was young it was warmed by the beautiful Goddess of the Sun whose name was Amaterasu. It was the warmth from her rays that made the rice and all manner of plants grow. She pleased both men and gods with the beauty of her radiant light.

The brother of the Sun Goddess was the Storm God. He was a mischiefmaker and had a violent temper. The Goddess loved and cared for him, but nothing would stop her brother from behaving badly.

One day, in a rage, the Storm God flooded the rice fields and tore the roofs from the houses. There had never been such a tempest before. It broke the Goddess's heart to see how many had been killed or injured by her brother's thoughtless act. Instead of begging forgiveness, the Storm God just blew into the Goddess's face and laughed.

It was the final straw. The Sun Goddess could stand her brother's unruly behaviour no more. She had had enough. She hid inside a cave and blocked the entrance with a rock. At once the world grew dark and cold. Evil spirits roamed the earth, and the voices of the people cried to heaven. But the Sun Goddess would not leave her cave. The world was dying. So the gods decided that something must be done.

They called a great meeting. What could they do to tempt the Sun Goddess out of her cave? The God of Thoughts helped them to make a plan. They brought with them to the cave many fine gifts. These included a rope of jewels, a great mirror and many pieces of silk cloth. The Storm God, ashamed of what he had done, brought as his gift a great sword. These gifts were hung on a tree outside the cave. Surely they would tempt the Sun Goddess to return? The gods waited and watched. Nothing happened. The cave stayed shut.

Then chickens were brought to the cave to set up a great crowing. Bonfires were lit and songs were sung. One of the goddesses began a merry dance. Soon the sound of laughter filled the air. Deep in her cave the Sun Goddess was amazed. What could she hear? What could it be that was making such noise? Curious to know what was going on she called out, 'What is making you so merry?'

'We have found a Goddess more beautiful than you,' the Gods replied. Very slightly the cave door opened. At once one of the Gods held up the mirror and showed it to the Sun Goddess. She was fascinated by her reflection. Gradually the rock door opened and light flooded into the world. The Goddess came out and gazed at the mirror. The God of Strength grabbed her and pulled her further out. Then another God placed a rope across the cave so that she could not go back.

The Sun Goddess promised that never again would she hide her shining face, and from that day to this she has kept her promise.

(Traditional Shinto story)

Grace Darling

Of all the stories of rescue at sea none is so famous as the true story of Grace Darling.

Grace was born in 1815, the year of the Battle of Waterloo. Her father was a lighthouse keeper on the wild Northumberland coast. As she grew up she learned how to clean the great lantern at the top of the house, and how to row the small lighthouse boat.

She came from a large family—with eight brothers and sisters. As they grew up they all left the lighthouse and went out into the world, except for Grace. Grace was not a very strong girl. She preferred to stay at home with her father and help him run the lighthouse.

One night in 1838 disaster struck. A great storm blew up. Great waves crashed on the rocks, the thunder roared and lightning flashed. Heavy black clouds rolled across the sky. This was a dangerous night for any ship at sea. They kept a small boat in the lighthouse, which it was Grace's job to look after. So, as the storm died down, she went out to see if the boat was still safe.

It was about five in the morning when Grace climbed down the lighthouse steps on her way to check the boat. She clambered across a rock and there was the boat still safely tied. Grace stared out across the sea, and saw a terrible sight. A ship lay wrecked upon the rocks, with people clinging onto its sides and shouting for help. Grace ran back to tell her father. The waters still raged and the winds blew.

'It is too dangerous for us,' said her father, 'we've only got a small boat.'

'Oh please, father,' Grace begged, 'if we do not try to save them they will all drown.'

Her father listened to her pleading and looked across at the desperate figures clinging on to the rocks. Should they take their small boat into the stormy seas and try to rescue the people from the wreck, or stay in the lighthouse where it was safe?

Grace and her father pushed their small boat out into the wild sea. The boat was tossed about on the great waves. The sea swamped in, and every now and then as a huge wave raised the tiny boat they could see the helpless people on the rocks. They rowed on nearer and nearer to the wreck.

At last Grace's father jumped out onto the rocks. Grace was left to manage the boat alone as her father helped the exhausted survivors. They rescued four men and a woman from the rocks, and rowed them to safety. Then back they went through the raging seas a second time for those who were still left. Then for a third time they made the awful crossing. Altogether seventeen people were saved. Had it not been for Grace's determination they would all have died.

The news of Grace Darling's brave rescue spread all over Britain. The Royal National Lifeboat Institution gave her a silver medal, and she was given a special reward. Hundreds of people wrote her letters after her story had appeared in all the newspapers. A famous poet called William Wordsworth even wrote a poem about her. Her night of courage had made the girl from the lighthouse famous.

Greyfriars Bobby

One of the famous sights of Edinburgh is the bronze statue of a dog, sitting on top of a granite fountain. The dog is a little Skye terrier, who, though small, became one of the most famous animals who ever lived. His name was Greyfriars Bobby.

The story of Greyfriars Bobby began in the middle of the last century. Wednesday was market day in Edinburgh, and every week on that day people would flock to the shops and stalls. Among them was Mr Gray, and his shaggy little Skye terrier called Bobby. At exactly one o'clock a gun was fired from Edinburgh Castle high above the town. This signalled lunchtime for Mr Gray, who left the market and went to his favourite restaurant, Traill's Dining Rooms.

Year in and year out it was the same. Mr Gray would hang his coat near the door, lean his stick against the wall, and choose something from the menu. Bobby would sit at his master's feet and have his lunch, usually a large bun followed by a big, meaty bone. They never missed a single Wednesday.

But in 1858 Mr Gray died. He was buried in the churchyard of Greyfriars in Edinburgh. Three days later it was market day again. At lunchtime people began to gather in Traill's Dining Room. The one o'clock gun boomed over the town. Then Mr Traill got a surprise, for there, coming into the restaurant, was the tiny, bedraggled figure of Bobby.

Mr Traill recognised him at once, and gave him his usual bun and bone. But instead of sitting under a table to eat it, Bobby carefully picked up the food and disappeared down the street with it. Next day exactly the same thing happened. On the third day Mr Traill followed Bobby. To his surprise Bobby hurried to the cemetery, sat down where Mr Gray was buried and ate his lunch.

Mr Traill found out that Bobby had run away from the relatives of his dead master who had taken him to live with them. So he was taken back. But he ran off a second time, then a third. It was no good. Nothing could stop Bobby staying with his master. The cemetery keeper tried. He said it was against the rules for dogs to be in the cemetery. It said so on a notice. But Bobby couldn't read, and when the gate was locked he just scrambled over the wall.

Some people tried to tempt him away with delicious food, but Bobby would never leave his master's grave except to fetch his food from Mr Traill.

In winter Bobby became cold and wet so someone gave him a comfortable kennel to sleep in.

For fourteen years Bobby kept watch by his master's grave. He became one of the 'sights' of the city. And when he died in 1872 he, too, was buried in Greyfriars, in a flower-bed near his master's grave. The grave can still be seen, as can his collar in the city museum. But his most famous memorial is the statue, a statue to one man's best friend.

Guy Fawkes

When Queen Elizabeth died in 1603 everyone wondered what the new king would be like. His name was James; he was already King of Scotland, so now he became King of both England and Scotland. James was not a popular king. He quarrelled with members of Parliament, and with anyone he did not agree with. Above all he quarrelled with Roman Catholics. He said that Catholics should not follow their religion, and threw many of their priests in prison. So a group of Catholics met in secret and they decided to kill the King. One of these Catholics was named Guy Fawkes.

Guy Fawkes was a soldier. He was a brave man who had fought in the Spanish army for ten years. But most important of all, he knew about gunpowder. For the men who were plotting to kill the King wanted to blow him up, and Guy Fawkes agreed to help them.

The plotters knew that the King was going to open Parliament on 5th November. That would be a good opportunity to kill the King and many of their other enemies as well. But how could they get the gunpowder into the Houses of Parliament?

They solved this problem by renting a house right next door to the Houses of Parliament. Under this house was a cellar. From here they could break into the cellars which ran beneath the House of Lords, right under the spot where King James would be sitting.

So the work began. They carried by night thirty-six barrels of gunpowder and hid them in the cellar. On top of the barrels they put loads of firewood. No one seeing the piles of firewood would ever think that two tons of gunpowder were waiting ready to be set off. Finally Guy Fawkes laid a thin trail of gunpowder which would burn for a quarter of an hour before the whole lot blew up. This would give Guy Fawkes enough time to escape once it was lit. At last everything was ready.

Guy Fawkes went down the dark cellar steps on 4th November, sat himself by the barrels of gunpowder, and waited for the morning when the King was due to open Parliament and he would light the fuse. The hours went by. It was cold and lonely with only a few rats for company. Not a sound was heard. Then at midnight there was a knock on the cellar door. Who could it be?

Suddenly the door flew open and soldiers appeared.

'I arrest you in the name of the King!' said a voice.

There was no escape. Guy Fawkes was grabbed by the soldiers. They searched the piles of firewood and soon discovered the barrels of gunpowder. Guy Fawkes and the plotters were taken to the Tower. They were all executed for treason. Nobody knows who betrayed them. Thus ended Guy Fawkes and the other men who were part of the Gunpowder Plot.

To this day a careful search is made of the cellars before the opening of Parliament but nothing suspicious has been found since. And every 5th November we burn the guy and set off fireworks in memory of the 'gunpowder, treason and plot' of the first Guy Fawkes.

Hans Andersen (1805–75)

More than one hundred years ago there lived a boy called Hans Christian Andersen. He lived with his family in a town called Odense in Denmark. He was the only child of a cobbler and his wife. They were very poor, so poor that all three of them had to live in one room.

Hans was a happy boy. When he was young his father made him a toy theatre, and his mother showed him how to make clothes for his cardboard actors and actresses. His grandmother lived nearby and she used to tell him stories whenever he visited her, tales of magic and adventure. Hans loved to make plays out of these stories and act them in his toy theatre.

This gave Hans an idea of what he would like to be when he grew up—an actor. But poor Hans was an ugly and clumsy boy. His feet were too large, and so was his nose. He looked so odd that the other boys would laugh at him. To make matters worse Hans began to have fainting spells, which grew so bad that his mother took him away from school.

Then when he was eleven years old his father died. This meant his mother had to find a job, or they would starve, and the only work she could get was washing clothes in a nearby river. To help out, young Hans went to work in a factory, but this was not to his liking. He wanted to work in a theatre, so when he was fourteen he set out to seek his fortune in the great city of Copenhagen. Just like in a fairy tale, he left home with only a few coins in his pocket, determined to be a success.

In Copenhagen Hans went at once to the Royal Theatre. There he met a famous dancer called Madame Schall, and told her that he wanted a job in the theatre. Using his top hat as a tambourine he started to sing and dance. He leapt wildly around the room beating his tambourine and singing in his croaky voice, 'He must be an escaped madman,' thought Madame Schall. She told him he was hopeless, and Hans went away in tears.

Everyone he went to told him the same. He could not dance, he could not sing and he would never make an actor. So what could he do? Hans Andersen decided to become a writer. To do that he had to go back to school for although he could read he knew nothing of grammar and spelling. At school they would laugh when he told them that his ambition was to be a great writer.

Hans Andersen wrote all kinds of books, he wrote about his travels, a book of poems and a novel. Then he remembered the stories he had enjoyed most as a boy—the tales that his grandmother had told him. So Hans Andersen began writing his own stories of magic and adventure. They were a great success, and his fairy stories made him famous, not only in Denmark but all over the world.

Later, when he wrote the story of his life, he said it had been just like a fairy tale. The boy who had been such an Ugly Duckling had grown up to be one of the most famous writers who ever lived.

Hans of Harlem

Hans lived in Holland where the land is flat and low, so low that much of it is under sea level. By the side of the fields there are high banks which hold the water back. These banks, made of rocks and earth, are called dykes. Hans walked past them every day on his way to school in the town of Harlem.

Late one afternoon as the sun was beginning to set, Hans was on his way home from school. By the side of the path was a dyke, and behind the dyke was raging sea. Hans knew that without the dyke, the fields and the town would be flooded. He walked on, listening to the waves beating against the dyke.

Suddenly Hans saw something on the path in front of him. It was a trickle of water. Where had it come from? Hans looked carefully and saw a trail of water running down the side of the dyke. It was a leak, a leak in the dyke! The water was coming through faster as the earth wall broke away. Soon the leak would be a flood. He must act quickly, but what could he do? Hans pushed his hand into the hole to stop the stream of water. Behind his hand he could feel the great force of water pushing against him. Wildly Hans looked round and shouted, 'Help, help! There is a leak in the dyke!' The sound of the wind carried his words away. There was no answer, only the sound of the waves crashing furiously against the walls of the dyke. But there was no water coming through, because Hans was holding it back.

Again he shouted for help, but there was no one to hear. Hans began to tremble. It was getting cold and dark, the wind howled, and Hans began to feel hungry and afraid. There was no one to help him, he was all alone and beginning to feel very tired, but he knew he had to keep his arm in that hole.

The night grew dark, stars appeared in the sky. Hours passed, but at last they found Hans. His mother and father had brought their friends to join in the search. Hans was found lying against the dyke, still blocking the hole.

His mother wrapped him up warmly, and in no time Hans was carried home and up to bed. His father and friends at once set to work and stopped the leak in the dyke. When the people of Harlem heard of their narrow escape from flooding, Hans became their hero.

(Dutch legend)

Hereward and the Witch

In 1066 William, Duke of Normandy, defeated King Harold at the Battle of Hastings. William was crowned King of England, but for several years Saxon soldiers continued to fight him. The most famous of the rebel leaders was Hereward the Wake. Hereward wanted to keep England free from the Normans, so William led a large army of soldiers determined to hunt Hereward down and kill him.

At last William succeeded in cornering Hereward on the Isle of Ely. Ely is built on a hill and at that time it was surrounded by marshes which were dangerous to cross. It was all right if you knew the way, but if you put a foot wrong you would sink into the marsh and drown. William and the Normans did not dare try. There was only one path or causeway across the marshes, and this was well guarded by Hereward. Hereward had escaped and was safe. But William had other ideas.

In those days everyone believed in magic and the power of witches. William's friends suggested that he should use magic to defeat Hereward the Wake. They told him of a witch who lived nearby and who was famous for her curses and magic spells. They said she was in league with the Devil and could turn the Evil Eye on anyone she chose. She would be sure to help William defeat Hereward and his Saxons. So William agreed to employ the witch, and built a high wooden tower so that the Saxons would see her and hear the curses she would hurl at them. They would be so terrified that the Norman soldiers would defeat them with ease.

Hereward was a brave and clever man. He knew that if he was to fight a far stronger enemy he must use his intelligence. So he decided to go and find out for himself what William was planning. He disguised himself as a poor Saxon potter, was carefully led through the marshes by a local guide, and made his way to the Norman stronghold. Here he found lodging for the night in the house of a woman who happened to be a friend of the very witch that William had decided to employ. During the night Hereward overheard the two women discussing their plans and calling upon evil spirits to help them. Hereward lost no time in getting back to Ely to warn his followers what to prepare for.

Early next day the attack came. The Normans poured into the causeway, and as the Saxons came out to defend it the witch appeared on top of the tower, she raised her arms and in a weird, terrifying voice called on the evil spirits to defeat the Saxons. At the sight of the witch the Saxons stopped in fear. Hereward gave a signal and his men lit blazing torches. At once they set fire to the marsh reeds. The witch's voice was drowned in the crackle of flames. The fire swept quickly towards the Normans, who fled in panic. Many fell into the bog and drowned, some were caught by the flames, others by arrows shot by Hereward's men. The witch fell from the tower with a great scream and broke her neck.

William himself was lucky to escape in the confusion. Hereward had defeated the witch. Never again would William try to gain his ends by the use of magic.

(Historical legend)

How Diogenes Found Happiness

Over two thousand years ago there lived in Greece a rich man named Diogenes. He lived in a lovely house with servants to look after him. He owned vineyards and orchards. He had dancers and musicians, and singers to sing for him. But none of this made Diogenes happy. He was always so busy seeing people and doing things. There was the farmwork to be done, and the house to be kept in order. There were things to buy and things to sell. His servants would quarrel, and his fields would get flooded. He had plenty of money but people kept telling him what he should and what he shouldn't be doing with it. There seemed to be no end to his problems.

What Diogenes really liked doing was to walk in the forest—there he felt free. Perhaps he would sit under a tree and read, or just look at things for a long time and think about them. But even in the forest his happiness never lasted long, for his servants and advisers would follow him and pester him with their questions.

So one day Diogenes called all the servants of his household together. 'I cannot find happiness here,' he said. 'Everything I own gives me trouble. I want to travel so that I can see things and talk to people.' Diogenes had decided what to do. He gave away everything that he owned, his house and his furniture, his fields and his farm, all that he owned, even his clothes.

His servants were worried. 'And what will become of us?' they cried.

'Men should not be slaves,' said Diogenes. 'You are free to go.'

'But how will *you* live,' they asked, 'now that you have given everything away?'

Diogenes pointed to his dog, 'I will live a simple life as he does,' said Diogenes. 'He is happy yet he does not own a thing.'

Taking with him only his drinking cup Diogenes set off. There was a ship in the harbour and he decided to go wherever it took him. 'From now on,' said Diogenes, 'I am a citizen of the world.' Eventually Diogenes arrived at Athens, the capital of Greece, and there by a well he saw a young boy drinking water with his cupped hands. Diogenes looked at the only thing he carried. 'Why, I don't even need my drinking cup,' he said, and threw it away. Now he had nothing.

Diogenes had nowhere to sleep, so he found an old barrel and made it his home. People came from far and wide to see Diogenes living in his barrel. He loved to sit in the sun and talk to them. Soon he had many friends and he became famous for the wisdom of his words. The people of Athens offered Diogenes a fine house to live in. 'No thank you,' he said, 'I'd rather stay here in my barrel.'

One day the king, Alexander the Great, got to hear of this strange man called Diogenes. Alexander was the greatest king the world had known. His army had won great battles, and the lands that he had conquered stretched further than the eye could see. Men trembled with fear at the sound of his name. This great king went to see Diogenes, and found him lying outside his barrel, fast asleep.

'Wake up, Diogenes!' ordered Alexander. Diogenes opened one eye and then shut it again.

'I can give you anything in the world,' said the king. 'Tell me what you want and you shall have it.'

'I want you to step aside,' said Diogenes. 'You're blocking out the sun.'

'Is that all?' asked Alexander. Diogenes smiled and nodded. Without another word Alexander walked away. The sun shone down on the face of Diogenes. He had found happiness . . . in a barrel.

(Traditional Greek story)

How the Guru Chose Five Lions

In a Sikh temple the Holy Book is guarded by five men holding swords. Here is the story of how Guru Gobind Singh chose the first five men to protect the Holy Book. It happened in the year 1699 when the leading Sikh, whom they called Guru, asked all the Sikhs to meet him in a town called Anandpur.

The Guru, with a sword in his hand, stood before the huge crowd. 'I have called you here,' he said, 'to find the bravest of my followers. These I need to guard our Holy Book, and for that only the bravest will do.' The crowd stirred. Many of them thought they were brave enough to serve the Guru. But how was he to find out which of his followers was really the bravest? The Guru decided on a clever plan. Lifting his sword he asked, 'Who is prepared to have his head cut off?'

No one moved. Three times he repeated the question. At last a man spoke. 'I am,' he said. 'I cannot think of a better way of dying.'

As the people watched the man went to the Guru's tent. The sword was heard to fall, and the Guru came out with his sword dripping with blood. Again he asked for another brave man. There was a short pause, then another Sikh stepped forward and disappeared into the Guru's tent. Then a third, a fourth and a fifth man offered their lives and were taken into the tent of death.

Once more the Guru appeared, still carrying his sword. Behind him the tent flap opened and out came the five men, alive and unharmed. The Guru had found his five bravest men.

'From this day I will call these men Singh,' said the Guru, (Singh means lion), 'for they are as brave as lions.'

The Guru then told the people that they should all be brothers and sisters, and to show this it was only right that they should share the same name. He declared that every Sikh man should add Singh to his name*. That way they would remember to be as brave as those five brave men who were his first 'Lions'.

(Traditional Sikh story)

*Note: The Guru said that every female Sikh should add the name Kaur after her first name. Kaur means princess, showing that women too have a proud and important position among Sikhs.

How Prometheus Brought Fire to Man

There were many Greek gods but Zeus, their king, was the most powerful of all. He sat on a gold throne high in the mountain called Olympus. From there he could see over the whole world. But there was not much to see since neither man nor animals had yet been created. Zeus was feeling rather bored staring down on a lifeless world. So he said to Prometheus, 'Go and take some clay from the earth and make me a man. Make him in the shape of the gods, and I will breathe life into him.' Prometheus did as he was told. From the red clay of the earth he fashioned man, and Zeus breathed life into him. 'Now,' said Zeus, 'you may teach him all the things he needs to know, but you must not give him fire, since fire belongs only to the gods. Remember my words.'

So man when he was first created was little more than a wild animal. He did not know how to think or how to use the things he saw round him. He lived in caves, eating only herbs and raw meat. When he was wounded or ill, he died, for he knew no cures. But the good, kind Prometheus taught man how to live. He taught him to speak. He taught him how to tame animals, and how to sow seed. He showed him how to build houses and make tools. But it was slow work since the most important help to man was missing. Without it food was eaten raw, no bread could be baked, no houses could be warmed, and tools were only stone.

Prometheus looked up at the sun as it was driven across the sky in the chariot of Helios the Sun God. He knew that somehow he must give man the greatest of all gifts, the gift of fire. But how was he to do it? The chariot of the sun returned every night to the home of Zeus on the top of Mount Olympus. Prometheus realised that the only way to bring fire to man would be to climb up to the home of the Gods and steal it.

So Prometheus set out for Olympus. With him he carried a long stick of fennel which he knew would burn slowly. Prometheus climbed up the secret paths of the great mountain until he was outside the palace of the Gods. There by the gateway he hid until night fell and Helios drove up in his shining chariot. As the golden wheels sped by, Prometheus stretched out his stick of dry wood. As the wood touched the wheel it sparked into flame. Holding the burning stick under his cloak Prometheus sped down the mountainside back to the world of men.

The people were amazed to see their first fire. How the flames danced, how warm and gentle it was. One man even knelt down and tried to kiss the tallest tongue of flame. But he never did it again! Next day Prometheus set to work teaching men the uses of fire. He showed them how one fire could kindle another, how to cook meat and bake bread, how to hammer hot metal into tools and swords, and how to warm their cold homes. Cities grew, new inventions were made, everyone was happy. Everyone, that is, except Zeus.

When Zeus found that men had fire his anger was terrible. He sent at once for Prometheus who confessed that he and he alone had stolen the fire for man. Zeus thought of a terrible punishment for Prometheus. He had him chained to a rock, with a black bird flying round to peck at him. But there was one thing that Zeus could not do and that was to take away from man his greatest gift—the gift of fire.

(Greek legend)

How Winter Came to Earth

In the beginning, say the old Greek storytellers, it was always spring and summer. The sun shone and flowers were forever in bloom. If you felt hungry you just picked some fruit from the trees. There was always corn and vegetables growing in the fields. Leaves on the trees stayed green and never died. Man was happy, the weather was fine and there was plenty to eat. The Greeks called this the Golden Age. But it was not to last.

Farmers at that time enjoyed one good harvest after another. This was a busy time for Demeter since she was the goddess of harvest time. She kept the earth fertile and helped the corn to grow. Despite all she had to do, Demeter was as sweet and happy as a spring day. She had one daughter, called Persephone, whom she loved more than anything in the world.

One day Persephone was out in the woods with her friends picking some lovely spring flowers. Persephone had collected a basketful of white lilies, which grew of course all the year round. She wandered away from her friends as she looked for more lilies to pick. As she went further into the woods she had no idea that somebody was following her. Persephone was being watched by a man who was hiding in the shade of the trees. He was Hades, dark King of the Underworld, and with him was his chariot. He had seen Persephone in the distance, and had fallen in love with her. Suddenly he lashed his horses forward and drove his chariot swiftly towards her. She turned to see what the noise was. Too late. Hades leant out and dragged her into his chariot. Her dress was torn and her flowers were scattered on the ground. Persephone had no idea what was happening. She shouted for her friends and her mother, but no one heard. The ground opened up before them, and Hades drove down into the hidden Underworld where he was King.

Demeter searched for her daughter everywhere, but Persephone was nowhere to be seen. Demeter swore that she would travel to the ends of the world to find her daughter. Day and night she searched, without eating or drinking, calling out Persephone's name. This she did for nine days. A boy who saw her laughed at her and said she was mad. Demeter, in her fury, turned him into a lizard. It was the first unkind thing she had ever done.

On the tenth day Demeter found a forest nymph who told her that she had seen Persephone being carried off underground. Demeter was sadder then ever. No one who had gone into the Underworld had ever come back alive. What could she do? At last she decided to go to the greatest of the gods, Zeus and beg for his help. Zeus felt sorry for Demeter, and said he would help her on one condition, 'If Persephone has eaten any of the food of the Underworld, she will have to stay there forever.'

Now Persephone had been so sad in the Underworld that she had refused to eat any food. Hades had tempted her with the most delicious of things, but Persephone had always pushed them away. Then one day she walked under a pomegranate tree, and without thinking she plucked a fruit and bit it. Persephone had eaten of the fruit of the Underworld so Zeus could not let her go, but he did say that once a year she might come out of the Underworld to visit her mother. The rest of the time she must stay in Hades. When Persephone does return to see her mother they are happy and it is spring again. But when she returns to the Underworld the sun grows colder, the leaves fall from the trees, and winter is here once more.

(Greek legend)

The Impatient Jackal

A camel and a jackal once lived on the banks of a great river. The jackal often wondered what it was like on the other side of the river, but he could never get there as he couldn't swim.

So one fine morning he said to the camel, 'There is a big field of sugar cane on the other side of the river. Carry me on your back, brother camel, and I will show you where it is. You can eat all the sugar cane and I will find some crabs or fish.'

The camel liked this idea so he let the jackal climb on his back and then waded into the river. Slowly the camel plodded through the muddy waters with the jackal clinging to his hump.

'This is a fine way to cross the river,' thought the jackal, 'even if the ride is a bit bumpy.'

When they reached the other side the jackal jumped down and at once went on a search for fish and crabs. Soon the jackal was having a great feast. The camel found the sugar cane and he too began to eat. The jackal ate much faster than the camel and soon his stomach was full.

'Take me back now, brother camel,' he said. 'I've had enough to eat.'

'But I haven't,' said the camel, who carried on munching.

Now the jackal was a very impatient creature, and he was always annoyed when he was kept waiting. So he thought up a plan to speed the camel up.

The jackal gave one great howl, and then another. It was such a terrible noise that the men of the village came to see what was going on. When they saw the camel eating their sugar cane they beat him with their sticks and drove him out of the field.

'Can we go home now, brother camel?' asked the jackal.

'Yes, jackal, jump on my back,' replied the camel.

The jackal clasped the camel's hump and off they went across the river. On their way the camel said, 'Brother jackal, I think you have been rather unkind today. Why did you make such a terrible noise?'

'Oh, I don't know,' said the jackal. 'It's just a habit I have. I like to sing a little after my dinner.'

The camel carried on wading. When they came to the deepest part of the river, the camel stopped and said, 'Jackal, I feel like rolling over.'

'Oh no!' said the jackal. 'Why do you want to do that?'

'Oh, I don't know,' said the camel. 'It's just a habit I have. I like to roll a little after my dinner.' With that, the camel rolled over, and the impatient jackal fell with a great splash into the river.

(Indian folktale)

Isambard Kingdom Brunel

In 1806 was born this country's greatest engineer. He had an amazing name, Isambard Kingdom Brunel. He not only designed new inventions, but he built them as well. Not all his inventions were a great success. In fact many of them were disasters, But he never gave up trying. He was quite a small man but he had enormous energy and enormous ideas.

His first big project was a tunnel to go underneath the River Thames. It was to be the first tunnel to run underneath any river. People thought he was mad. 'It cannot be done,' they said. 'It's bound to collapse under the weight of water.' They were very nearly right, for just as it was being completed water seeped through and the tunnel was flooded. It had been meant for horse traffic, but it was never used. Not, that is, until years later when it became part of London's first underground railway.

Although the tunnel had not worked as he had planned this did not stop Isambard. In 1831 he achieved his greatest success—the Clifton Suspension Bridge. There was a huge valley near Bristol, over 200 metres across and nearly 70 metres deep. Isambard designed a bridge without any supports to cross the valley. He built a huge tower each side of the valley. 'How will it stay up,' people asked, 'without anything to support it in the middle?' The bridge was suspended across the valley by thick steel cables. You can still see it at Clifton, near Bristol.

After bridges, Brunel turned to railways. He built the Great Western Railway (now the Western Region). You may have been through the tunnel he built under Box Hill in Surrey, which is two miles long. Another interesting invention of Brunel's was the result of a near disaster. He loved doing conjuring tricks for his children. During one trick a half sovereign coin got stuck in his throat. He nearly choked to death. The doctors could do nothing to get it out. So Brunel set about trying to invent something that would get the coin out. His invention was a machine to which he was strapped. The machine swung Brunel upside down until all at once the coin dropped out.

Brunel was most famous for his ships. He built three great ships, and all were disasters in a way. First was the 'Great Western'. Fire put her out of action in 1837. Then there was the 'Great Britain'. She was longer than a battleship, with 64 staterooms and over 1000 metres of carpet. By 1846 she was a wreck. Brunel repaired her and you can still see her today at Bristol docks. Finally in 1858 he built the 'Great Eastern'. For fifty years this was the largest ship afloat. It was almost too big to launch, and on its first voyage the boiler room blew up, killing six sailors. She did not put to sea again for another year. But by the time this happened Brunel had died—of overwork.

Although Brunel was dead, his example lives on. Despite disasters and setbacks he kept going. His favourite saying was that he designed things the *best* way, not the cheapest. Perhaps this is why so much of his life's work— railway lines, bridges and tunnels—are with us today.

The Jester Who Fooled the King

There was once a King who was served by an old jester called Matenko. It was Matenko's job to keep the King happy, and to cheer him up when he felt gloomy. To do this Matenko dressed in strange clothes and told funny stories. After many years Matenko found it hard to think up new jokes and the King no longer found him very funny. The King decided therefore to find himself a new court jester. Matenko would have to retire.

As a parting gift the King gave Matenko a small tumbledown cottage on the far edge of the royal estate. Matenko took his wife to see their new home.

'Is this all the King gave you after being in his service for thirty years?' she asked, pointing at the dingy cottage.

'I am afraid so,' said Matenko. 'But I'm sure with a bit of paint it will look very nice.'

'We can't afford to buy paint,' complained his wife. 'We haven't even got money to buy food.'

This was true. The King had not given Matenko any money since he retired. What were they to do? Who would employ Matenko now? How were they to live? Matenko had an idea.

'Listen wife,' he said. 'Go to the palace and tell the Queen that I have died of a broken heart. Rub your eyes with onions, that will make you cry. When the Queen sees your tears I am sure she will take pity on you and give you some money for food.'

The wife did as she was told. She rubbed her eyes with onions and with tears streaming down her face went to see the Queen. Sure enough the Queen was very sad to hear that poor Matenko had died. With kind words she gave the wife a bag of gold to take back with her.

When Matenko saw his wife returning with the gold he was overjoyed. It gave him another idea. 'This time, wife, we'll pretend that *you* have died. I will go to the *King* and tell him that you have died of a broken heart. I am sure he will be just as generous as the Queen when he hears my news. Now where are those onions?...'

Matenko made sure that the King was alone and went to see him with tears in his eyes. When the King heard how Matenko's poor wife had died of a broken heart he felt very sorry for the old jester and handed him a heavy bag of gold. The trick had worked! Matenko made his way happily back to the little cottage.

That night the Queen happened to mention to the King about her visit from Matenko's wife, so the King told the Queen about Matenko's visit.

'They can't both be dead,' said the King. 'I think someone has been playing a trick on us. We'll go first thing tomorrow and find out!'

The next morning the royal carriage headed towards Matenko's little cottage. Matenko's wife looked out of the window and saw who was coming. 'Oh dear, what are we going to do, we shall be found out.'

'Don't worry dear,' said Matenko. 'I've got an idea. Quick, wipe some flour over your face and lie there. I'll lie over here. They're sure to think we are *both* dead. Remember don't move!' As soon as Matenko and his wife had whitened their faces and laid down on their beds the door swung open. In came the King and Queen.

'Oh dear, they *have* died,' said the King.

'I wonder who died first,' said the Queen.

'I did,' said Matenko.

'No I did!' said his wife.

The King and Queen both laughed. Matenko and his wife looked at themselves and began laughing too. The King realised how mean he had been, and gave Matenko a proper pension. It was the least he could do for a jester who had fooled a King.

(Polish folktale)

Johnny Appleseed

Over one hundred years ago in the United States of America lived a farmer who was to become famous. His name was John Chapman. Year after year he watched the ploughing, planting and harvesting just like any other farmer. But one year, while he sat peeling an apple he had an idea! Instead of throwing the core away, why didn't he plant the pips and see what happened. He did. Within weeks four or five little apple trees began to sprout. This set him thinking. America was a huge country ... why were there so few apple trees when they were so easy to grow? All it needed was someone to plant the seeds. Then, where nothing had grown, there could be fruitful trees right across the country.

So John Chapman sold his farm, packed his bags and set off. At every farm he came to he would ask the farmer for a few apples. He carried no gun or hunting knife with him. Just his seeds, his shovel for planting, a pot for cooking, and a Bible to read. Where there were no farms he planted his seeds. In valley forest and plain, wherever Johnny went, there grew apple trees.

At first people didn't understand, they shouted 'Johnny Appleseed!' at him and laughed. Johnny didn't mind because he knew that planting apple trees was important. The trees would provide beautiful blossom in the spring, and ripe fruits in the autumn. There would be apples in plenty for everyone to eat. He was a strange sight to see, wandering alone in the forests planting his seeds. When his clothes became ragged he wore an old coffee sack with holes cut in it for his arms and legs. When he lost his cap he wore his cooking pot for a hat. When his shoes wore out he went barefoot, even in winter.

As time went on his fame spread. People stopped laughing. They invited him to stay for the night in their log cabins. He rewarded them by telling stories of his adventures, of the Indians he had met and of the wild animals he had seen. Johnny was given pears, plums and peaches. These too he would sow on his travels, and fruit trees grew where none had been seen.

One day he came across a wolf caught in a trap. He set the wolf free and it ran away. Not long afterwards Johnny was captured by some Indians. They got ready to scalp him with their tomahawks, when all of a sudden there was a fierce snarling noise. The Indians stopped and ran. Johnny saw that the noise had come from a wolf. It was the same wolf that he had saved several days before. The wolf came up to him like a friendly puppy and licked his hand. It followed Johnny for some time, before one day disappearing back into the forest.

The Indians thought that Johnny must be some kind of medicine man. In a way he was, for he could cure any disease with his knowledge of herbs and forest plants. Once he cured an Indian chief of a fever, and was made a member of the Shawnee Tribe. They asked him to stay with them. But Johnny had work to do, and more trees to plant.

Now he was welcomed wherever he went. For forty years he travelled and planted trees. They say that when he died an apple tree grew over his grave. And old men would tell the tale of when Johnny Appleseed came by, with little more than a few pips in his pocket.

John Bunyan and his Flute

John Bunyan wrote a famous book called *The Pilgrim's Progress*. It tells the story of Christian and the adventures that befell him on his journey through life. John Bunyan believed that people should be free to worship in whatever way they wished. The rulers of England did not like these ideas so they put John in prison. They kept him in Bedford Jail for twelve long years.

Although he was in prison, John Bunyan made the best of his time there. He worked hard to keep his family by making shoe-laces and selling them at the prison gate. In his spare time he went on writing, and doing something else rather more mysterious. From time to time the prison warder would hear the sound of music coming from John Bunyan's cell. It sounded like someone playing a jolly tune on the flute. But the prisoners were not allowed to have musical instruments in their cells; that was strictly forbidden. Whenever he heard the music the jailer would rush along to John Bunyan's cell and look through the door. But all he could see was John sitting on his little wooden stool, working away making shoe-laces. The jailer would search the cell carefully but found no sign of a flute or any other musical instrument. Yet as soon as the door was closed there was that flute again, as loud and as clear as ever. Where could that music be coming from?

John played many kinds of tune on his flute. He had no music to play from so he had to make up tunes himself. Sometimes he would write the words for a hymn, and then compose a tune to go with it. Here are some words from John Bunyan's most famous hymn. Perhaps you will know it:

'He'll fear not what men say,
He'll labour night and day
To be a pilgrim.'

John Bunyan laboured night and day making his shoe-laces and, when he could, composing beautiful tunes on his flute. You may be wondering why the jailer never found the flute on which John was playing. Where could he have hidden it in his tiny cell? In fact he was sitting on it! For John had taken one of the legs from his wooden stool, and hollowed it out with his knife. Then he had cut finger holes so that he could play upon it. When the jailer came to search he made such a rattling with his keys that John always had time to put the leg back on the stool before the jailer could catch him!

Note: You may prefer to describe John Bunyan's flute as a recorder, and illustrate the story with some flute or recorder playing.

The Justice of Dick Whittington

Before there were newspapers and radios to bring us the news, towncriers walked the streets of London ringing their bells and calling out the news of the day. On one particular day the towncrier was shouting, 'Oyea! Oyea! Oyea! A bag of 200 gold coins has been lost. A reward of half this money is offered to anyone who finds it!'

All who heard the towncrier kept a special lookout for the lost bag. It so happened that a poor young sailor found the bag lying on a bench in a tavern. The bag was indeed full of coins. Though he was poor, the sailor was honest. He knew what he should do. He hurried after the towncrier to tell him that the bag had been found.

'You're a lucky man,' said the towncrier. 'Take the bag to a merchant named Andreas who is staying at the Tabard Inn in Southwark and a reward will be yours.'

The young sailor took the bag with him to the inn where the rich merchant was staying. The merchant was overjoyed to get his bag of gold back. He poured the coins out onto the table, and slowly counted them.

'I suppose you'll be wanting your reward?'

'If you please, sir,' said the sailor. 'My mother is a widow and we are very poor. With a little money I could give her a home and perhaps start myself up in a trade.'

But as the merchant counted his coins, greedy thoughts began to enter his head. Now the money was safe how could he avoid giving the sailor his reward? He had an idea.

'You thief!' he cried. 'Where's my diamond? My diamond was worth ten bags of gold. It was here in my purse with the coins. Now it has gone. What have you done with it?'

The poor sailor did not know what to say. 'There was no jewel there,' he replied. 'I am no thief.'

'Either you give me back the diamond and take your reward, or begone from here, you thief!'

The sailor felt angry at being called a thief. 'We shall see who is the thief,' he cried. 'Come with me to the Lord Mayor. He shall judge my case. Although I am a poor man he will treat me fairly.'

'Huh! Put you in jail more likely,' sneered the merchant, and off they went to the court.

At this time the Lord Mayor was Dick Whittington, the most famous Lord Mayor of London. First the merchant, then the sailor, told their stories. Dick Whittington listened carefully and looked closely at the two men; the mean greedy face of the merchant, and the honest open face of the sailor.

'Why,' he asked the merchant, 'did you not tell the towncrier that the bag also contained a valuable diamond?'

'Ah,' said the crafty merchant, 'it was to test the honesty of the finder, my Lord.'

'Do you swear that the bag you lost contained 200 gold coins *and* a diamond?' he asked the merchant.

'I do,' said Andreas.

'And do you swear that the bag you found held only 200 pieces of gold?' he asked the sailor.

'I do,' he replied.

'Then the problem is solved,' said the Mayor. 'This cannot be the merchant's purse since there is no diamond in it. So it must belong to someone else. If it is not claimed within forty days the bag and the money belong to the sailor!'

The merchant's face turned very white, his mouth dropped open but no sound came out.

'I do hope,' said the Mayor, 'that someone will find your bag with the diamond in it.'

The sailor went home with the money, and the merchant resolved never again to be so greedy.

(English legend)

King Alfred Learns to Read

King Alfred was born over a thousand years ago and grew up to be one of England's greatest kings. He fought many battles with the Danes who were trying to conquer England, and eventually forced them to make peace. This is the story of another kind of battle which he fought when he was a boy—the battle to learn to read. This is how it happened.

One day the Queen of Wessex was in her palace watching her three sons playing together. She knew that one of them would one day be King. She wanted her boys to be good and wise as well as brave. So she went to a shelf and took down a large book. As she opened the first page she called the boys over, 'Come my sons and look at this treasure I have got.' The boys gathered round their mother and gazed at the book. They had never seen such a big book before. They could not read because no one had taught them, but they liked the pictures and the coloured letters which appeared on every page.

'This is the most valuable book in the world,' said the Queen. 'It is a Bible and it is full of wonderful stories. I will give this book to the first one of you who is able to read it.'

Each of the princes went away determined to win the prize, but soon the eldest prince grew tired. It was hard work learning to read. 'Who needs a book?' he said, 'I'm going out to practise sword fighting. A king needs to fight not read.' So he gave up.

T... but he too became lazy. 'Why should I sta... n is shining? I'm going out to play.' And he too stopped learn...

O... ng the shape of each word and saying its s... for he too wished to fight with his swo... play ... but ... pt trying. It took a long time but ever... he thought he could read the great book...

O... Bible from its shelf and called the prin... page and first she asked the eldest prin... looked at the lovely pictures in the book... read one single word. The second prince tried next, he coul... read a few words, but did not know what they meant. Now it was the turn ... the youngest prince. The Queen pointed to the words and the prince read... the heavens and the earth...' The prin... at first but as he grew ... confident his reading got better and bette... The Queen tried him on other pages. Yes, he could read all the wonderful stories of the Bible. At last the Queen was satisfied.

'Well done, my son,' said the Queen. 'You have worked hard and won the prize. The book is yours.'

And who was this young prince? His name was Alfred, the only English king to be called the Great.

(Historical legend)

The Lady of the Lamp

Nurses are among the most important people that help us in our society today. The most famous nurse of all time was Florence Nightingale, the 'Lady of the Lamp', and this is her story.

Florence Nightingale was born in 1820 in Italy. She was named after the city that she was born in called Florence. Her father was a rich man so his daughter Florence did not have to work for her living, but from an early age she wanted to help others.

She looked after her first patient when she was still a girl. One day she was out riding her pony when she saw a sheepdog lying by the roadside. Florence went over to see what was wrong. The dog had a broken leg. Its master, an old shepherd, came over to say that he did not think his dog would ever walk again. The poor dog would have to be destroyed. Florence decided she would try to help. She found two straight sticks which she made into splints and bandaged the leg up. The broken leg mended, and the dog was soon running again as fit as ever. Years later the old shepherd would say that his sheepdog had been Florence Nightingale's first patient.

In those days hospitals were dirty places, nurses knew nothing about looking after sick people, and few of those who went into hospital expected to come out alive. Florence decided that she wanted to be a nurse. Her parents were horrified and said that they would not let her. For years they said no, but at last when Florence was thirty years old they let her start her study of nursing.

Soon after, in 1854, a terrible war broke out. It was called the Crimean War, and was fought against the Russians. The Crimea was a long way from England, and the wounded soldiers had no one to nurse them. Florence Nightingale read in the newspapers about the soldiers who were dead and dying, and decided that she would go and help them. With a party of a few other women Florence set off on the long and dangerous journey to the Crimea. People jeered at her and thought she was mad.

When Florence arrived in the Crimea she found the hospitals old and dirty. Rats ran across the floors, and there were no beds to sleep on. There was blood and mud all over the floors, and not enough food to eat. The doctors were not pleased to see Florence. They told her to go back home. But Florence was a determined woman, and she knew what she had to do. Beds were found, the floors were scrubbed, and the injured men were made more comfortable. These wounded men, instead of hoping to die, began to get better. Other women nurses went out to help. News came back to England of the wonderful work that Florence Nightingale and her nurses were doing. They heard how, late at night, Florence would still be walking through the quiet wards tending the soldiers, carrying a lamp to light her way. Those rough soldiers called her the 'Lady of the Lamp', and would kiss her shadow as she passed.

When the war was over Florence Nightingale returned to England. The Queen had heard of her good work, and she gave Florence a diamond brooch with the words 'Blessed are the merciful' engraved upon it. Florence Nightingale started a school for nurses, and she became famous the world over. Because of her life's work, sick people are properly cared for by both men and women in hospitals and nursing homes today.

Little Girls Are Wiser Than Men

It was an early Easter. Snow still lay in the gardens and water ran in streams down the village street. A large puddle had formed in the road between two farms, and two small girls were playing by the muddy water. Their mothers had given them new dresses to wear. The smaller girl was dressed in blue, the other had on a yellow dress. They had just come from church, and showed off their new dresses to each other. Then they began to play. Soon they had the idea of splashing about in the water. The younger one was about to step into the puddle with her shoes on, but the older one said, 'Don't Malasha! Your mother will be angry. Let's take off our shoes and socks.'

So they did. Then they held their skirts above their knees and walked towards each other through the pool. When the water reached Malasha's ankles she said, 'It's deep, Akulina—I'm scared.'

'Don't worry,' said Akulina, 'it won't get any deeper.' As they got near each other Akulina said, 'Look out, Malasha, don't splash. Walk carefully!' Just as she said that Malasha plopped one foot in the water, splashing it all over Akulina's dress. Her face was also splattered with water. When she saw the dirty spots she became angry with Malasha, and went to hit her. Just then Akulina's mother happened to be passing. She saw her daughter's dirty dress.

'Where did you get so dirty, you little wretch?' she said.

'Malasha did it on purpose,' answered the girl.

Akulina's mother grabbed Malasha and hit her on the back of the head. Malasha howled all the way down the street. Out came Malasha's mother.

'Why did you hit my girl?' she said, and began shouting angrily at her neighbour.

Soon they were quarrelling fiercely. Their husbands came out and a crowd began to gather in the street. They were all shouting, and no one was listening to anybody else. They were about to start fighting when Akulina's old grandmother came out. She tried to stop them, 'Come my friends. Remember what day it is. Easter is a time for joy, not quarrelling.'

They didn't listen to the old woman, and nearly knocked her off her feet. She couldn't quieten the crowd, until Akulina and Malasha helped. While the men and women were shouting at each other Akulina had cleaned her dress and gone back to the puddle. She took a sharp stone and began digging away the earth round the puddle to let the water run into the street. Malasha soon joined her, and helped her to dig with a small stick. Just as the men were starting to fight the water streamed into the street. Malasha's stick was carried off by the water. It ran towards the old woman who was still trying to calm the men. 'Catch it, Malasha, catch it!' shouted Akulina.

The girls were so happy watching their stick being washed along by the water that they ran straight into the group of men. The old woman saw them and said to the men, 'Don't you see how silly you are? Here are you fighting for these girls while they have forgotten all about it, and are playing happily together. Dear little things! They are wiser than you!'

The men looked at the little girls and felt very silly. They burst out laughing and each went back to his home.

As Jesus said, 'Unless you become as little children you shall not enter the Kingdom of Heaven.'

(Abridged from Tolstoy)

Louis Pasteur (1822–95)

Louis Pasteur was a Frenchman who lived a hundred years ago. He was a famous scientist who fought all his life against germs and disease. It was from his name that we get the word 'pasteurised' which means that milk has been made free from germs.

When Pasteur was alive thousands of sheep and cattle died each year from a disease called anthrax. One day Pasteur told a French farmer that he was working on a way to protect his cows from this deadly disease. The farmer did not believe him. 'I wish you could help,' said the farmer, 'but there is nothing that can stop anthrax. We don't even know what causes it. One day a cow is healthy, the next day it is dying. Then it spreads to the others. There is nothing you can do about it.'

Pasteur had other ideas. For many years he had been studying germs. People did not believe that such tiny things as germs existed. 'You can't see them,' they said. But Pasteur could, through his microscope. He knew that not all germs are harmful, and he proved that many could be killed by great heat. This is how we kill the germs in milk. Milk is made so hot that harmful germs die, then we call the milk 'pasteurised'.

Louis Pasteur became convinced that germs caused anthrax, but how could you kill the germs in a cow? You can boil milk, but you can't boil a cow! There was one clue. If a cow ever recovered from the disease, it never caught it again. Pasteur thought about this, and then he had an idea. If he gave the cows a small dose of the disease, they would recover, and never catch it again! In this way they would be protected from more deadly attacks in the future.

Pasteur now had to test his idea. He took some anthrax germs from a dying cow. He kept these germs in a laboratory, in the cold, until they were very weak. Then he put some in a hollow needle and went along to a nearby farm. A great crowd of people gathered to see what was going to happen. Pasteur knew that people would only believe he could protect cows from anthrax if they saw it with their own eyes.

Pasteur took fifty sheep and four cows, and divided them into two groups. The first group of animals was injected with a dose of weak anthrax germs. The second group wasn't. A month later both groups of animals were injected with a deadly amount of anthrax germs. 'Come back in three days,' said Pasteur. 'You will see that one group of animals has been protected, the others will be dying like thousands of sheep and cattle are dying all over France.'

The third day came. A big crowd had come to see the result. Pasteur took them to the barn where the first group were kept. No one spoke as the door was opened. Then everyone cheered as out came twenty-five healthy sheep and two healthy cows. But what of the other animals? They were a sorry sight. When Pasteur opened the barn door only two sick-looking sheep staggered out. The rest were dead or dying.

Once again Pasteur had won his fight against germs. Whenever we drink our milk we should remember that it is safe because it has been pasteur-ised.

The Mark on the Donkey

When God made the world he first planted a garden. There were flowers and trees of every kind. The animals roamed free and everything was at peace. The tiger was friends with the deer, and the lion lay down with the lamb. The world was a happy place—even the camel smiled. And the donkey walked among them with a voice like a golden bell.

Then God created man and sent him into the garden. The animals were amazed to see this strange new creature who walked on two legs, and had no tail. But they were too polite to say anything—except for one animal. Peals of laughter echoed through the garden. The donkey was laughing at the man. Suddenly his golden voice changed into a horrible braying sound.'Eeor! Eeor!' The garden went quiet, and God spoke, 'You shall bray until the end of the world, and forever be the servant of man.' And so it was.

For hundreds of years the donkey continued to make his ugly braying sound and had to carry man and the weight of his belongings. This was his punishment for laughing at the man God had created. The donkey was patient and did his work well. But God did not forgive him until one day . . .

A man came walking along the dusty streets of an Eastern village until he came to a young donkey who was tied to a post. The man untied the donkey and led him to his Master. The little donkey was frightened because he had never been ridden before. Suddenly he heard a gentle voice and a kind hand stroked his neck and ears. A rough blanket was thrown over his back, and gently he was ridden towards a great city.

There were great shouts and cheers as the donkey entered the city gate. 'Hosanna! Hosanna to the Son of David!' Palm leaves were thrown before his feet. But the donkey was not afraid because there were calm hands guiding him.

And when Jesus climbed down from his back a new mark could be seen on the donkey's grey coat. It was a brown cross which ran down the donkey's back and across his shoulders.

The mark of the cross has been seen on the back of every donkey to this day—a sign that God has forgiven him. The donkey had played his part for one glorious hour in a day that will never be forgotten.

(A legend from Italy)

Mary Jones and Her Bible

There was once a little girl named Mary Jones who lived in a small village in the Welsh hills. Her parents were very poor, but they were happy in their tiny stone cottage. Every Sunday the family went to church where Mary heard Bible stories read by the preacher. 'Oh, I wish I could read the Bible,' she would say. But there was no one to teach her to read, and Bibles were very expensive. In those days only the rich could afford them.

Mary was quite a big girl when a school was started in the village. She went every day, and soon she had succeeded in one of her great ambitions. She had learnt to read. One of her neighbours from a nearby farm invited Mary to the farmhouse to read her Bible. But what Mary really wanted was a Bible of her own. Her parents could never afford one, so Mary decided to earn the money herself.

In the holidays, and at weekends, Mary worked hard to earn the money. She ran errands, weeded gardens, fetched and carried, helped to mind babies, and all the while stored away the precious pennies that she was given. It took her six years to save enough money to buy a Bible—a Bible that she could read, a Bible in her own language.

'Where can I buy a Bible?' she asked her neighbour.

'The Reverend Thomas Charles sells them,' said Mrs Evans. 'But he lives in Bala, and that's a long way away.'

'I'll get there,' said Mary.

So early one morning Mary set out across the hills to walk to Bala. It took her all day. She often felt tired, but she plodded on. Eventually she got there, and bought her Bible. A Welsh Bible, a Bible that she could read, of her very own. The man in Bala, Mr Charles, was amazed when he heard how far Mary had come. It started him thinking. How many poor people all over the world would like a Bible of their own, a Bible they could afford. So he helped to form a Society that would print Bibles, not only in Welsh, but in all the languages of the world.

Now the Bible Society has translated the Bible into over a thousand languages so that more and more people in the world can read it. And all because a little Welsh girl went for a very long walk.

Note: A full version of this story appears in *Mary Jones and her Bible* by June Bosanquet, published by The Bible Society, 146 Queen Victoria Street, London EC4V 5BX.

Mercury and the Axe

Long ago in Greece there was once a man who was cutting wood by a river when his axe slipped from his hand and fell into the water. The river was deep and the current ran fast. Hard as he looked the man could see no sign of his axe. It had disappeared forever beneath the swirling waters. Or so he thought. There was nothing he could do. As he sat on the bank, he thought of his lost axe and began to cry.

Mercury, the winged messenger of the gods, happened to be passing by, and saw the man crying by the riverside. He stopped and asked the man what had happened. When he was told, he felt sorry for the man, and so he dived into the fast flowing river. Soon he came up with a golden axe in his hand, and asked the man whether this was the axe he had lost. No, said the woodcutter, this was not the axe he had lost. So Mercury dived down again, and this time came up with a silver axe. No, said the man, this was not his either. So the winged god went down for a third time, and came up with the woodcutter's own axe. 'That's the one!' he said, and then thanked Mercury for all the trouble he had taken. Mercury was so delighted with the honesty of the man that he made him a present of the gold and silver axes as well.

When the woodcutter had finished chopping his wood for the day he went back to his mates who were working in another part of the forest, and told them of his good luck. As they listened, one of the men thought that he too would like to get a golden axe from Mercury.

So the following day he went down to the river's edge, and deliberately threw his axe into the fast flowing waters. When it had disappeared he sat down on the bank and, loudly as he could, began to cry. In a little while Mercury appeared again, and asked the man what was troubling him.

'I've lost my axe,' said the man. 'It just slipped out of my hand as I was cutting wood. It's fallen in the water and I can't reach it.'

Mercury felt sorry for the man and once more dived into the cold waters of the river. He soon reappeared and shouted to the man, 'I can see something down there. Does you axe happen to be a golden one?'

The eyes of the man lit up. 'Oh yes,' he said, 'solid gold.'

The god was angry for now he knew that the man was lying. 'What a shame,' said Mercury, 'the axe that I have found is just an ordinary one. I cannot find your golden axe anywhere in the river. As this is not *your* axe I'm afraid I cannot help you. I must go and find out who this axe belongs to.' With that the god and the axe disappeared.

Left on the bank, without any axe, was a sadder but wiser man.

(*Aesop*)

Midas and the Golden Touch

Many years ago there lived a King named Midas. King Midas was very rich, but like many rich people today he was not content with the wealth he had. He wanted more, and all his time was spent in trying to get richer.

One day Midas saw an old man being made fun of by his gardeners. They had found him in the King's rose garden lying fast asleep, and had tied him up with rose branches, weeds and flowers. Midas released the old man, only to find that he was Silenus, servant of the god Dionysus. When Dionysus heard how Midas had freed his old servant, he told the King that he would reward him with any favour that he wished. Midas thought quickly and said, 'I wish that everything I touch would turn to gold!'

'Your wish is granted,' said Dionysus. 'I hope it will make you happy.'

From that moment everything that Midas touched turned to gold. For the next hour or two the King had a wonderful time turning everything that he wished into gold. The flowers and trees in his garden, the marble benches, the statues that stood in the hall, vases and ornaments all changed to gold. How they shone with just one touch of his hand! He sat in a chair and smiled, at once the chair turned to gold.

Midas was delighted with this gift from the gods. Now surely he was the richest King the world had ever seen. The gold glittered around him. Midas began to feel hungry, it was time for lunch. He sat down at his table, which shone before him at his touch. The plates and dishes too turned at his touch to golden metal. Food was placed on golden dishes, and wine was poured. He raised the goblet to his lips but the wine became solid gold. Neither wine nor water could pass his lips. The bread turned gold under his fingers. The meat turned hard and yellow and shiny. There was nothing he could eat. Midas was amazed. What use was his wonderful gift if even the food he touched was turned to metal. Just then his little daughter came running in from the garden. Of all living things he loved her most. Gently he kissed her hair. At once she turned gold, and stood still as a statue. All his joy was gone. The world was now a cold and lonely place for Midas.

Rising from his golden chair he left his golden palace, and hurried away to find Dionysus to beg him to take back the terrible gift. 'I will give all my gold,' said Midas, 'for the chance of having my daughter back.' Dionysus felt sorry for the foolish King, and told him to bathe in a special river. The King did so. When he came out of the water Midas touched the grass. To his joy it still stayed green. The golden touch had gone. He bathed his daughter with the water and to his joy she returned to life. They say that you can still find gold at the bottom of the river where Midas bathed. But that would not interest Midas for he knew that there were things in his life more valuable than gold.

(Greek legend)

The Mirror of Truth

The King was once the most handsome man in his kingdom. But as the years passed he grew fat and lazy. He had big meals and always ate two of everything he liked. He never walked when he could ride in one of his carriages. He was in fact a very happy man until one day he looked into the mirror.

'Who is that ugly man staring at me in the mirror?' he wondered. 'It's me!' he thought, 'that pale face, those puffy cheeks, those dark bags under the eyes. Quick, servants, change my mirror, I don't like the look of this one at all!' The King tried every mirror in the palace, but in each one he looked the same.

At last he called for his butler. Pointing to himself in the mirror the King asked, 'Am I really that ugly?'

The butler thought for a moment, and then said to the King, 'Oh no, Your Majesty, there must be something wrong with the mirrors. What you need is the mirror of truth. My old grandmother told me about it. It's magic, and only in *that* mirror can you see yourself as you really are.'

'Good,' said the King. 'Go quickly and fetch me that mirror.'

'I am afraid it is not as easy as that,' said the butler. 'For the magic to work you must fetch it yourself, Your Majesty.'

'Really?' said the King. 'Oh well, send for my best carriage.'

'Ah,' said the butler, 'I remember my grandmother telling me that one could only find the mirror of truth if one goes to fetch it on foot.'

'You mean *walking*?' said the King.

The butler nodded.

'All right,' said the King wearily, 'we will go after I've had a nice big lunch.'

'Ah,' said the butler. 'The magic mirror can only be found very early in the morning when the sun has just risen.'

'But I'm still asleep then,' groaned the King.

'I will wake you, Your Majesty. By the way there are some magic exercises we must do before we set out. Then we are sure to find the mirror of truth.'

So the next day the faithful butler woke the King at dawn, and showed him the magic exercises, which included touching the toes. The King was rather surprised. He hadn't seen his toes for many years. They strode out of the palace together and into the hills. But sad to say they did not find the mirror that day. The next day they did the same. Then the next day, and the next. Still they found no mirror.

For six months they continued their search. The King by now had become fit and healthy, but he was very disappointed at not finding the mirror. Then one morning just as the sun was peeping over the hills, the King saw something glistening in the grass. It was a mirror! Excited, he called the butler over.

'Yes, Your Majesty,' said the butler. 'It must be the mirror of truth.'

The King picked it up with trembling fingers and looked into it. What a tanned and handsome face he had. Gone was the pale skin and tired eyes. This must indeed be the mirror of truth.

It was then that the butler confessed. 'Your Majesty, the mirror is not magic at all. It's the same mirror that you saw in the palace. I hid it here for you to find. It is not the mirror that has changed, it's you!'

The King realised he had been tricked but he forgave his faithful butler. He felt fitter and healthier than he had ever done before. He continued to walk in the hills with his butler, and to do his magic exercises, and whenever he saw a mirror he remembered the mirror of truth and smiled.

(European folktale)

The Monster of Padstow

Each May Day at Padstow in Cornwall, an old custom is revived using a hobby horse. This strange creature is made from a hoop covered in black tarpaulin, which hides the legs of the wearer, with a horse's head and long hairy tail. This horse has another head as well, made from a coloured mask with great staring eyes, rolling tongue and sharp snappy teeth. This hobby horse monster gallops the streets guided by a man who is called the 'teaser'. The 'teaser' carries a large club which he waves at the horse to steer it through the streets. Many others join in the procession—musicians, Robin Hood and his men, and morris dancers.

This custom is thought to bring good luck to the people of Padstow. There is an old legend which explains how the custom started. The story takes place in the year 1346. England was at war with France at the time, and Cornish men had gone to help the king fight at the seige of Calais. All the able-bodied men from Padstow had gone to join the King's army and the local fishermen had taken the boats to help. Only the old and the sick were left with the women and children. Life was very quiet when all of a sudden a strange ship was sighted sailing towards them. From its mast flew a French flag. It was an enemy ship, heading straight for their harbour. What could the women and children do without their menfolk to protect them? One brave and quick-thinking woman had an idea. She got the others together and as quickly as they could, they made between them a huge and fearful looking monster. Many women hidden under colourful sheets carried its long body. Its great head rolled, its eyes blazed and its teeth were sharp. Strange noises came from its open mouth.

As the French came into the harbour of Padstow the sailors were ready to attack the undefended town. But coming towards them was a strange sight. A weird and frightening monster came rolling through the streets heading straight for the ship. The monster stopped at the harbour entrance, daring the sailors to set foot on land. Slowly the French ship turned and sailed away. The monster had looked so evil and terrible that the raiders had thought they had seen the Devil himself. Padstow was saved.

The Moon Festival

Once there was a lady called Cheng O who lived with her husband Hu Yi in the reign of the Perfect Emperor about 2000 B.C. Cheng O was the most beautiful lady in the whole Empire, and her husband was the greatest archer. But there was one thing in China which was valued more than beauty or strength and that was life itself. They wanted to live forever, and they believed that somewhere in the world was something that would make them immortal. So they hunted for some pill or some drink which would make this possible. Cheng O and Hu Yi searched for flowers, ate herbs and mixed strange drinks, but nothing worked.

Then one day a strange thing happened. The sun rose as usual but it was followed by another sun, then another, then another, and soon ten suns were shining in the sky. The heat was unbearable, rivers dried up and the rocks began to melt. Plants drooped and died, the earth turned black. There was panic everywhere. What could be done? Hu Yi, the greatest archer in China, had an idea. Fixing an arrow to his great bow Hu Yi shot it at the first sun. The sun exploded and disappeared. Hu Yi shot again and again. One by one the suns were shot out of the sky—until only one remained. The Queen of Heaven from her palace high above the clouds saw how Hu Yi had saved the world. As a reward she made Hu Yi lord of the one remaining sun, and she gave him a pill. 'This,' she said, 'is the pill of everlasting life!'

Hu Yi rushed home to tell his wife. 'I am the god of the sun,' he said, 'and I have been given the pill of everlasting life.' Cheng O the beautiful gasped in wonder. Carefully Hu Yi hid the precious pill in the roof where none should find it, then he went out again with his bow to hunt. When Hu Yi had left the house his wife Cheng O went to where the pill was hidden. She took it out and looked at it lovingly. Above everything this was what she wanted—everlasting life. Then she swallowed the pill. At first she felt rather strange, but the feeling soon wore off. Then she felt afraid. What would Hu Yi say when he found that she had taken his precious pill? What would he do? She had better escape quickly.

As Cheng O fled from the house a wonderful thing happened. The wind swirled in her dress and she began to fly. Up and up she went until she was skimming the clouds. This pill had certainly had a magical effect. Higher and higher she flew, until the world was just a globe in the sky, until she reached the moon. The moon was a lonely place, but she did find one other creature there, and that was a rabbit. The Chinese believed that if you looked hard at the moon you could see the shape of a rabbit.

When Hu Yi discovered that his wife had stolen his pill he glowed with rage. 'I will go to the sun,' he said, 'and search the skies for that wife of mine, for although she took my pill I still love her.' Hu Yi made the sun his home, and ever since has pursued the moon across the sky. When the moon is full they meet, and this meeting is celebrated during the moon festival. It is then that the Chinese take their lanterns to look at the moon as it glows with the light of the sun.

(Chinese legend)

The Story of Muhammad

Fourteen hundred years ago in the country now called Saudi Arabia a boy was born. His parents died when he was very young, and he was brought up by his grandfather and then his uncle. His name was Muhammad. He belonged to one of the Arab tribes that lived near the Red Sea.

Muhammad worked as a shepherd boy, and sometimes he went with the camel caravans across the great desert to trade in the big cities. This was dangerous work for there were many different Arab tribes, and they were always fighting each other and raiding the caravans. At that time they worshipped all sorts of gods and demons, but there was one thing they all thought of as holy. This was a house called the Kaaba. Kaaba is an Arabic word which means cube. It was not really a cube, but a box-like building which measured about 12 metres by 6 metres by 15 metres. It was covered with black material and built into one corner was the famous Black Stone*. The Black Stone was the only thing which united the wild and warlike Arab tribes.

At this time the holy Kaaba was being rebuilt. But, as so often, the Arabs began to quarrel about it. Who was to have the honour of putting the sacred Black Stone back into place in the wall? The arguing got worse and worse. They couldn't agree who was to do it, then someone suggested that the next person to pass through the unfinished door would be the man to replace the stone. They agreed. All eyes turned towards the door. The Arabs waited, and in came Muhammad.

When Muhammad was told that he could have the honour of putting the Black Stone in place, he showed what a wise man he was. He sent one of the Arabs to fetch him a large piece of cloth. Then he asked one member of each tribe to hold part of the cloth with one hand. When they were all holding the

*Probably a huge piece of black meteorite.

cloth Muhammad placed the Black Stone in the middle of it. Then he told the Arabs to lift it all together. Slowly the stone was raised on the cloth and put in its place. What Muhammad had shown was that if people work together they can achieve great things. From then on Muhammad spent his life trying to unite the Arabs.

Muhammad spent a great deal of time alone in a cave on Mount Hira thinking how he could bring all the wild tribes together. One day a shaft of bright light pierced the dark cave and in its dazzling beam Muhammad saw a vision of the Angel Gabriel. The angel was holding a length of beautiful silk, and on it there were some words in Arabic. Muslims often say these words which sound like, 'La ilaha illal hah,' which means 'There is no god but God'.

Today many millions of people in the world live by the rules laid down by Muhammad. They are written in a book called the Koran. The Koran says that, no matter where they are, at certain times of the day followers of Muhammad must turn towards Mecca, kneel down and pray. In Mecca is the Kaaba, and in the Kaaba is the Black Stone which Muhammad used to show how men should work together for God.

The Mystery of the Mary Celeste

There are many mysteries connected with the sea. One of the greatest mysteries of the sea concerns a sailing ship called the *Mary Celeste*.

The *Mary Celeste* set sail from New York on 7th November 1872. It was bound for Italy and on board was a full cargo. The ship was commanded by Captain Benjamin Briggs who took with him his wife and two-year-old daughter. There were seven men in the crew. As the ship sailed out into the Atlantic Ocean no one would have guessed how the voyage would end.

Nearly one month later, on 5th December, the *Mary Celeste* was sighted by the lookout of another ship called the *Dei Gratia*. 'Ship on the starboard bow, Captain!' shouted the lookout. The captain of the *Dei Gratia* came on deck and looked carefully through his telescope.

'I can see the name on the side,' said the captain. 'It's the *Mary Celeste*. My old friend Benjamin Briggs is the captain. I shared a dinner with him the night before he sailed.'

So the captain of the *Dei Gratia* ordered a signal of welcome to be flown from the highest mast. But he was puzzled when his signal was not answered. The *Mary Celeste* sailed slowly past. Strangely, although its sails were full, they were not catching the wind.

The captain of the *Dei Gratia* called for his most powerful telescope, and peered closely through it. What he saw surprised him. There was no one steering at the wheel of the *Mary Celeste*. There was no lookout. In fact there was no sign of life at all. The captain ordered his ship to turn and sail towards the *Mary Celeste*. As the *Dei Gratia* came close the captain sent his mate in a small boat to investigate what was happening on the strange ship.

The mate rowed across and then pulled himself up the side of the Mary Celeste. When he climbed on deck he found the ship deserted . . . and so began the great mystery. Captain Briggs, his family and the crew had all disappeared. Everything else was just as it should be on board ship. There was food still left on the captain's table. By the men's bunks there were personal belongings, including their pipes and their money. The beds were still neatly made. One small boat was missing, and one strange object was found. There was a sword left lying on the deck covered in brown stains. The *Mary Celeste* was like a ghost ship. What could have happened?

Perhaps they were all washed overboard. But there was no bad weather or rough seas, so that could not have happened. Perhaps they sailed off in the small boat, but why would they leave all their clothes and money behind? Perhaps they had all been murdered. There was no sign of fighting. The brown marks on the sword were checked. They were not blood, only rust. None of those who had sailed on the *Mary Celeste* were ever seen again, and no clues were found to explain the mystery. Whatever the truth was, it remains one of the secrets of the sea.

Nail Soup

One day a hungry old tramp knocked on the door of a little red house It was a chill winter evening and the wind cut through him like a cold knife. An old woman who lived in the house opened the door just a crack.

'Good lady, I am tired and hungry,' said the tramp. 'Will you give me something to eat and somewhere to sleep for the night?'

The old woman laughed at him. 'Go away,' she hissed, 'I am poor and have nothing to give the likes of you.' And she started to close the door.

'We should help one another,' persisted the old tramp. 'Can you give me just one crust of bread to eat?'

The old woman was really quite rich and she had a full larder of food, but she was very mean. She hated to give anything away.

'No, I haven't even got a crust of bread for you.'

The door was about to close when the tramp tried once more. 'Wait! I'll show you how to make a lovely soup. It's called nail soup and all I need is a pan and some water.'

The old woman rather liked getting something for nothing, so she opened the door and let the tramp in. From one of his pockets he pulled out a nail and showed it to the old woman.

'Are you sure it will make a good soup?' she asked.

'The best nail soup you ever had,' said the tramp.

The old woman put a saucepan of water on the hot stove, the tramp dropped the nail in, and the water began to boil. After a while the tramp picked up a spoon, and took a sip of the hot water. 'Delicious!' he said. 'But do you have an old onion or carrot, just one that you were going to throw away? That would make the soup even better.'

Now the old woman never threw anything away if she could help it. She found a fat onion and a big carrot, which the tramp dropped into the bubbling water. The old woman was growing curious.

'What's it like now?' she demanded.

The tramp sipped it again. 'Lovely, it just needs a little something to make it perfect. Perhaps a bit of bacon or an old bone, just something you might give to the dog.'

The old woman never gave anything to dogs, indeed she did not give anything to anyone. But her mouth was beginning to water at the prospect of this soup, so she gave a piece of bacon and an old bone to the tramp. Into the pot they went.

'Isn't the soup done yet?' she asked.

'Almost,' said the tramp, tasting some of it with his spoon. 'It might cook faster if we added a few old potato skins.'

The old woman had no potato skins, so she gave the tramp a couple of potatoes which he popped in. 'And a little flour,' he added, 'just to finish it off.' This too the old woman provided.

When the soup was cooked the old woman put milk, fresh bread and butter on the table. Then she and the tramp sat down and shared the lovely soup.

'I never knew,' said the old woman, 'that you could make such a tasty soup with only one nail.'

The tramp smiled and nodded. He did not tell the old woman that it was the onion, carrot, bacon, bone, flour and potato that had made the soup taste so good. All he said was, 'It's surprising what you can do with a little help.'

(*Swedish folktale*)

The Old Woman in the Vinegar Bottle

Once upon a time there was an old woman who lived in a vinegar bottle. It was rather a small bottle to live in, and much of the day the old woman spent cleaning and polishing the glass walls. This made her very grumpy.

'Oh dear,' she would say, 'what a terrible life I lead, stuck here in this vinegar bottle. Always polishing the glass, and everyone looking in. I wish I could live in a nice cottage with a little garden, and lace curtains at the window. I'd be happy then!'

One day as she was saying these things to herself an angel happened to be flying by and heard the old woman's words. The angel felt sorry for the old lady, and in a flash the vinegar bottle was turned into a lovely little cottage with lace curtains at the window and a pretty garden. The old lady looked around her in wonder. Gone were the glass walls. She now had everything she had wished for. The angel smiled and flew on its way.

Some time later the angel was flying back over the old lady's cottage when it heard a familiar sound. The angel stopped and listened. It was the voice of the old lady.

'Oh dear, what a terrible life this is. Just a poky little cottage, a tiny garden and no room in which to put anything. I wish I had a proper house with an upstairs, and a nice long garden, and a spare bedroom to put all my things in, and proper lined curtains for my windows. How happy I'd be then!'

The angel heard the old woman's words and felt sorry that she was not happy. In a flash the cottage was transformed into a big house on two floors, with a large garden at the back, and lined curtains at the windows. The old woman looked pleased. The angel smiled and flew on its way.

Not long after the angel was flying that way again, and heard a voice that it recognised.

'Oh dear, what a terrible life this is. A huge house and only me to look after it. All those stairs to go up and down, all those rooms to clean. A large garden to look after and no one to help me. Oh, how I wish I had a palace to live in, with servants to look after me, lovely clothes, and people to visit me. How happy I'd be then!'

The angel sighed as it heard the old woman's words. In the twinkling of an eye there was a flash, the house was replaced by a great palace, with crystal chandeliers, and an army of servants to wait upon her. There were lovely gardens full of flowers, with trained gardeners to look after them. There were cupboards full of dresses to wear, and many different bedrooms to choose from. The kitchens could provide any food wanted. All who saw this wonderful palace wanted to meet the lucky person who lived there. The old lady blinked in wonder. The angel smiled and went on its way.

Some time later the angel found itself flying again over the high turrets of the palace, when ... 'Oh dear, what a terrible life this is. So many people to see and clothes to wear. So many servants to look after. Such a long way to have to walk, so many rooms and corridors and hallways. All this food is making me fat, so many flowers I can't think what to do with them, everyone polishing floors and making them slippery, or not polishing them and leaving them dirty, so many doors to open and close, all those funny beds, what a life! ...'

Before another word could be spoken there was a flash of light, and the old lady found herself back inside the vinegar bottle—and for all I know she is still there today.

(European folktale)

Pandora's Box

Long ago the world was a happy place. No one had ever heard of sickness or disease. There was no anger or hatred, no one was lazy, hungry or cruel. Everyone was so happy that the gods themselves became jealous. Zeus, the king of the gods, decided that he would punish mankind with all kinds of trouble. So Zeus made a clay model of a beautiful young woman. When she was finished Zeus ordered the four winds to breathe life into her. The chief goddesses dressed her in beautiful clothes and jewels and called her Pandora, the most beautiful woman ever created.

Pandora was sent to earth. She had with her a strange box. When a young man called Epimetheus saw Pandora he fell in love with her, and she agreed to become his wife.

'What is in that box you carry with you?' asked Epimetheus.

'It was given to me by Zeus, king of the gods,' said Pandora. 'I do not know what is inside it.'

'Then promise me that you will never open it,' said Epimetheus, 'for it might bring us trouble.'

Pandora put the box in a corner and promised never to touch it.

After a while Pandora became curious about the box. She sat and looked at it, wondering what was inside. Surely it wouldn't matter if she had a quick look inside? She bent down and was just about to open the box when she remembered her promise not to touch it. 'A little peep could not do any harm,' she thought. Her fingers touched the lid. Should she open it or not?

Slowly and carefully she lifted the lid. With a scream she tried to shut it again. Too late. Out flew a swarm of ugly looking creatures. They were the spites that trouble mankind. There was anger and greed, hatred and cruelty, old age and disease, fear and jealousy and many more. Try as she might, Pandora could not stop them. They swarmed around like angry wasps, pinching and stinging her. Then they flew out into every corner of the world.

At last Pandora managed to close the lid of the box. Then she heard a soft tapping, and something whispered, 'Let me out, let me out.' It was coming from inside the box. Pandora was frightened and would not listen. Then it came again. 'Let me out, let me out!' What should she do? Pandora once more opened the lid. Out flew the last thing left in the box—a beautiful bird with shining wings. It was hope. And hope too flew out into the world.

Troubles fly everywhere giving people sickness and selfishness, unhappiness and disease, but no matter where troubles go, you will find that hope is there also.

(Greek legend)

The Pardoner's Tale

There were three men who sat drinking in a tavern early one morning. And as they sat they heard a bell ringing outside. One of the men called to the boy of the house to go and see why the bell was ringing. The boy was soon back with the answer.

'Sir,' said the boy, 'it is a funeral going by. A friend of yours, Sir, has been killed by a secret thief that men call Death. Death has killed many people in this land. He is our great enemy. Be prepared to meet him at any time. That is what my mother taught me.'

'By Saint Mary,' said the innkeeper, 'the boy speaks true. This year Death has killed man, woman, child, servant and page in a village only a mile away. I think he lives there, but it's as well to keep out of his way if you can.'

'Why?' said one of the drinkers. 'Is it so dangerous to meet him? Let us go and search for him, my friends. Let's kill this treacherous villain called Death.'

The three men swore an oath that they would be as brothers, ready to live and die for each other. Without delay they set off for the village of which the innkeeper had spoken. They were determined that Death would die, if they could catch him.

They had gone nearly half a mile and were about to cross a stile when they met a poor old man. The old man was wrapped completely in black, except for his face.

'How now, old man,' said the first drinker. 'Perhaps you can help us. We are looking for Death. We have heard that he lives somewhere in these parts, and we mean to find him.'

'God bless you, Sirs,' said the strange old man. 'I know the very place that you will find him.'

'Where, where?' said each of the men.

'You will find him in that field yonder,' said the black figure pointing his finger.

The three men went straight to the field and there under an oak tree they saw something which amazed them. A huge pile of coins lay there waiting for them. The coins were gold, and they glittered in the sunshine.

'We're rich, we're rich!' cried one of the men.

'Wait a minute,' said another, 'we'd better not let anyone else see this. Let's wait until nightfall and carry it home when no one else can see us.'

They all agreed that this was a good idea. While they waited they sent the youngest man back to the village to buy some food to eat and some wine to drink. The young man set off for the village. When he was gone the two men who had stayed to guard the treasure began plotting. Which would be more, a third share—or a half? They soon agreed that when the young man returned they would kill him and take his share of treasure for themselves. 'It'll be easy,' they thought, 'there are two of us and only one of him.'

It so happened that as the young man walked to the village a wicked idea was planted in his mind. He went to an apothecary's shop (a kind of chemist) and said he wanted to kill some rats. Back he went with two bottles of poison and a bottle of wine for himself.

As soon as the young man got back the other two leapt on him and stabbed him to death. The two murderers felt very pleased with themselves and turned their greedy eyes on the piles of gold. 'Let us drink and make merry,' said one, 'before we share our treasure.' He picked up one of the bottles, took a long swig and handed it to the other man who also drank deeply. It was a bottle of poison. Within seconds the murderers fell upon their gold . . . dead.

The greedy men had found what they were looking for.

(Adapted from Chaucer)

The Story of Prince Sana

In a country long ago lived a prince called Sana. He fell in love with a princess from a neighbouring kingdom. They married and lived happily together. But soon there were dark clouds on the horizon. News came that an army of Moors was on its way to attack their kingdom. The King himself was now too old to lead the army. 'Don't worry,' said his advisers. 'Your son Prince Sana will lead us. He will drive out the enemy.' But no one knew that although Sana was a big and brave-looking prince, in his heart he was a coward.

'What shall I do?' he said to the Princess. 'They all expect me to lead the army and fight the Moors, but I am too scared to fight. I just want to run away.'

The Princess was sad to see her husband so frightened. She wanted to help him so much, but what could she do? An idea came to her.

'I shall wear your armour, and ride at the head of the army. Everyone will think it is you.'

So that is what they did. The Princess put on Sana's armour and rode out on his horse, while Sana hid himself in the palace. The Moorish army made a ferocious attack. The Princess drove her men on and forced the Moors back. The Moors attacked again, but again the army led by the brave Princess drove them back.

The Princess had led her soldiers well, but some had begun to suspect that the person who led them was not really the Prince. True, it was the Prince's horse, but the person riding it seemed much smaller than the Prince, and why was his face always covered by his helmet? And where was the Princess? Rumours began to spread. So the Princess rode back to the palace.

'Here,' she said to the Prince, 'put on your armour. Go out and show yourself to the soldiers. They are beginning to suspect who I am. We'll change back later.' The Prince agreed. He put on his armour and the Princess put on one of her long dresses. Together they rode out to show themselves to the soldiers. The King also was there. All of a sudden the Princess whipped Prince Sana's horse. It bolted forward. The soldiers followed, cheering for the Prince. Poor Prince Sana could not stop the horse. He was heading straight towards the enemy camp, with his soldiers following fast behind. The Moorish lookouts were amazed to see Prince Sana on his white horse riding towards them. They fell into a complete panic. Prince Sana took out his sword. He did not really know what to do with it, but he had to fight. When the battle was over the Moorish army had fled. They had been defeated and driven out of the kingdom. Prince Sana was a hero.

The old King was pleased and proud of his son. Prince Sana told the King, 'My wife is the one who deserves our thanks. It was she who taught me never to hide from danger but always to ride at it!'

(Legend from the Sudan)

The Quack Doctor

There was once a cobbler who earned his living by mending shoes. He was a lazy man, and never finished a job properly. The shoes that he repaired always came unstuck. People got to know that he was a bad workman and stopped bringing their shoes to him. So the cobbler decided that he would move to a new town. There he could pretend to be whoever he liked, nobody would know. He decided to make some easy money by becoming a quack doctor.

He rode into a new town, and stuck up notices everywhere proclaiming that he was a great doctor and could cure any ailment—for a price. His first visitor was a woman who told him that her friend was suffering from bad eyes.

'Ah,' said the pretend doctor, 'I'm very good at eyes. I'll cure her in no time with my special ointment.'

So the quack doctor went to the woman's house, and out of his black bag took a jar of ointment, which was nothing more than grease.

'Close your eyes,' he said, 'while I rub the ointment in.'

She closed her eyes while he rubbed the grease on.

'Good,' he said, 'now keep them closed while the medicine does its work.'

The woman sat there with her eyes tight shut, and while she did, the quack doctor helped himself to the silver candlesticks that were on the mantlepiece, then the ashtrays, the crystal vase, and some precious ornaments. When his bag was full, he said to the woman, 'Now you can open your eyes. I'm sure you feel much better. That will be ten pounds, please.'

The old woman rubbed her eyes. They felt as bad as ever.

'I'm not going to pay you,' she said. 'My eyes are as bad as ever.'

'Oh well,' said the quack, 'cures always take a time to work. You can have the rest of the ointment for only five pounds. That'll be twenty pounds, please.'

'Twenty pounds!' exclaimed the woman.

'Well it is a rather expensive jar you see.'

'No I don't see,' said the woman, 'that's the trouble. I'm going to tell the King about you.'

'Oh well, please yourself,' said the doctor, as he picked up his bag of loot and quickly left.

The old woman went to see the King and complained, 'Before I could see everything in my house, and now I can't see anything—not my silver candlesticks, nor my ashtray, nor my crystal vase, nor my ornaments. I can't see a thing.' The King was suspicious, and sent for the quack doctor.

The quack doctor came, and as soon as he saw the King said, 'Oh dear, Your Majesty, you don't look too well. I've got something that will cure you in no time.'

'Oh yes?' said the King. 'Can you cure poisoning?'

'Certainly, Your Majesty, I have a cure right here in my bag.'

'Good,' said the King. 'Send in my servant.'

In came the King's servant holding two large cups.

'Please put your cure in this cup of water.' The doctor shook a bag of coloured powder into it.

'Good,' said the King. 'Here is some deadly poison'—he took out a small bottle of red liquid, and poured it into the other cup—'Now you drink it,' the King ordered the doctor, 'and then you can cure yourself. If it works I will pay you well.'

The servant handed the doctor the cup of poison. The doctor began to tremble, his hands started to shake and his cheeks quivered. He wasn't feeling very well. He looked at the poison. There was nothing for it, he had to confess. He couldn't cure poison, he wasn't a proper doctor, and could he have a lie down? The truth was out. The old woman got all her possessions back, and the quack doctor was thrown into jail. Never again would he pretend to be something that he wasn't.

(European folktale)

The Quarrelling Quails

There was once a fowler who made his living by catching birds and selling them in the market. He was an expert in catching a small and beautiful bird called the quail. To do this he used to imitate the cry of a quail, which would attract other quails, and when they came close he would catch them in his net. The quails who were caught were put into the fowler's basket and would never again be seen in the forest.

The King of the quails was worried about the loss of his friends, so he called all the quails to him and gave this order: 'If any of you are caught in the net you must spread your wings and fly upwards. That way you will carry the net with you and so make your escape.'

The quails agreed and so it happened. The next time the fowler flung his net over a flock of quails, they lifted their heads and flew off with the net.

The fowler was rather surprised and returned home empty-handed that day, and from then on whenever he tried to catch some quails the same thing would happen. The birds flew off carrying his net. The fowler's wife began to grumble at her husband's failure. 'You don't love me any more,' she complained, 'or you would bring home some quails to sell in the market.' The fowler explained to his wife how the quails were making their escape, and then added, 'My dear, don't worry, they get away now because they all pull together, but I'm sure it won't last.' And so it happened.

One day, as he was landing, one quail trod on the head of another.

'What do you mean by that?' demanded the offended quail.

'Oh, I'm sorry,' was the reply. 'I didn't see you there.'

'You must have done it deliberately,' said the quail who had been trodden on, and they began quarrelling. Soon their friends joined in, all the quails began to quarrel, each taking one side or the other. Only the King remained calm, but he could not stop the quarrels.

The next day the fowler once more attracted some quails with his call, and then threw his net over them. This time he caught quails in the middle of their argument. Instead of flying off at once they began to quarrel. 'Let me be first!' 'Stop pushing!' 'You can't even fly properly!' 'Move over!' 'Stop flapping like that!' The quails were not thinking of each other but only of themselves.

And while they quarrelled the fowler rolled up the net and carried all the quails back home to his wife. The quarrelling quails were never seen in the forest again.

(A Jataka Story)

Note: The Jataka stories were written in India about 300 B.C. They are stories about Buddha's previous lives, when Buddha was born as some animal or bird. Buddhists believe that you will be born again in some living form according to the manner in which you have lived your life.

The Story of Rama

Over 3000 years ago there lived in India a handsome prince called Rama. He fell in love with a beautiful princess named Sita, but Sita's father wanted only the best of men to marry his daughter. So a proclamation went out saying that the King would give his daughter to the first man who could bend the mighty bow of Shiva. Many tried but no one was strong enough to bend the bow. But Rama managed to bend the bow, and so won the hand of the girl he loved, the beautiful Sita.

Rama took Sita with him to live in the forest, and with them went Lakshmana, who was Prince Rama's brother. The three of them, Rama, Sita his wife, and Lakshmana his brother, lived together doing good to others whenever they could, and driving out evil spirits and demons from the forest.*

Now the demons had a King who was the lord of all evil. His name was Ravanna. He had twenty arms and ten heads, and like all demons he could change himself into any form he wished. Ravanna heard about the good deeds of Rama, and swore to get revenge. In his dark mind the demon King thought of a plan, a plan to get his revenge on Rama. His ten heads smiled as he changed his form and headed for the forest where Rama lived.

As Sita gazed out of her bedroom window she saw in the forest a golden deer, flashing between the trees. She called for Rama who stared out at the golden deer.

'Stay here, Lakshmana,' he said to his brother, 'and guard Sita, while I go and hunt that golden deer.'

Rama took his great bow and disappeared into the trees on the track of the deer. A little while later a voice came from the trees. 'Lakshmana come and help me I am wounded!' Was it the voice of Rama? Lakshmana went to see.

Sita, all alone in the house, heard a knock on the door. She opened the window to see who it was. There before her stood a poor holy man, old and bent, and dressed in rags. In his hand he held a begging bowl.

'Give me a little water,' he cried.

Sita leant out to take the bowl, and in a flash the old man was transformed into the demon King in a golden chariot. Ravanna grabbed fair Sita and carried her far into the sky in his chariot of gold, back to his island palace of Sri Lanka. As they flew over the mountains Sita ripped the jewels from her necklace and flung them out. And the heads of Ravanna laughed in triumph.

Back in the forest Rama had lost the trail of the golden deer when Lakshmana found him. They rushed back to the house, but Sita was gone. Rama and Lakshmana were heartbroken. How would they ever find her? Which way did she go? Whoever they asked, nobody knew. Rama left the forest and went into the mountains where the monkeys lived. There in the

*See *The Story of Divali* which explains why Rama was living in the forest.

mountains a clue had been found. Some jewels dropped from the sky as a golden chariot flew by. The monkeys had found them and showed them to Rama. At once he knew the necklace was Sita's. The monkeys had seen the chariot heading over the sea towards the island of Sri Lanka where the devils lived.

One monkey, braver than the rest, went as a spy to the city of the demons and there he saw the beautiful Sita, now a prisoner of the demon King Ravanna. So Rama and Lakshmana, with an army of monkeys, had a mighty battle with Ravanna's demons. Rama destroyed Ravanna and rescued his dear wife Sita. Once more the forces of goodness had defeated the forces of evil.

(Adapted from the *Ramayana*—the great Hindu epic c. 1000 B.C.)

Rip Van Winkle

Many years ago there lived a lazy man called Rip Van Winkle. There was nothing he enjoyed more than settling down into a corner and having a good sleep. His poor wife had to do all the work for him, cleaning the house and caring for the children.

Despite his faults Rip was a kind man, always ready to help anyone who was in trouble. He was a great friend of children and would always mend any broken toys for them. But Rip's wife could not see this good side. She was always scolding him for being so lazy, though it never did any good. Whenever his wife began to grumble Rip would call his dog and walk him off to the woods.

One day Rip and his dog went for a long walk up the side of a high mountain. Rip had never been this way before. It was a warm day so he lay down under a tree to rest. Suddenly he heard a voice calling out to him, 'Rip, Rip, come and help me.' Rip looked down the mountainside and saw a little old man with a long beard. The little man was carrying a barrel on his back. Again he called, 'Rip, Rip, come down and help me.'

Rip went down to help the little man and lifted the barrel onto his shoulders. 'Follow me,' said the old man, and he led the way up and up to the mountain top. Once there he saw twenty more little old men just like the old man with the barrel. They were bowling great balls at a line of skittles, making a noise like rumbling thunder. Rip put the barrel down onto the grass and the little men emptied it into huge mugs. The little men drank in silence and when they had finished began once more to play their game of skittles. Rip was feeling rather thirsty so he picked up one of the little men's mugs and tried a taste. He went on drinking until he had emptied several mugs. All at once his eyes began to feel very heavy. He tried to keep awake, but he sank slowly to the ground and into a deep sleep.

When he woke Rip found himself under the old tree. The day was bright and he rubbed his eyes sleepily. 'I must have slept all night,' he thought. 'I should never have touched that drink. What will my wife say when I get home?' He whistled for his dog but the dog never came. As he got up his limbs felt stiff. Slowly he made his way down the mountainside. As Rip came near the village he met some children. He did not recognise any of them, and their clothes seemed very strange. They looked at Rip and began to stroke their chins. So Rip did the same, and found he had grown a beard.

Rip walked into the village and all was changed. The village had grown, with new houses, strange names over the shops, and people he had never seen before. His own house was now a ruin, the roof had fallen in, and its windows were broken. He saw a dog which looked like his, but it growled at him when he came near.

'Who are you?' asked one man.

'I am Rip. I'm looking for some of my old friends.' But when he told the man his friends' names, he found that they had died or left the village years ago. 'Does no one remember Rip Van Winkle?'

An old woman came up and cried, 'It is Rip Van Winkle himself! But where have you been for the last twenty years?'

Rip told his story, and now whenever they hear thunder in the village, the people say that the little men must be playing at skittles.

(*Adapted from Washington Irving*)

Robert the Bruce and the Spider

One of the great Scottish heroes was called Robert the Bruce. He fought against the English King Edward I to keep Scotland free. He was descended from a line of Scottish kings and wanted to drive the English out so that he could become once again the true King of Scotland. Many stories are told of his brave deeds in fighting the English, but no story is so famous as that of Robert the Bruce and the spider.

Robert's army was defeated by the English at the Battle of Perth, and he escaped with only a few hundred of his men. His wife and sisters were soon captured by the English, and he was hunted through the wild hills of Scotland. Anyone suspected of helping Robert the Bruce was hanged. His enemies were everywhere. It was a hard life, travelling by night and hiding by day. Robert lived in caves or under rough shelters made from branches and the skins of deer. He was often cold, wet and hungry. At last he reached the Western Islands with a handful of his followers. What hope was there now that Scotland would be free? Robert the Bruce, lonely and dispirited, lay in his cave and wondered what he could do next. His friends had been killed, his family put in prison, and his army defeated. All seemed lost.

As Robert was sitting in his cave wondering what to do, something caught his eye. Something moved. There it was again. A small black object swinging on a thread. A spider! Robert looked to see what it was doing. The spider was hanging on a long silken thread which dangled from the roof of the cave, and was trying to swing across to another rock. 'Just a spider weaving his web,' thought Robert. The spider swung across but couldn't quite reach the rock on the other side of the cave. It swung again and again, to and fro, but still could not reach the other rock. Robert looked closely at the spider as, hanging from its slender thread, it tried again and again to reach its target. Each time it failed. Robert began thinking to himself how like the spider he was, failing time after time. At last with one great swing the spider reached the other rock, and succeeded in weaving a great web. This gave Robert new hope, for if the spider could succeed, why shouldn't he?

It was this one spider, so the story goes, that encouraged Robert to continue his fight to keep Scotland free. Instead of giving up he persevered. With a few friends he sailed across to the mainland to continue the struggle. After many more adventures he gathered an army ready to fight the English. The two armies met at a place called Bannockburn on a lovely June day in 1314. The Scots won a great victory. King Edward was defeated, and Robert the Bruce became King Robert of Scotland once more. Greater success was yet to come, for his wife and family were freed, and a peace treaty was signed which meant that Scotland was free at last, and at peace with England. All because Robert the Bruce had never given up, even when everything was against him, and perhaps also because of the perseverence of one small spider.

(*Historical legend*)

St Andrew

St Andrew is the patron saint of Scotland, and we celebrate St Andrew's Day on 30th November. St Andrew lived in Galilee at the same time as Jesus. He and his brother Simon Peter were fishermen, and they were the first two men to follow Jesus.

When Jesus fed the great crowd of five thousand who had come to hear him, it was Andrew who found the small boy with the five barley loaves and two fishes. Andrew was a great preacher. He persuaded many people to become Christians, and founded many churches.

How did Andrew become the patron saint of Scotland? The story begins with St Andrew's death. He had managed to convert many Romans to the Christian faith, including the wife of a Roman Senator. Andrew was arrested and the Senator ordered him to be put to death. Like many saints St Andrew was crucified—not on an upright cross like Jesus, but one in the shape of the letter X. This is the shape that you see today on the Scottish flag.

Many years later the remains of his body were taken to Constantinople to be buried. And there a man named Regulus, who looked after the graves, had a very strange dream. He dreamed that an angel appeared to him and warned him to take the bones of Andrew to a safe resting place. So Regulus took the bones and began travelling from country to country wondering where he should bury the saint's remains.

One day he landed in Scotland, and in a dream the angel said that here was the place that he should bury the saint. But first Regulus had to ask the king's permission. The king at that time was Angus, and King Angus was busy preparing to fight off an English army. Before the battle Angus had a vision. In the blue sky he saw a white diagonal cross. It was the Cross of St Andrew. The Scottish army won a great victory. So King Angus built a church where the saint could be buried. And the place became known as St Andrews. There is a town of that name today on the East Coast of Scotland.

So, in the 8th century St Andrew became the patron saint of Scotland. The flag of Scotland, a white diagonal cross on a dark blue background is called St Andrew's cross, and it can be seen on every Union Jack.

(*Traditional Christian story*)

St Christopher the Bearer

Long ago there lived a giant of a man who was called Offero. He was the strongest man in the whole country. He was proud of his powerful arms and of his mighty chest. 'I will only serve the greatest and bravest of all kings,' said Offero, and so he began to travel from place to place seeking the mightiest of rulers.

Everywhere Offero went he asked, 'Who is the greatest king in the world?' At last he heard of a great king and hurried to join his army. Before long a minstrel came to sing to this king. One of his songs was about the devil. Offero saw the king make the sign of the cross with his hand every time the minstrel sang of the devil. 'Why is the king making that sign?' asked Offero.

'To protect himself from the devil,' one of the king's men replied.

'That means the devil is more powerful than the king,' said Offero. So he gave up his job and set off to look for the devil.

Some time later Offero was riding across a desert when he met a band of horsemen. The leading horseman stopped him and said, 'What are you doing here?'

'I am looking for the devil,' answered Offero. 'I want to serve him.'

'Then look no further,' said the man, 'for I am the man that you are looking for.'

So Offero rode off with the band of horsemen. In a while they came to a white cross which had been set up by the roadside. At once the leader stopped and set off along a different road.

'Why did our leader turn away from that cross,' asked Offero. 'Oh, our leader is afraid of that cross—it's the sign of Jesus Christ.' Offero still had not found the mightiest ruler. He set out at once to look for Jesus Christ.

For many days Offero travelled but he met no one who could tell him where Christ could be found. Then one evening he stopped at a cave where an old holy man lived. Offero told the old man that he was searching for Jesus Christ. The old man replied, 'You will only find Christ by being kind and unselfish. Are you willing to use your strength to help other people?' Offero said he was. So the old man showed him a broad, fast-flowing river.

'Many people pass over this river, but the current is strong and in bad weather they are swept away and drowned. You are tall. Will you stay here and help people across the river?'

Offero said he would. He built himself a shelter and for many days he helped travellers to cross the river. He helped the old and the sick by carrying them on his back. While he was there no one ever drowned.

One night there was a great storm. The rain beat down on the roof of his small hut. The wind roared and all of a sudden he heard a small voice calling him. Outside was a little boy sitting by the side of the swift-flowing river.

'Please carry me across,' said the child. Offero bent down and lifted the child onto his huge shoulders, and waded out into the river. The storm grew worse, the waters swirled around him and as he went the child grew strangely heavy. Offero struggled on, hardly able to bear the great weight on his shoulders. At last he reached the other side.

'You felt as heavy as the whole world,' said Offero to the child as he put him down.

'I bear the weight of all the cares of the world,' said the child, 'for I am Jesus Christ. Your name, Offero, means bearer, but from today you will be Christoffero, the bearer of Christ.'

So the great giant Offero became Saint Christopher, and from that day on he has been the patron saint of all travellers.

(Traditional Christian story)

St Columba and the Loch Ness Monster

In Scotland there is a huge lake called Loch Ness. It is very beautiful, but its waters are dark and mysterious. It is also very deep, well over 300 metres at its deepest part. Many strange stories have been told of the lake. Here is one of them.

About fourteen hundred years ago St Columba came to Scotland where he travelled around trying to make the wild Scottish people into Christians.

One day he came to the side of Loch Ness. There he expected to find a boat waiting, but instead found some men digging a grave. 'Who is that grave for?' he asked.

'It is for someone who is dead,' came the answer.

'How did he die?'

'He died from the bite of the monster who lives in these waters—the monster that swims like a whale and bites like the devil!'

'Nonsense!' said Columba. 'There is no such thing.'

There was a boat on the other side of the lake, so the saint ordered one of his men, named Lugue, to swim across the water to fetch the boat.

'Wha ... what about the monster?' asked Lugue.

'Have faith,' said Columba. 'Nothing will harm you.'

So Lugue waded in and started swimming. When he was about half way across there was a terrible commotion in the water. Suddenly the long neck of the monster rose up, with a gaping mouth and two staring eyes. It drew back its head and darted at Lugue. Lugue's legs turned to jelly.

The onlookers were terrified. But the saint was not afraid.

'Leave that man alone!' he shouted. 'Go back to where you belong!'

At once the beast obeyed and sank slowly beneath the waves. Lugue swam to the shore, still shivering.

'There wa ... was a monster!' he cried.

'Nonsense!' said Columba. 'There is no such thing.'

And from that day to this no one has been harmed by the monster of Loch Ness.

(Scottish legend)

St David

Long ago in a valley in Wales lived a boy who was to become the patron saint of his country. He was named after a famous king in the Bible, called David. Like the David of the Bible he grew up tall and strong, with a fine singing voice.

St David led a simple life. He travelled through Wales teaching people the stories of Jesus. Like Jesus he was a poor man. It is said that his only food was of the simplest kind such as bread and leeks. The leek was his favourite plant, and one day he was to make it famous. This is how it happened.

The Welsh people at that time had many enemies, and one day St David was called upon by his people to help them fight an army that was attacking them. The battle started in a narrow valley and soon there was a mass of shouting and fighting bodies. Such was the confusion that it was difficult to see who was friend and who was foe. There was blood and bodies everywhere. St David wanted to help, but how to tell which side was which? He was near to despair, when looking across the fields to a nearby farm he was struck with an idea. For there growing in the winter soil were the long green stalks of his favourite vegetable. Row upon row of leeks!

At once he called out to his men, 'Over here, pick these leeks and stick them in your helmets.' So the soldiers fell back as best they could, picked the leeks from the fields where they grew and stuck them in the bands of their helmets. With their leeks waving in the wind they returned with fresh heart to the fight, and at last the battle was won. From that day on, the wearing of leeks has always been associated with St David.

The story may just be a legend, but to this day soldiers in Welsh regiments are presented with leeks on 1st March, which is St David's day. And even if you think the leek of St David is not a very pretty thing to wear—you'll find it very good to eat!

(Traditional Christian story)

St George and the Dragon

Once upon a time there was a city ruled by a King whose only child was a daughter. The King's daughter was a beautiful girl. She was the pride and joy of the old King. All was well in the kingdom until the day that a terrible monster came. It was a dragon of gigantic size and strength which made its home in a lake at the foot of a nearby mountain. Every day it heaved itself from the water and slithered towards the town, roaring and bellowing and seizing in its jaws anything it could catch. No one dared to go out of the city gates, and the people were in a state of terror and despair.

At last they made a bargain with the dragon. Every morning, very early, two lambs were left outside the city gates. The dragon would seize and eat them, then slither back to the lake until the next day, when it would be hungry again. This continued for some time and the people began to feel safe. But soon there were no sheep left in the city.

The dragon refused all other food. The only things it wanted to eat were children and young people. So the people drew lots to see which child would be fed to the dragon that day. There were so many children in the town that the King agreed that his daughter's name should join all the others in the lottery. And one day, to his horror, he found he had drawn out the name of his own lovely daughter. In despair the King offered his fortune to save her, but no one would agree to let their child go instead.

So when morning came the princess was put outside the gates to await her fate. Soon the bellowing of the hungry dragon could be heard, drawing closer and closer. But at that very moment a knight on a white horse was seen riding towards the city. It was St George, wearing as his sign a red cross on a white background. Seeing the young girl he rode towards her and asked her what she was doing there all alone. The princess told him about the dragon. 'Do not be afraid,' said St George. 'I will fight the dragon, God will help me.' Just then the dragon arrived, breathing great clouds of fire and smoke. The knight knew what he must do. He lowered his lance and charged at the monster full tilt, thrusting his spear deep into its throat. The dragon roared and thrashed the ground with its tail. The beast was badly wounded. St George called to the princess, 'Take your belt and tie it round the dragon's throat. You shall lead it back to the city.'

Many people were watching from the city walls. Now they saw the princess leading the dragon towards them, as if it were her pet dog. Those who watched ran in panic, but St George called to them saying he was a Christian, the servant of a living God who had given him the strength to defeat the dragon. If the people only became Christians they too would have the power to overcome evil. St George ended their fears by killing the dragon and cutting off its head. The people of the city became Christians, and the King offered the Saint the hand of his daughter in marriage. But George was a true and gentle knight. He left the princess with her father, and rode away to seek new adventures.

(English legend)

St Patrick

We do not know where Patrick was born. Some people say it was Scotland, others say it was Wales. His father was a Roman, and he grew up as a Christian. While he was young something terrible happened. One day pirates from Ireland sailed up the river near Patrick's home and raided his father's farm. Patrick was captured and taken to Ireland. He was sold as a slave to an Irish king. His job was to look after the pigs and sheep. It was a hard and lonely life. No one expected to hear of Patrick again.

But Patrick remembered that he was a Christian. He prayed to God. His favourite prayer was one that had been taught to him by his Roman father— 'Deo Gratias' which means 'Thanks be to God'. Even in that wild country, with no one to care for him, he remembered God and one day his prayers were answered.

One night he had a dream. It seemed to be a message from God. The voice said, 'You will soon return to your native land. Go. Your ship is ready.' It was 200 miles to the sea, but Patrick set off. After many adventures he reached the coast, at a place we now call Dublin, and there in a harbour was a ship ready to sail. The captain let him aboard and Patrick sailed to freedom.

When Patrick grew up he decided to become a priest. He studied in France, and after many years became a bishop. But Patrick always remembered the days he had spent in the wild country of Ireland. He heard voices in his dreams telling him to go back and teach them of God. So he sailed once more for Ireland.

At that time the Irish were not Christians, they were a wild and warlike people. Their priests were called druids. At springtime the druids held a great festival when they lit a huge bonfire in honour of the Sun God. The fire was to be lit outside the King's castle at a place called Tara. The King said that no other fire was to be lit but his fire. But at midnight flames leapt into the sky from a nearby hill. Patrick had lit his own fire to show that it was Easter Day. The King sent at once to find out who had dared to light the fire. Patrick was captured and brought before the King. Patrick was not afraid. He told the King about the life of Christ. 'I bring the true light,' he said. 'The light of Jesus.' The King saw what a brave man Patrick was and allowed him to preach to the people of Ireland. While he was preaching Patrick picked a small green plant called a shamrock, saying, 'There are three leaves on this one shamrock, just as God is three persons in one—Father, Son and Holy Spirit.'

Many stories are told of St Patrick. One tells of how he rid Ireland of all its poisonous snakes and reptiles. People lived in fear and dread of these deadly snakes, so Patrick decided to do something about it. He climbed a high mountain and using all his saintly powers drew the snakes and reptiles up the mountain after him. Then he drove them down the other side and did not stop until they reached the sea where they were all drowned. It is said that one old serpent resisted, but Patrick overcame it by cunning. He made a box and invited the snake to enter it. The snake refused, saying it was too small, but Patrick insisted that the snake would find it quite large enough to be comfortable. After a long argument the snake said it would climb in and prove to Patrick how small the box was. As it did so, Patrick slammed down the lid and threw the box into the sea. The legend says that the waves of the sea are made by the writhing of the snake, and the noise of the sea is that of the snake begging Patrick to release it. True or not, to this day there are no snakes living in Ireland.

(*Traditional Christian story*)

St Valentine and the Birds

Birds can be quarrelsome creatures. One day a great row broke out among the birds as to who should be King. Every kind of bird thought he should be King. So they decided to hold a competition.

'Let us see who flies the furthest,' said the pigeon.

'No,' said the swift, 'let us see who flies the fastest.'

'I think the King should be the *strongest* bird,' said the eagle.

'The bird who is most beautiful should be King,' said the peacock.

'Let us choose the best singer,' said the blackbird.

'The one who is wisest should be King,' said the owl.

No one could agree. So at last they decided to ask St Valentine, the friend of the birds, to say which of them was best fitted to be King.

St Valentine thought carefully and said, 'He that flies nearest to heaven is best fitted to be King.'

The birds agreed and decided to put the matter to the test. A signal was given, up and up they went, big and small together. Each flew as best they could to outfly the others and reach nearest the sky. Higher and higher they flew, and soon the smaller birds found they could fly no further. One by one they dropped out of the race and sank down to earth, until only two birds were left, the lark and the eagle. At last the lark could fly no higher, and he too glided to the ground. The eagle soared still higher into the sky, before swooping down to land at the feet of St Valentine.

'I am the King of the birds!' he cried.

But little did the eagle know that there *on top of his head* stood the smallest of birds, a tiny wren.

The wren was so small and light that the eagle had not noticed his little passenger. No matter how high the eagle went, the wren was always higher. She had chosen the strongest bird to carry her into the sky, and so had risen higher than all the other birds.

'The wren did not fly at all,' hooted the owl. 'The eagle won for he not only flew highest of all, but he carried the wren as well.'

The other birds did not know what to think. So they waited to see what St Valentine would say.

'To rise to the top you must have the help of others,' said the saint. 'The wren relied on the strength of the eagle and rose to be highest of all. Just like the Christian must rely on the strength of Christ our Lord, if he wishes to reach up to heaven.'

Alas, the birds were no wiser.

The wren thought he had won, but the eagle was convinced that he was King of the birds. As for Valentine, he just carried on loving them all.

(Italian legend)

The Salmon of Knowledge

Long ago in Ireland there lived a great hero called Finn MacCool, though most people knew him simply as Fingal. His father was the chief of his clan, but he had been killed in battle before Fingal was born. So his mother had brought him up, and taught him how to hunt in the forest, as well as the poetry and history of his people. Fingal discovered many things in the forest, but nothing he found was as precious as the Salmon of Knowledge.

It happened like this. One day while Fingal was out hunting in the forest he was kidnapped by a giant named Blod, and was forced to be his slave. Fingal had to cook the giant's meals and clean out the cave in the woods where he lived. He was made to fetch wood for the fire, and in his spare time Fingal was told that he must dig for worms. These were for Blod who used them for fishing in the lake. Actually Blod did not much care for fish, and even less did he like fishing. But he did want to catch one special fish, a certain magical salmon with a silver mark on its forehead, which he knew would be the Salmon of Knowledge. Anyone who caught this salmon and ate the first piece of it would have knowledge of all things past, present and future. More than anything the giant wanted to catch this fish.

For seven years Blod tried every means he could think of to catch the Salmon of Knowledge, and for seven years young Fingal dug for worms. Still the salmon swam in the dark corner of the lake, where a great hazel tree bent its branches and dropped nuts of knowledge into the water. The salmon ate the nuts as they fell, and their power passed into him.

Then at last, on the very last day of the seventh year it happened! Blod could hardly believe his eyes as he felt a tug on his line and hauled out of the water a fat salmon with a silver mark on its forehead. Blod gave the salmon to Fingal and ordered him to cook it, shouting, 'And don't dare let anything happen to it, or I'll boil you in oil!'

Fingal felt his fingers tremble as he hung the salmon carefully over the flames of the fire. He felt his knees shake while the fish cooked. When he returned from bringing more wood his heart stopped beating, for there on the side of the salmon was a great blister where it had been burnt. Trembling all over Fingal reached out and tried to press the blister down with his thumb. Ouch! The fish was like a hot iron and he pulled his thumb back, thrusting it in his mouth to ease the pain. As luck would have it a piece of steaming fish had stuck to his thumb, and so by accident Fingal was the first person to swallow a piece of the magical fish. From that moment he was filled with the power of knowledge, and his eyes could see into the future. So that even before he heard Blod's footsteps he knew that the giant was, at that moment, coming towards him.

Fingal ran as fast as his legs would go, and behind him roared the giant. Just as Blod was about to lay his big hairy hands on the boy's shoulders Fingal would dodge out of the giant's way. He also knew how to get rid of the giant forever. Fingal raced to the edge of a great cliff, with Blod hard on his heels. Just at the edge Fingal jumped sideways. Blod was coming too fast to stop—over he went, and crashed on the rocks far below.

Fingal was safe. He now knew what people meant when they told him of the power of knowledge.

(Irish legend)

Salt Is Better Than Gold

There was once a King who had three daughters. He was growing old and began to wonder how much his daughters loved him. So one day he thought he would find out. He sat himself down on his throne in the great hall, and sent for the first of his daughters. She was his eldest. She knew her father very well and she knew what he liked best.

'Now tell me, daughter,' said the old King. 'How much do you love me?'

The eldest daughter thought for a moment before she replied, 'I love you more than gold, father.'

The old King smiled. There was nothing he liked more than gold. 'You have spoken well,' said the King.

Next he called for the second daughter and asked her how much she loved him.

'I love you, father, more than silver,' she replied, and her father smiled. He loved the shine of silver, the glint of coins and riches.

'You have spoken well,' said the King.

Finally he sent for the third daughter. She was the youngest, and she loved her father dearly.

'Now tell me, child,' said the King. 'How much do you love me?'

The youngest daughter thought carefully before she answered.

'I love you, father, better than salt.'

The old King blinked. 'Speak again, daughter,' he said. 'I don't think I heard you quite right.'

'I love you, father, more than salt.'

'Salt! Salt is nothing!' roared the King. 'You do not love me at all! Go, and never let me see you again!'

At this the youngest daughter burst into tears and ran from the room. She loved her father very much, but he did not seem to understand. What could she do? Where could she go?

Still crying she ran downstairs until she came to the palace kitchens. There the cooks were busy preparing the King's supper. An idea came to her. She ordered the cooks not to add any salt to the King's food, to add no salt to the soup, to put none in the vegetables when they were boiled, to mix none in the sauces, no salt in the gravy, no salt in the butter, no salt on the fish, no salt on the chips.

'No salt at all?' said the cooks.

'No salt at all,' said the princess.

So the cooks prepared the food as the princess had ordered.

That evening the King sat down to his supper feeling grumpier than usual. His knives and forks were of silver and his plates were of gold. But the King was thinking only of his food. In came the soup. The King tasted it. 'Ugh! Take it away,' he said, 'it's got no taste.' Then came the fish. That too was tasteless. The meat, the vegetables, even the chips, there was something wrong with all of them. 'Fetch me the cooks,' he bellowed. The cooks came trooping in. The King glared at them.

'Who cooked this dreadful meal?' asked the King.

'Your Majesty,' said the chief cook, 'we just followed the princess's orders. Leave out the salt she said, so we did.'

Slowly the King realised how wrong he had been. He sent at once for his youngest daughter.

'I never knew how important salt was,' he said. 'Please forgive me for being so angry. You love me like salt, and salt is better than silver or gold.'

(A folktale—note similarity to Shakespeare's King Lear)

Seeing the Light

Many years ago in India there lived a King who had two sons. Both boys were tall and strong, and the King wondered which of his two princes would be best suited to rule the kingdom when he died. They both were skilled with the sword. Each could shoot an arrow to its mark and ride the swiftest horse. The King could not make up his mind which of the sons should be chosen. Both were brave and strong, but which of the princes was the wisest? The King decided to give them a test.

Late one evening when the work was done he sent for the two boys and said to them, 'Tomorrow my sons, in the early morning before the sun has risen, I want you to go to the market and buy me something that will fill this great hall.' Then he gave each boy a small copper coin. 'This will be a test,' said the King, 'to see which of you is wise enough to rule my kingdom when I am gone.' With that he wished them goodnight, and the boys were left wondering how they could buy something to fill the great hall with just one small coin.

The next morning the princes rose early and made their way among the stalls and loaded wagons looking for something to buy. The market was crowded even at that early hour with plenty of things for sale. The first prince began to look around. There were great bags of rice, but a sackful cost more than one coin. There were piles of fruit, but they too were expensive. Bales of cotton, dried fish, bags of salt, sugar and spice—but one coin would not buy nearly enough to fill his father's hall. At last as evening shadows began to fall he saw a stall stacked high with straw. 'That will be cheap and light to carry,' he thought. So with the coin he had he bought as much straw as he could carry. But the straw was not nearly enough to fill the hall, for it barely covered the floor.

When the sun had set his brother returned. He too had spent the day searching the market with his one copper coin, but he had succeeded in finding something which would fill the great hall. When his father saw his gift he was well pleased. 'You, my son, are wise,' he said, 'and have shown me you are fit to rule my kingdom.'

The second son then lit the candle which he had bought in the market place with his copper coin, and he placed it carefully in the middle of the hall. The flame from the candle shone through the darkness and filled the great hall of the King with light.

(*Indian folktale*)

The Selfish Giant

Every afternoon as they were coming home from school the children used to go and play in the giant's garden. It was a large, lovely garden, with soft green grass. The flowers shone like stars and birds sang in the peach trees. The children were happy in their games in the giant's garden.

One day the giant returned from a visit to his friend the Cornish ogre. He had been away for seven years. When he arrived he saw the children playing in his garden. 'What are you doing here?' he cried in a gruff voice. The children ran away. 'My garden is my own garden,' said the giant. 'I won't let anyone play in it but myself.' So he built a high wall around it and put up the sign 'Trespassers will be Prosecuted'. He was a very selfish giant.

The poor children had nowhere to play. They tried to play on the road, but that was dusty and dangerous. They walked around the high garden walls when lessons were over, and remembered their games in the garden.

Then spring came and all over the country there were blossoms and little birds. Only in the garden of the selfish giant was it still winter. The birds did not sing as there were no children, and the trees forgot to blossom. Snow and frost lay on the ground and the north wind blew. 'I cannot understand why spring is so late,' said the selfish giant, as he looked out at his cold, white garden. 'I hope there will be a change in the weather.'

But spring never came, nor did summer—until one day. The giant was lying in bed when he heard some lovely music. It was the sound of a bird singing in his garden. 'I believe that spring has come at last,' said the giant. He jumped out of bed and looked out of the window. The children had crept through a hole in the wall and were playing in the branches of the trees. The trees were now covered in blossoms, birds were flying by, and the grass was growing green. Only in one corner was it still winter. In it was a little boy who could not reach the branches of the trees. The giant's heart melted when he saw the boy. 'How selfish I have been!' he said. 'Now I know why spring never came here. I will help that little boy to the top of the tree and then I will knock down the wall. My garden will be a children's playground for ever.'

When the giant went out into the garden, the children were frightened to see him and ran away. But the giant helped the small boy up into the tree. 'It is your garden now,' the giant said to the children, and with a great axe he knocked down the wall. So the children came back and they played with the giant in his beautiful garden. All day long they played, and in the evening they came to say goodbye. 'But where is your little friend?' asked the giant, 'the boy I put up into the tree.'

'We don't know,' said the children. 'He has gone away.'

They did not know where the small boy lived and had never seen him before.

Every afternoon when school was over the children came to play with the giant. Because the giant was no longer selfish he had many friends. But still he longed for his first little friend, the boy he had lifted into the tree. Then one day, many years later, the giant saw the little boy again—but if you want to hear what happened when he did, you will have to read the story for yourself, and see what happened at the end of the *The Selfish Giant* by Oscar Wilde.

The Seven Sleepers

Long ago the Romans were great soldiers and conquerors, but they were often very cruel. One day their Emperor Decius ordered that all Christians should be put to death. He used to travel far and wide to make sure his order was being carried out.

One day the Emperor arrived in Ephesus and ordered that temples should be built in honour of the Roman gods. There were many Christians in Ephesus. So the Emperor gave them a choice. Either they could worship the Roman gods, or die. The people chose to live, all except for seven friends. They were Christians and did not want to worship Roman gods. Decius was angry with these troublemakers so he sent for them.

'Give up your religion,' he said to the seven friends, 'or I will have you killed.' The young men stood bravely before the Emperor and refused to give up their religion. Like all Romans the Emperor admired courage, so he said, 'I will give you one chance. If you have not changed your minds by the time I return to Ephesus you will be seven dead Christians.'

The young men wondered what to do. One of them knew of a secret cave in a nearby mountain where they could hide. So off they went to live in the cave where they thought they would never be found. When the Emperor returned and heard that the seven had disappeared he started a fierce hunt for them. Roman soldiers searched the mountainside, and soon the cave was found. The Emperor was sure that the seven friends were hiding inside it, so he ordered his soldiers to block up the entrance with stones and rocks, leaving the seven young men to die of hunger and thirst.

Years passed by and the cave was forgotten by everyone. Then one day a shepherd decided to build a hut on the mountainside and began to use the stones that he saw lying there. As the stones were taken by the shepherd a hole was uncovered in the mountainside.

Next morning as the first rays of the sun pierced the darkness of the cave, the seven men who were sleeping inside woke up. To them it seemed as if only a night had passed. But when they came down to the city they were in for a big surprise. Christian crosses and churches were everywhere. They went into a baker's shop to buy some bread. When the baker saw their money his eyes bulged in amazement. 'These coins are 400 years old,' he said. 'Where did you find this treasure?' The seven friends denied knowing anything about treasure. So they were taken to the Governor.

'Where do you come from?' asked the Governor.

'We come from Ephesus,' said one of the men. 'If this is Ephesus, it seems to have changed a lot since yesterday.'

'These coins were minted 400 years ago, in the reign of the Emperor Decius,' said the Governor.

'Oh no,' said one of the seven friends, 'that can't be right, because only yesterday we were hiding from the Emperor in a cave on the mountainside.'

'Either you are mad,' said the Governor, 'or a miracle has taken place.'

Everyone from far and wide came to see the Seven Sleepers and listen to their strange tale. Bishops came, even Emperor Theodosius himself came, and all thought the story must be true.

(*Traditional Greek story*)

Silent Night—1914

Imagine living in a hole in the ground. All around you there is mud and water. There are other people lying with you in this small hole but some of them are wounded, some of them are dying. There are bombs falling and bullets flying. It was like this for thousands of men during the First World War. 'It will be all over by Christmas,' they said, when Britain went to war with Germany in the summer of 1914. But by Christmas Eve they were still fighting and dying.

At first there had been soldiers galloping across country on horseback, but machine guns and bombs had stopped all that. Men and horses had been blown to pieces. So they had decided to dig holes in which to hide. These were called trenches. Here the soldiers could fire at each other without being seen. All through the autumn the German and British soldiers dug trenches and waited there in the mud and water for the bombs to fall. The trenches of the two armies stretched for hundreds of miles. There was only a short space of ground between the trenches of the two armies. Nothing grew there and the ground was full of holes. They called it 'no man's land'.

It was Christmas Eve and both armies were waiting in the trenches for the other to attack. The soldiers were feeling homesick. They thought of their family and friends, and wished they were back home. What a strange way to spend Christmas, hiding in a muddy hole waiting to shoot and be shot at. The night grew dark and still. All the shooting had stopped. The British soldiers lay shivering in their trenches.

Suddenly they heard a strange sound. Very softly at first, then louder and louder, came the sound of singing. It seemed to be coming from the German trenches. The words were German, but the tune was familiar. The enemy, the hated 'Huns', were singing a carol—'Silent Night'.

As the British listened, first one and then another began to join in. Soon all the British soldiers hidden in the trench were singing with the Germans. 'Silent night, holy night . . .' The waves of the song flowed across 'no man's land', the German words mixing with the British. It was then that the miracle happened. Not only were the two armies singing together, but soldiers began to climb out of the trenches and come towards one another. In their hands, instead of guns some of them held little gifts of chocolate or cigarettes.

This is how a reporter of *The Times* newspaper described it:

'The men rose and advanced to meet each other as if they had been released from a spell . . . and some say that the darkness became strange and beautiful with lights as well as music, as if the armies had been gathered together not for war but for the Christmas feast.'

Unfortunately it was the only time that the two sides came together in peace. For four long years there was fighting and killing. But in that silent night of 1914 the soldiers had remembered the Christmas message, 'Peace on earth, and goodwill toward men.'

The Sorcerer's Apprentice

Long ago in a country far away there lived a boy named Peter. Peter was an apprentice to an old magician. The magician did not think much of the boy, for Peter was lazy and did not like work.

Peter's master worked his magic in a cellar where he was always mixing things in a big black pot. For years the magician had been trying to make gold, mixing all sorts of things together with buckets full of water. It was Peter's job to fetch the water. But Peter was tired of walking backwards and forwards to the river. He was tired of having to keep the pot filled with water. He wanted to do magic himself.

One day the magician had to go out. He still had not managed to make gold and was going into the country to search for rare plants and herbs for his magic. 'Fill all the tubs with water from the river while I'm gone,' he said to Peter. 'I won't be long.'

Peter was now alone in the magician's cellar. He looked round. Books of magic were piled up against the walls, covered in dust and cobwebs. There was a stuffed crocodile hanging from the ceiling and bottles of strange liquids on the shelves. An old broom stood in the corner. Peter looked into the big black cauldron. 'Oh dear,' he said to himself, 'this will take hours to fill. Backwards and forwards, backwards and forwards. I wish I could find some quicker way to do it!' Peter looked round, saw the broom, and then he remembered. A few days before, the magician had used some special words to make the broom walk. And not only walk, he had also made the broom carry a bucket. If the broom could walk and carry a bucket it could fill the big black pot too. But what were those words? Peter went up to the old broom and mumbled some words that sounded like his master's. The broom did nothing. 'Oh I forgot to tell him what to do,' thought Peter. 'Broom! Broom!' cried Peter. 'Fill the tubs with water from the river!'

There was a short strange silence. The air was full of magic. Then slowly the broom stood up straight. Its bristles divided into two legs, two arms sprouted from the handle. Suddenly it began to walk. It picked up a bucket and went to the river. Soon the broom was back with a bucket full of water, which it tipped into the big pot. And off it went back to the river again. Back and forth the broom went, bucket after bucket of water, until the pot was full.

Off went the broom again. 'Oh dear,' thought Peter. 'I'd better stop that broom.' But before he could speak the broom was back, splashing water all over the cellar floor. 'Stop Broom! Enough!' shouted Peter. But on it went, spilling water everywhere. 'I'll stop you, you silly broomstick,' cried Peter. He went to the woodshed and brought an axe. As the broom came splashing through the door . . . chop! The broom was split in two. But to Peter's horror he saw two halves of the broom slowly rising from the ground. The two brooms took two buckets and went off towards the river. Water was pouring in twice as fast. Tables and chairs were beginning to float. The whole cellar was flooded. Peter tried mumbling all the spells he knew, but to no avail. There was water rising everywhere, the books began to float off the shelves, when suddenly the magician appeared in the doorway. He was hopping mad. In a voice of thunder he stopped the brooms, in a flash of light the water vanished.

Peter had learned his lesson—never again would he meddle with magic!

(*Adapted from Goethe*)

The Stolen Tulip

Ever since tulip flowers were found growing in far off Turkey man has been trying to grow one special tulip—a *black* tulip. Many tulips have been very dark brown, or the deepest blue, but none has been truly black. None, except perhaps the one in this story.

Many years ago there was a competition among the bulb growers of Holland. A prize of one thousand golden crowns was offered to the first person who could grow a black tulip. There was great activity among the bulb growers. They tried every way they knew to grow a black tulip. They produced blue and brown ones, shimmering purple and bottle green ones, striped ones and blotchy ones.

At last one of the keenest growers produced a small bulb which was a mixture of all the darkest colours he had ever grown. 'This surely,' he said, 'is the first, the one and only *black* tulip.'

It was still just a small bulb, but he could see it in his mind's eye growing and opening into a velvety black flower. He didn't even think of the handsome prize that he would win. The black tulip would be the most valuable flower in the world, but it would also, he thought, be the most beautiful.

The bulb grower knew that he had better keep the news of his bulb a secret. The only people he told were his family and his closest friends. But like many a well kept secret it travelled from person to person, until it reached the ears of a bulb grower who was his greatest rival. Now this man had for years been trying to grow a black tulip, without success. He would dearly like to get his hands on that prize—a thousand gold crowns! Now he had been beaten to it. Or had he? A plan began to form in his mind. Perhaps he would win the prize money after all.

That night when all was dark he slipped out of his house and made his way to the garden where he thought the black tulip bulb would be kept. In through the gate he went and up to the great glass greenhouse where all the bulbs sat ready for planting. There they lay in rows, each one neatly labelled. His hand reached down for the latch. Just as he thought—not locked! Quietly he let himself into the greenhouse. It was quite dark so he struck a light and moved quickly along the rows of bulbs. Yes, there it was—'The Black Tulip', on a special shelf all to itself. With the bulb safe in his pocket the thief placed another bulb where the black tulip bulb had been, and hurried home in triumph.

Back in his own house the thief placed the bulb carefully on his mantelpiece. The black tulip! It looked like any other tulip bulb, but this one would make him rich. The following day his housekeeper found what she thought was an onion lying there on her master's mantelpiece.

'Funny place for an onion,' she thought. 'Oh well, it'll make a nice omelette.' So she took the precious bulb out into the kitchen. There she cracked two eggs, chopped up the bulb and proudly presented it to her master for his next meal—an onion omelette.

The thief, his mind still on the money he would win, tucked into his supper. When he had finished the omelette, he glanced over to the mantelpiece. The bulb! Where had it gone? In a panic he searched high and low, to no avail, it had quite disappeared. He questioned all his servants. No they hadn't seen a tulip bulb. Had they seen anything unusual?

'Well,' said the housekeeper, 'only an old onion, but you ate that for your supper!' All of a sudden the thief began to feel rather ill, and from that day on he vowed that he would never steal again.

And we are still waiting for the first black tulip.

(Dutch folktale)

The Strange Treasure

There was once an old farmer who had two lazy sons. The old man worked hard to look after his crops, but his sons were of little help. All they wanted to do was to play, and they left the old man to do all the work. 'What will become of the farm when I die?' thought the old man. 'Who will care for it then?'

One day the old man became ill so he called his two sons to his bedside. 'My sons, I have not very long to live. Listen carefully to what I have to say.' The two sons bent down to listen to their father's feeble words. 'There is a great treasure hidden in the vineyard,' he whispered. 'Do not tell anyone, but if you search hard enough, one day you will find it.' So saying the old farmer died.

The two sons started to hunt for the treasure. They went out into the vineyard with their spades and plough, and began turning the earth. They pulled up any weeds in their way, and trimmed the branches of the vines. They dug between all the vines but found neither gold nor precious stones.

The vines however were strengthened by this tending and the careful ploughing, and that autumn they yielded the richest harvest of grapes the brothers had ever seen. It was hard work picking the grapes, but when they took them to market they found that their fine, ripe grapes fetched a good price.

The following year they continued the search. They tried digging in other fields, but could not find the treasure their father had spoken of. Once more at harvest time their vineyards and orchards were ripe with fruit, and as they gathered their fine harvest the oldest son suddenly realised what their father had meant.

'I think I have discovered our father's treasure,' he said. 'It was right in front of us all the time.'

He pointed to the grapes on the vines and the fruits on the trees.

'This vineyard is the treasure which our father left us.'

'Yes,' said the younger son, 'and it has taught us a lesson. If you want rich rewards you must work hard.'

(European folktale)

The Story of Swan Lake

There was once a Prince called Siegfried. He was a handsome young man, full of the joy of living.

It is his twenty-first birthday, and all the people of the village are holding a party for him in the castle grounds. There is merry music, dancing and the sound of laughter. Suddenly all goes quiet as the Queen Mother arrives. She soon reminds Siegfried that now he is twenty-one he has come of age and must choose a bride. She announces that a ball is to take place the following evening when the Prince must choose from six noble young ladies which one is to be his bride. The Queen Mother leaves and Prince Siegfried sighs. He realises this is the last evening he will share with his friends. At that moment a flock of white swans flies over their heads. 'Look!' says the Prince to his friends. 'Let us chase those swans.' So they all return to the castle to prepare for the hunt.

Deep in the forest lies a lake, silent, and bathed in moonlight. 'Hush!' calls Siegfried, 'be on your guard'. Slowly the hunters creep forward, taking care to make no noise with their crossbows. One of the hunters indicates that he has seen a swan, the others follow after him to hunt the swan, but Siegfried stays behind, alone at the edge of the lake.

All is quiet, there is magic in the air. Suddenly a beautiful white swan appears on the lake, and glides to the shore. To Siegfried's amazement from out of the lake steps a lovely young girl.

'Who are you?' gasps the Prince.

'I am Princess Odette,' she whispers. 'I have been put under a spell by a wicked magician. By day my friends and I become swans, only at night can we become ourselves again.'

'I will save you,' cries Siegfried. 'Where is this magician?'

'You will never find him,' says Odette. 'He hides by day, disguised as an owl. The spell can only be broken when I fall in love with a man who has never said that he loves another.'

At this, the Prince falls in love with Odette, and they begin to dance with happiness. But suddenly there is a frightening hoot, a sinister owl appears in the trees, with huge staring eyes. The prince grabs his crossbow and shoots. The owl flies off into the wood with the Prince chasing him.

Odette, the swan Princess, is joined by her friends. The hunters see them and aim with their bows to kill them. 'Siegfried stop them! They think we are swans!' cries Odette. Just in time Siegfried arrives to stop them shooting. The swan maidens soon realise that they are among friends and start to dance beautifully.

'Promise me you will come to the ball tomorrow,' says Prince Siegfried.

'I will tell everyone that I love only you, and then you will be a swan no more.'

Happily, Odette promises that she will come.

'My lords, ladies and gentlemen! Pray silence for the Queen Mother and Prince Siegfried.'

It is the night of the ball. Siegfried dances in turn with each of the six chosen girls, but all he can think of is Odette. Then the wicked magician arrives at the ball, disguised as a nobleman, with his daughter Odile dressed as a black swan. By magic the magician has made Odile's face look just like Odette's. The Prince thinks that she is his swan princess, and tells everyone that he loves her. Too late Odette herself appears at the window. In an agonising moment Siegfried realises he has been tricked. Frantically he rushes from the ballroom, but Odette has vanished.

Siegfried chases through the forest until he finds Odette, standing by the lake. He begs her to forgive him, but as he speaks there is a flash of light and the evil owl appears in the trees. A storm breaks, Odette gives a loud cry, and throws herself into the waters of the lake. Racing to the lakeside Siegfried too plunges in, choosing to die with her. By this the spell is broken, the magician who is hidden nearby falls dead. The storm ends and the swan maidens return. Gliding across the lake, as if in a dream, they see Odette and Siegfried, saved by their love for one another.

(German legend)

The Talking Turtle

There was once a fellow called Cary. The trouble with Cary was that he could not keep anything to himself. He was a great chatterbox. Whenever anybody had done something which was not right, Cary would run and tell everyone about it. He never told lies, he just told the truth and that's what made it so bad. Everyone believed what Cary said, and there was no way you could pretend he was making it up.

When he was young he would always tell the teacher if he saw somebody pinch someone else, or if they had said a rude word. He would always tell who it was that made a rude noise. He was always talking when he should have been listening. When he was alone he would even talk to himself. The sure way to spread a story about someone was to tell it to Cary.

As Cary grew older he got no better. No secrets were safe when he was around. No boy could have a girlfriend, and no girl could have a boyfriend, without Cary spreading the word. Nothing seemed to stop Cary's gossiping, nothing, that is, until the time he found a turtle in the road.

The turtle was bigger than the common kind, so Cary stopped to look at it. The old turtle winked its eyes and said, 'Cary, you talk too much!'

Cary jumped four feet into the air, and then just stood there with his mouth hanging open. He looked all round, but there was nobody in sight. 'My ears must be back to front,' he said to himself. 'Everyone knows that turtles are dumb.'

The old turtle winked its red eyes again. 'Cary you talk too much,' said the turtle. With that Cary spun round like a top and headed back for home.

When Cary told his friends about the turtle they just laughed in his face. 'You come with me,' said he, 'and I'll show you!'

So the whole crowd went along but when they got there the turtle never said a word. It looked just like any other turtle, only bigger than the usual sort. Cary tried talking to it, but the turtle's mouth never moved. The crowd of people were fed up having to go all that way for nothing. The jeered at Cary for telling tall stories, and left him standing there. Cary looked sadly at the turtle, and the old turtle winked its red eyes and said, 'Didn't I tell you? You talk too much.'

Some people said the whole thing was a joke, because it isn't possible for turtles to talk. Perhaps someone was hiding in the bushes and throwing his voice so it just sounded as if the turtle was talking. Everyone knows that ventriloquists can make dummies talk well enough to fool almost anybody. But none of Cary's friends were good enough for that; in fact no one in town could throw his voice like that.

Whether it was a joke or not, the turtle stopped old Cary's chatter. Whenever he came up with one of his stories, his friends would just laugh and say, 'Go and tell the turtle, Cary, go and tell the turtle.'

(American folktale)

Thinking for Yourself

A True Story

Four small girls were walking home one afternoon from their infant school when a car drew up beside them. The man inside the car called the girls and said to them, 'Your father says you are to come with me at once. He sent me to fetch you.' The man held the back door open and three of the girls got in. They had always been taught to do as their father said. But the fourth girl did not get in. She had been taught to think for herself. So she did. And ran.

The car drove off, while the fourth girl ran as fast as she could to a nearby police station. She told her story to the policeman, describing the colour of the car and direction it was going. At once a call went out to all patrol cars in the area. Within a short while the car in which the man and girls were travelling was stopped, and the girls were soon brought back safely.

The girl who raised the alarm was questioned by the police.

'What made you run off instead of going too?'

'I don't know, but Daddy and Mummy are always saying 'Think!' They say 'You've got a mind of your own, use it'. So I thinked. I thinked that if Daddy really wanted us he'd have come himself, and I thinked that the man only said one Daddy and we've got three Daddies, all of us I mean. So I ran.'

Reported in *Baby and Child* by Penelope Leach, (M. Joseph)

The Heron Who Liked Crab

An old heron lived by the side of a pond. He used to eat fish, but his favourite food was crab. He was getting too old to catch fish, so he thought he would play a trick on them. He pretended to be very sad, and did not even try to catch the fish which swam near him.

The heron thought that someone would notice, and sure enough along came a crab.

'Old heron, why don't you catch fish any more?' asked the crab.

'Alas!' said the bird. 'I am so sorry for all of you that I can catch no fish.'

'Why are you sorry?' asked the crab.

'I heard some fisherman say that they are going to come along and catch all of you in their nets.'

'Alas! Alas!' cried the crab. 'What is to be done?'

'I know a way out,' said the heron. 'Tell the fishes that I can take them to a bottomless pond so deep that no net could catch them.'

'Yes I will,' said the crab. 'Thank you, heron, for your kindness.'

The heron stood on one leg and smiled.

The crab crawled away to tell the fishes of their great danger and how the heron could help them. So the fishes went to the heron, and every day the heron chose a few to be saved. The crafty bird took them on his back to a nearby rock, threw the fish against it, and ate them. The fish in the water thought their friends had escaped disaster, and every day they fought with each other to be saved. The crab also waited for his turn.

One day the heron thought, 'I'm tired of fish. Today I'll have my favourite food.' So he took the crab. Up flew the heron with the crab on his back. After a while the crab noticed that they were not flying towards any water.

'Where are we going?' he asked suspiciously.

'Hee, hee, hee,' screeched the heron. 'You're going the same way your friends went.'

Before him the crab could see a rock, and all around it were the skeletons of fish. At once the crab realised what was going to happen and stretched out his claws in anger and terror.

'Wretch!' he hissed, and caught the neck of the heron in a vice-like grip. The heron struggled and stretched, trying to throw the crab against the rock. The crab clung on and his sharp claws cracked the heron's neck. The heron fell and the crab crawled slowly back to the pond.

The fish were very surprised to see him back, and soon the whole story was told.

'That will teach us,' said the fish, 'not to listen to others but to think for ourselves.'

(an Indian fable adapted from the *Panchatantra*)

The Thorny Devil

Many years ago in the great Australian outback there lived a boastful lizard. More than anything else this lizard loved to throw his boomerang. Day after day he would practise, throwing his boomerang high into the sky. The lizard would watch it fly in a great circle scattering the birds as it went, and then catch it as it came whizzing back. 'Just watch me,' said the lizard. But you know how dangerous throwing boomerangs can be . . .

One day as the lizard was showing off as usual, he saw a cockatoo sitting on the branch of a nearby tree. 'Look at me!' shouted the lizard. 'I am the best boomerang-thrower in the bush!' Then he threw his boomerang again as far as he could. The cockatoo just sat in the tree and blinked. The lizard caught his boomerang and waited for the bird to say how clever he was. The cockatoo said not a word; she didn't seem to have noticed.

'This time,' thought the lizard, 'I'll show her!' With a mighty heave the lizard sent the boomerang flying towards the gum tree where the cockatoo sat. It was meant to fly in a great circle round the tree. Instead it flew closer and closer to the cockatoo.

'Squark!' screamed the cockatoo as it hit her on top of her head. A shower of feathers came fluttering down. 'Look at me!' she screamed. 'You've knocked off my best feathers and given me a great bump on my head.'

The lizard gazed up at the cockatoo. Sure enough most of her beautiful head-feathers had gone. There was only a crest of them left standing on top of her head. 'I'll teach you to throw boomerangs!' screamed the cockatoo.

The lizard looked at the cockatoo's hooked beak and sharp claws, and decided to leave his boomerang where it had fallen and head for the nearest bush. The cockatoo swept down towards him. The lizard dived into the bush. Unfortunately, it was a thorn bush. Prickles stuck into him like a thousand needles. The more he wriggled the more they pricked him. 'Ow, ow, ow!' cried the lizard.

'Let that be a lesson to you,' squawked the cockatoo, as she flew back to her tree. 'Never show off when you are playing with boomerangs.'

Out from under the bush limped the lizard. His smooth shining skin was now a mass of prickly thorns. No amount of rolling about or shaking himself would get rid of them. Slowly and painfully the lizard crawled home. And he never threw the boomerang again.

To this day, in Australia, there is a kind of lizard with a knobbly, spiky back. Its skin is so prickly that they call it 'the thorny devil'. And if you see a cockatoo you will notice the crest on its head, those few tall feathers which escaped the boomerang all those years ago.

(Australian Aborigine legend)

The Three Wishes

There was once an old man. Although he had worked hard every day of his life, he was very poor. One day as he was walking home from another hard day's work he said to himself, 'If only I could have three wishes, then all my troubles would be over.'

All at once a small man dressed in green appeared before him. 'I am here to help you,' said the Elf. 'I will grant you your three wishes. Whatever you wish will be yours. But take care what you do with them.'

The old man could not believe his luck. He ran all the way home to tell his wife, without stopping even to say 'Thank you' to the Elf.

'Wife! Wife!' shouted the old man. 'Good news! The little people have granted us three wishes. We can have anything we like.'

'Oh good,' said his wife. 'We can get out of this little old cottage and get ourselves a lovely new house.'

'Oh no,' said the old man. 'We need some horses first. We'll be able to ride everywhere.'

'I shall have a lovely new dress,' said the wife. 'In fact a whole new wardrobe of dresses.'

'Oh no you won't,' said the old man. 'I need clothes more than you do. I shall get myself a new suit—you've got plenty of dresses.'

'Oh no I haven't,' said the wife.

'Oh yes you have,' said her husband, and soon they were in the middle of a flaming row.

After a while the old man said, 'Let's stop arguing and have something to eat. We can decide what we really want after supper.'

The wife agreed. The old man sat down at the table, and his wife brought out their evening meal. One well cooked sausage each. The old man was hungry. He licked his lips as the sausage sat sizzling on the plate.

'Ooh, I wish this sausage was as big as my arm!' he said.

Wham! The sausage swelled and swelled until it was as long and fat as the old man's arm.

'Now look what you've done,' scolded his wife. 'You've wasted one of your wishes on a sausage!'

'It wasn't my fault,' moaned the old man.

'Oh yes it was,' said the old woman, and she continued her scolding.

At last the old man could stand it no more.

'Oh I wish that sausage was on the end of your nose!' he said.

Wham! The long sausage hung on the end of his wife's nose. It certainly stopped her grumbling. Instead she burst into tears. She cried and she cried. And still the sausage hung from the end of her nose. At last the old man said, 'Oh I wish that sausage would *go!*'

Wham! The sausage flew from the wife's nose right out of the window. Instead of being pleased his wife was more angry than ever.

'Look, you've used up *all* our wishes,' she said.

The old man sat there scratching his head. 'Why,' he wondered, 'did it all go wrong?'

(Folktale)

Till Eulenspiegel

Over six hundred years ago there lived in Germany a boy called Till Eulenspiegel. In English his name means Owlglass. Throughout his life Till hated work. In fact, he used to work hard to avoid work. He loved jokes and tricks of every kind. And he was clever at making money in the most unusual ways. Often his tricks worked because the people he tricked were bad-tempered or greedy. As in this story.

One day Till was passing a baker's shop when he saw a large notice in the window—'Skilled Baker Required. Apply Within.' Till went in and persuaded the baker to give him the job. 'For many years,' said Till, 'I've kneaded the dough.' So Till began work for the baker, but it wasn't long before he was up to his tricks.

Once a month the baker had to go to the big city of Hanover to buy flour. He said to Till, 'I am going to Hanover tomorrow, so *you* will be in charge of the baking.'

'That's easy,' said Till. 'What shall I bake?' The baker was a grumpy man, and it didn't take much for him to lose his temper.

'Idiot!' he shouted. 'What do you think you should bake—owls and monkeys? Just get on with it!'

Then off stomped the baker, slamming the door behind him. But he had given Till an idea.

Owls and monkeys! That's what the baker had said. So Till set to work mixing the dough, then shaping the loaves into owls and monkeys. When the baker returned he couldn't believe his eyes. Instead of loaves his shop was filled with bread owls and monkeys.

'You fool!' he shouted. 'Have you gone mad?'

'I only did as you told me,' said Till, with wide innocent eyes.

'Take them and get out!' roared the baker. 'They can be your wages. And don't come back!'

Till quickly filled a sack with the owls and monkeys. Then he made off, dodging the baker's kick as he went. Till knew just what to do with those owls and monkeys. He sat outside the church in the market square. It was coming up to Christmas, and everybody was in a good mood. Till soon had his owls and monkeys on display.

'Buy a lucky owl or monkey for Christmas!' he shouted.

People were curious and soon a crowd gathered. What a novelty! No one had ever seen such strange loaves before. In a short time they were all sold, and Till had a pocketful of money.

That year Till and his mother celebrated Christmas in grand style—all because of the trick he played on the bad-tempered baker.

(German legend)

You can hear how a famous composer called Richard Strauss celebrated the tricks of Till in his music, which is called 'Till Eulenspiegel's Merry Pranks'. When we listen to the music Strauss reminds us that the spirit of mischief and harmless fun lives on.

The Tinkling Medals

There was once, in Russia, a girl who was always winning prizes at school. The prizes that she won were little silver medals which she pinned to the front of her dress. Some prizes were for good behaviour, others were for working hard. She was very proud of all the medals she had won, and never stopped telling others how clever she was.

'Look at my medals,' she would say. 'No one has got as many medals as I have.' This was true. But nobody liked her for boasting about it. When other children won medals they took them home, but this girl would always wear hers, so that everyone could see how clever she was.

One day the headteacher announced that a wolf had been seen wandering around the wood near the school. It was winter, and the wolf was probably feeling hungry.

'It has come to the village looking for food,' said the headteacher. 'You must be very careful when you go home. Always walk with some of your friends. You must not go home alone.'

When school was finished for the day everyone went home with their friends. Everyone except the girl with the medals. She was so bossy that she had no friends. She wasn't going to ask anyone to walk home with her. They could if they wanted. But none of them wanted to. So she set off alone on the path through the woods back to her home. As she walked along she felt a little lonely. It was beginning to grow dark, and the wind whistled through the trees. But she could hear the medals chinking on her chest, and she knew that no one was as clever as she was.

Suddenly she saw a grey shadow in the trees. It disappeared, and then she saw it again. It was the wolf! She stopped and looked around. There was no one to be seen. Then she began walking quickly. She glanced back. The shadow was following her. 'I'd better hide,' she thought. So she ran through the trees as fast as her legs would carry her. Her heart was pounding. She saw a large bush and crouched quickly behind it. The leaves covered her completely. Here she would be safe.

The shadow of the wolf moved past where she was hiding, then it stopped. The wolf's ears pricked up listening. The girl lay quite still in the bushes. She did not make a movement or a sound, but as she breathed the medals on her chest began to tinkle. The wolf had heard the sound of tinkling medals.

Although they searched the whole forest, the girl was never seen again. All that was found, beneath an old hedge, were three shining medals.

(Adapted from Saki)

The Troll's Share

There once lived a farmer who was a very hard worker. He was most careful to get everything he possibly could out of his land. One year when he was sowing his crops he noticed a small hill in the middle of one of his fields. Nothing was growing on it but weeds and grass. 'That'll never do,' he said to himself. And at once began to plough over the mound.

Scarcely had he pulled the plough across the hill, when it suddenly began to shake. Then it rose like a mushroom, held up by four red pillars. The farmer knew at once that he had been trying to plough up the roof of a Troll's house. The Trolls were ugly monsters that hated the sunshine. They lived underground, but at night they raised the roofs of their houses on pillars and crawled out. The Troll who lived in this hill-house was sitting there, shaded by his earthy roof. He peered angrily at the farmer, and bellowed, 'Who has dared to plough up the roof of my house! How dare you meddle with us earth-dwellers!'

The farmer crept up to the edge of the house, making sure he kept well out of the reach of the Troll.

'I beg your pardon, Mister Troll,' said the farmer, as politely as he could.

'I had no idea that this hill was your roof. It was sitting here doing nothing and it seemed a pity to waste good ground.'

'Hmmm,' grunted the Troll, 'and what were you going to do with it?'

'Why, plant crops on it,' said the farmer. 'I could grow plenty of good food up there on the roof of your house.'

'Well it's *my* house,' grumbled the Troll, 'and the only person who should grow things on it is me.'

'You're quite right,' said the farmer. 'But it would mean a great deal of trouble for you, and hard work which I know you won't like. And there is the sunshine. I know that gentlemen like yourself who live underground hate to work in sunlight. Why not let me sow the crops for you and we can share whatever grows on your roof. One year I'll take the part that grows above ground, and you can have what grows under it. The next year I'll have what's under the soil and you can have what's above it.'

The Troll scratched one of his heads. He had three of them, but none had many brains inside.

'That seems fair,' he muttered. 'You seem a good strong fellow. All right, it's a deal. I shall have the first crop which grows above the ground, and you can have the roots. Next year I'll have the crops beneath the soil and you'll have what grows above it.'

The farmer promised that he would keep his side of the bargain. The Troll thanked him, his mouths began to yawn and he settled down to sleep again. Slowly his house sank under the ground until nothing showed but the little hill which was its roof. The farmer went on with his ploughing, smiling to himself at the thought of the bargain he had made with the ugly Troll.

After he had finished ploughing the farmer sowed carrots all over the hill. They grew well and at harvest-time he gathered a heavy crop. According to the bargain the farmer kept the carrots themselves, since they grew underground, while the Troll had the useless tops. Next year the farmer sowed a fine field of wheat across the roof of the Troll's house. When it was ripe he harvested the crop for himself, according to the bargain, and dug up all the roots for the Troll.

So the farmer had a harvest of carrots and a harvest of corn in alternate years, and the Troll had his share of carrot tops and corn roots. The farmer was pleased, and the Troll was content, since he knew no better even though he had three heads.

(Danish folktale)

(Follow up: Carrots are a root crop, what other root crops might the farmer have sown, and what above-ground crops could he have alternated them with? Is it good for the soil to grow one kind of crop one year, and another kind the next? This story is about a harvest, what other kinds of harvest are there?)

Tulsi the Peacemaker

Long ago in India there lived a very fat Maharajah. He was the richest and most powerful King in the whole of India. He ate off gold plates, dressed in the finest silks, and his palace was crowned with ivory towers. Peacocks roamed the palace gardens. His vast army included spearmen and bowmen, chariots and elephants. More than all these things he loved his daughter, the beautiful Princess Tulsi.

One day the Maharajah was inspecting his army, riding high in his howdah past rows of bright uniforms and sharp pointed swords. As he rode past the lines of soldiers he thought to himself, 'Why have a large army and never go to war?' On the following day he ordered his chief minister to send a letter to the neighbouring King. The message read: 'Send me fifty blue pigs or else!' As the messenger hurried off, the Maharajah tapped his tummy and smiled.

Some time later the messenger returned with a note from the neighbouring King. The Maharajah blinked when he read the message: 'We have got no blue pigs for you, and if I had . . .' So the King was *refusing* to give the great Maharajah those fifty blue pigs!

'This means war!' shouted the Maharajah.

His great army marched forth with flying banners, the chariot wheels rolled and the earth trembled with the tramping of elephants. The war was as cruel as all wars are. Death and injury made the land wretched. Corpses were left rotting in the fields and houses were burnt. Mothers cried for their dead sons, and waited for fathers who would never return. The war dragged on. What could be done to end it? Only one person knew, and that was the Maharajah's daughter, the beautiful Princess Tulsi. She was determined that the fighting must stop.

'But what can you do?' said her friend. 'How can one person stop two great armies?'

'You are only a girl,' said another. 'No one will listen to you.'

'You are too young to do anything,' said a third.

But all this made Tulsi more determined than ever. She swept past the guards and burst through the great doors of the council chamber.

'I want to see the King,' she said. 'I want to see the King.'

The Maharajah stared in surprise. 'Go . . . go to your room, daughter!' he bellowed. 'War is a business for men not girls.'

'My dear father,' said Tulsi. 'I do not want to speak of war, I want to talk of peace.'

The Maharajah could hardly believe his ears. No one had ever spoken to him like this before—let alone a mere girl. But before he could speak, Tulsi was saying, 'Why don't you go and speak with your enemy. Ask the King that you are fighting what he meant by his letter. It wouldn't hurt just to talk, would it?'

The old Maharajah could not think of an answer. So it was not long before the Maharajah rode forth to meet his great enemy, the neighbouring King. And Tulsi went too.

When they met, the other King spoke first.

'What did you mean, Maharajah, by your message—"Send fifty blue pigs or else"?'

'Fifty blue pigs,' explained the Maharajah, 'or else white pigs or black pigs, or any other colour that you might have. I would have paid you a good price. But what did you mean by, "We've got no blue pigs for you, and if we had . . ."?'

'Oh,' replied the King. 'If you had carried on reading you would have seen. My message was, "We have got no blue pigs for you and if we had I would be most pleased to send them to you."'

At once the Kings realised their misunderstanding. The war was stopped, the soldiers came home, and the country returned to peace and plenty. The Maharajah grew in riches, but of all his treasures the one he loved best was his daughter, Tulsi the peacemaker.

(Indian legend)

The Two Friends

Once many years ago in the city of Syracuse lived two men who were the best of friends. One was called Damon, and the other Pythias. Whether it was work or play Damon and Pythias were always together.

The ruler of Syracuse at that time was a cruel man named Dionysus. The people of Syracuse lived in fear of him. Damon was one of those who plotted to overthrow Dionysus. For this he was thrown into prison. 'In three days,' said Dionysus, 'you will die.'

Now Damon's wife and child lived far away from Syracuse. Damon begged Dionysus to let him go and see his family one last time before he died.

'All right,' said Dionysus. 'But I will put your friend Pythias in prison while you are gone. If you do not come back he will die at sunset on the third day.'

Pythias agreed to go into prison in his friend's place, so Damon set off to see his family for the last time. As he hurried away Dionysus turned to Pythias and said, 'He'll never come back. In three days you will die. Then it will be Damon's turn. I'll hunt him down and kill him. That way I shall be rid of both my enemies.' Pythias also wondered if he would ever see his friend again.

After a day's journey Damon reached the home of his wife and child. He stayed with them another day. On the morning of the third day he kissed them both and said 'Goodbye for ever'. Then he ordered his servant to bring his horse for the journey back to Syracuse.

'Your horse, master?' said the trembling servant. 'Did you say your horse?'

'Yes,' said Damon, 'my horse. I must hurry back to Syracuse. Where is my horse?'

'Something has happened master. Your horse has run away.'

'Run away?' said Damon. 'Then you must have let it go.'

'It was only to save you master,' cried the servant. 'Stay here with us, no one will ever find you here.'

'Fool!' said Damon. 'You have not only lost my horse, but you have killed my friend Pythias.'

Both his wife and child begged him to stay. What should Damon do? Stay free and let his friend die, or rush to try and save him? Off he went on foot back towards Syracuse. Down valleys, through woods, over fields he ran. Across rivers and raging torrents he swam. He ran until his strength was almost gone. Then he saw a man riding by on a horse. He begged the man to sell his horse.

'Why should I sell him to you?' asked the man.

'It is a matter of life and death,' said Damon. 'Will you sell?'

'No I won't,' said the man.

Damon pulled him from his horse, threw him all the money he had, and rode off at full speed for Syracuse.

The sun was setting on the third day. The crowds had gathered outside the gates of Syracuse. Pythias was led out of prison. Dionysus spoke to him, 'Your friend has not returned. Now you must die.'

Pythias was taken to the block where he was to be beheaded. The executioner picked up the axe. Dionysus smiled. Suddenly there was a stir from the crowd. A cloud of dust was coming towards them. It was Damon on his horse. The crowd cheered. Pythias was saved.

'Release the prisoner,' said Dionysus. 'Now I know what true friendship is. From this day there will be three friends, Damon, Pythias and myself.'

(Traditional Greek story)

The Two Metre Chopsticks

Once upon a time in far off China there lived a brave warrior, who met his death in battle, fighting for his country. He had lived a good life. He had been afraid of nothing, not even of the arrow that had pierced his heart. When he died he expected to be laid in one of the cold tombs on the hill. Instead he found himself outside the gates of Heaven.

A man was waiting there ready to receive him. 'Welcome,' he said. 'I was told that you were coming.'

'But where am I?' asked the warrior.

'This is Heaven, of course. The home of all good and brave men after they have lived their earthly life.'

'Tell me,' said the warrior, 'where do all the others go?'

'Oh, they go to the other place. Don't worry, you won't be bothered by them.'

'I'd like to see this other place,' said the warrior. 'Take me down to Hell.'

'All right, come with me,' said the guide. 'But you won't like what you see.'

So off they went, and soon arrived at the gates of Hell. Carefully they pushed the gates open. Inside the warrior could see a table, and on this table was a bowl piled high with freshly cooked rice. There were people sitting round the table, but the warrior was amazed to see that they were all starving. They looked thin, and mean, and miserable. The warrior soon saw why. For each person had in his hands chopsticks which were two metres long! Only by using the chopsticks could they reach the rice. But the chopsticks were so long that no matter how much rice they picked up they could never get the food into their mouths. It dropped on their heads, and in their eyes, and all over the floor. There was a terrible mess. Squabbles kept breaking out, food was flying, the noise was unbearable. The warrior looked at his guide. 'Can we go back now?' he asked.

So they did. The gates of Heaven opened wide and the warrior was led through. Once in Heaven the warrior was amazed to see the same table as he had seen in Hell, and there was the same bowl piled high with tasty rice, and sitting round the table were people holding two metre chopsticks. The warrior could hardly believe his eyes. 'But this is just what it was like in Hell,' he moaned.

'Really?' said his guide. 'Can't you see any difference?'

The warrior looked again. There was a difference. There were no sad, starving faces here, the people round the table all looked healthy and jolly. They were laughing and munching at the food. The warrior soon saw the reason why. Instead of each trying to grab what he could for himself, the people in Heaven were helping to feed each other. Although the chopsticks were too long for their own mouths, they were not too long for helping others. Each of them was using his chopsticks to feed someone else.

Now the warrior understood. Heaven and Hell were the same places, it was just that in Hell the people were selfish, and starved, while in Heaven they helped each other, and were happy.

(*Chinese folktale*)

The Two Painters

Many centuries ago the greatest country in the world was Greece. When people in Britain were still living in mud huts and dressing in animal skins the people of Greece had fine buildings and led the world in the arts of painting and sculpture. They loved beauty in all its forms and tried to find the best in all things.

They held the Olympic Games to find out who was the best in every sport, they held competitions in poetry, music, painting and sculpture. This story is about a competition to find the best painter in Greece.

Nobody could decide which out of two painters was the better artist. Some people preferred one artist, others preferred the other, so they agreed to ask an old man who had once been the best painter of his day, to judge between them. The old man told the two young painters to paint a picture that was as true to life as they could make it. They were to return in three months and when the paintings were unveiled he would judge which was the best.

The two artists went away and after three months returned, each bringing with him a finished picture. The crowds gathered in the market place eager to see which of the two painters would be the winner. The old man who was to judge stood in front of the two paintings, each of which was covered with a curtain. A signal was given. The first painter stepped forward and pulled back the curtain which was covering his picture. The crowd cheered for the painting was beautiful and very life-like. It showed a bowl of grapes which looked so ripe and juicy that one could hardly believe they were not real. All of a sudden some birds who had been flying nearby swooped down and began to peck at the picture. They were trying to eat the grapes. The crowd clapped with pleasure. If the painting was good enough to fool the birds it must surely be the winner.

Now it was the turn of the other painter. The old man gave the signal for the curtain to be pulled back so that all might see for themselves what this artist had painted. The young man smiled but did not move.

'It's your turn,' said the judge. 'Let us see your painting so that we can judge which is best.' But still the painter did not move. The old man was getting impatient. He stepped forward to pull back the curtain himself. His hand went to the curtain, but he did not seem able to get a grip on it.

'There is no curtain here,' he said to the crowd. 'The curtain is the painting. It's a painting of a curtain. It looks just like a real one!'

The crowd gasped with surprise.

When he had recovered the old man turned to the young artist and said, 'You are the winner. For although the other painting deceived the birds, your picture is better because it has deceived the eyes of man!'

They had found out who the best painter was. Or had they? I wonder which of the two paintings you would have chosen.

(Adapted from Herodotus)

256

The Ugly Duckling

The old duck was rather bored sitting on her eggs. It was summertime, and the sun was warm. Other ducks were swimming up and down the river, but none of them stopped to talk to her. Still, the eggs would soon hatch and she would be able to leave her nest and swim along with the other ducks.

One after another the eggs began to crack, and little fluffy heads peered out. The chicks struggled out of their shells as best they could. All the eggs had hatched except for one—the biggest egg of all.

'Well, and how are you getting on?' asked an old duck who had come to pay her a visit.

'I'm all right,' said the mother duck, 'except for this big one here.'

'Ah,' said the old duck, 'I bet that's a turkey's egg. Leave it and teach the others to swim.'

But the mother duck did not leave it; she stayed and kept it warm. After a while the great egg burst, and out of it came the biggest and ugliest chick the mother duck had ever seen. 'Well, we'll soon see if it is a turkey,' she said, as she led all her chicks into the water. In they went—even the great ugly grey one. So the family of ducks swam out into the river.

They were soon spotted by some rather proud Spanish ducks. 'Look at that strange ugly duckling,' one of them shouted. 'Let's go and tease him.' So they flew after him and pecked him on the neck.

'Leave him alone,' said the mother duck. 'He is not doing you any harm.' But that did not stop them making fun of the ugly duckling just because he looked so different from the rest. 'Never mind,' said the mother duck, 'I'm sure you will grow like the others in time.'

As each day passed things got worse. The ducks bit him, the hens pecked him, and the girl who fed the farmbirds kicked him. They all said he was the ugliest duckling they had ever seen. At last the ugly duckling could no longer stand the spiteful words, the teasing and the bullying. He swam away up river by himself and hid among the reeds.

The days grew shorter, the leaves turned yellow and the air grew cold. Autumn had come and the poor duckling felt lonely and uncomfortable lying by himself in the reeds. One evening, just as the sun was setting, a flock of large beautiful birds rose into the sky over the woods. The duckling had never seen anything so beautiful before. Their feathers were a dazzling white and they had long slender necks. They flew so high, spreading out their long splendid wings and uttering a strange cry. The duckling strained his neck to see them, but soon they disappeared and the duckling once more felt very alone.

The winter was so cold. The water froze and the ice crackled underfoot. How long it lasted the ugly duckling never knew. He lay among the bushes in the new-fallen snow, as if in a dream. The days and the weeks passed. He was still lying among the reeds when the sun began to shine again, the birds began to sing, and the spring had returned.

Once more he shook his wings. They were stronger now and before he knew it he was out in the open water. And there out of the reeds came three beautiful swans. To his surprise they swam around him and began to stroke him with their beaks. Some children were running along the river bank. 'Look, there's a new swan,' one of them cried. The young swan fluffed his feathers and flapped his great white wings. It was true, he really was a swan. How little did he dream when he was an ugly duckling that he would grow into a proud, happy swan.

(*Adapted from Hans Andersen*)

Varenka

Long ago there lived a little widow called Varenka. She lived in the great forests of Russia all alone in a cottage. Every night before she went to bed she prayed before an icon. She always liked to keep a vase of fresh flowers before her icon. One winter's day as she was arranging her flowers she heard the sounds of people passing her house. She went out to see who it was.

A group of travellers was walking by, each one carrying a bundle of clothes.

'Where are you all going?' asked Varenka.

'Haven't you heard?' said a traveller. 'War has broken out. Soldiers are coming this way and we are trying to escape. Get your things together and come with us.'

When Varenka heard this she thought, 'Who will look after the travellers as they pass? Who will look after the motherless children? Who will shelter the animals and feed the birds?' So she said to the travellers, 'No, I must stay, but you my friends should hurry on, and God be with you.'

Varenka returned to her house and bolted the door. As the sun went down Varenka knelt down and prayed, 'Please God, build a wall round my house so that the soldiers will not see me.' But in the morning God had not built a wall round her house, and in the distance she could hear the sound of gunfire. 'When the soldiers come,' she thought, 'what will become of me?'

She went into the forest to gather firewood, and there met an old man with a goat. The old man said to Varenka, 'My name is Peter. I am a goatherd. My cottage has been burnt down by the soldiers. They have taken everything from me except this white goat. Please give us shelter for the night.'

Varenka knew that there were wolves in the forest, so she said to the old man, 'Come with me, Peter. I will take care of you and your white goat.'

So Varenka took Peter and the goat, made them comfortable, and before they went to sleep she prayed, 'Please God, build a wall round my house so that the soldiers do not see Peter, the goat or me.'

But the next day there was no wall. Everything was the same. Varenka went out to gather mushrooms and herbs, and came across a young man asleep in the hollow of a tree.

'Wake up! Wake up!' she said. 'You cannot sleep here. The soldiers will find you. Listen! Can't you hear the gunfire?'

The young man was an artist, he had escaped from the fighting and carried with him all he had in the world—a painting and a flower. Varenka took the young man home. That night she said her prayers again. But still nothing happened. No wall was built around Varenka's house.

The next day as Varenka baked bread she heard the sound of crying from outside her window. It was a small child dressed in rags. Her mother and father had been killed by the soldiers. She was running away, and had smelt the bread that Varenka was baking. The sound of gunfire was getting closer. Varenka took the little girl in. That night Varenka prayed again, 'Dear God, please build a wall around our house and save us from the soldiers.'

The night was very still, but a gentle sound came all round the house. Varenka looked out and saw the snow falling heavily. It was up to the window sill and still falling. Deeper and deeper it became until at dawn the small house was quite hidden. The soldiers came that day. Inside the house they could hear the marching of feet and the firing of guns. But the house was hidden under the snow and the soldiers passed by. When the snow melted the people came out of the cottage, and thanked God for saving them.

Varenka's prayer had been answered, though not in the way she had expected.

(Russian story)

The Village of Eyam

Many of you will remember the nursery rhyme, 'A ring a ring of roses, a pocket full of posies, Atishoo, atishoo, we all fall down.' This rhyme was made up more than three hundred years ago, at the time of the Great Plague. The 'ring a ring of roses' were the spots which looked like red roses on the skin of anyone who caught the disease. The 'pocket full of posies' were the posies, or bunches of sweet smelling flowers, which people held to their noses to stop the nasty smells which they thought carried the plague. 'Atishoo, atishoo' were the first signs that anyone had the plague, and of course their sneezes soon spread the germs. 'All fall down' meant that whoever got the plague soon fell down—dead.

They called this plague the Black Death. In London during the August and September of 1665 nearly 50,000 people died of it. This was almost one out of every three people. As many as could tried to escape the disease by fleeing into the country. They thought they would be safe in the clean country air. But they often took the plague with them, and thousands more died in villages throughout the country.

It was not only people that carried the plague; rats also carried it, and not only rats. One day a box of fine clothes arrived at the tailor's shop in the small village of Eyam in Derbyshire. The clothes had come from London, and were once owned by someone who had died from the plague. Soon after unpacking the clothes the tailor fell ill, and within days he was dead. The plague had come to Eyam.

What were the villagers to do? Run away perhaps, as fast as they could from the terrible disease, like others had done. There was something special about the people of Eyam for they decided that they would not run away but would stay in their village, and risk their own lives rather than pass the plague on to other people. They would cut themselves off from the outside world until the disease had burned itself out. That way other villages might be spared. No one was to enter or leave the village. No letter or message was sent out, except for the one to arrange for food to be left by a lonely well outside the village.

There were no more contacts with the outside world—except for one. A girl called Emmot Sydall slipped out of Eyam to a small wooded valley where she met her sweetheart from the next village. His name was Rowland Torre. He begged her to come away with him to safety, but she said that she could not. She did not want to risk passing on the disease to him or to anyone else. They would meet again when the plague was over, and then they could marry. He begged and pleaded with her to go with him, but she went back to Eyam.

For six long months the people of Eyam saw family and friends dying one by one. Nobody knew who would be the next to die. No matter how healthy and strong you were, in a few days you might be dead and buried. Out of the 300 people who lived in Eyam, only thirty-three were left alive when the plague was over.

The church bell rang out the news that the plague had ended. One of the first visitors to the village was Rowland Torre, seeking the girl he was to marry. But she was dead.

The simple villagers of Eyam had given their lives rather than pass on the Black Death to their neighbours. They had given their lives but the plague was beaten and the people of Eyam were not forgotten.

When Fingal Faced a Bully

Fingal was proud to be the fastest runner and the strongest fighter in the whole of Ireland. He became the chief of his clan, and with his men built a huge bridge across the channel between Ireland and Scotland. It was called the Giant's Causeway. But the bridge was to mean bad news for Fingal.

Fingal learned that a Scottish giant, greater than any man had ever seen, was on his way across the bridge to challenge Fingal to a fight. The giant's name was Cucullain, and he was bigger than a bear and more bad tempered. He made mud pies out of mountains, and the stamp of his foot was like an earthquake. 'Glory be,' said Fingal to his wife Oona. 'What shall I do? I am about to be turned into a string of sausages by the biggest bully in Scotland!'

'Oh, come now,' said Oona his wife, 'every man no matter how big he is has some weakness. I am sure this Cucullain of yours is not as frightening as he sounds.' And Oona, who was a sensible woman, carried on with her knitting.

'Woman,' said Fingal, 'this man is as big as a mountain—he's going to mash me, indeed he will. They do say, though, that all his strength is bound up in the middle finger of his right hand. But what good is that to me?'

'Is that so?' said Oona.

She stopped knitting for a moment and looked very thoughtful. Soon a mighty roar and a thump of heavy footsteps told them that Cucullain was coming.

'Where shall I hide?' shouted Fingal.

'Quick,' said Oona, 'put on the baby's nightgown and his nightcap and climb into the cradle. Pretend to be the baby!'

Fingal blinked and his mouth dropped open, but before he had time to think Oona was squeezing him into the cradle, and covering him with the baby's nightclothes. Just as Oona had popped the baby's bonnet on Fingal's head there was a great crashing on the front door.

Oona opened the door and there before her stood the great Scottish giant. Before she could say, 'Good morning', Cucullain snarled, 'Where is he? Let me get my hands on him, I'll grind his bones to butter!'

'I am afraid he's out,' said Oona, 'but you can come in if you want to. You'll be seeing him soon.'

Cucullain stamped into the house and growled.

'Oh please tread quietly,' said Oona, 'or you'll wake the baby.'

The giant looked at the cradle in the corner, 'Och what a bonny little bairn you have.' Fingal squeezed down into the cot, and felt the sweat drip from his forehead as the giant came closer.

'My baby is three months old,' said Oona, who never told a lie.

'What a sweet little thing he is,' said Cucullain reaching out to tickle Fingal under his chin. With that Fingal opened his mouth and caught Cucullain's finger in his teeth, crunching it with all his might. The great finger which held all Cucullain's strength was bitten clean off. Fingal sprang out of the cradle but already the Scottish giant was on his way. Neither Fingal nor his wife saw the great Cucullain again. Sad to say, in his haste to return, the Scottish giant trod most of the Giant's Causeway back into the sea, so if you go there today only a few miles of it remain.

But from that day on Fingal was never troubled by bullies again.

(Irish legend)

Why the Sea Is Salt

Once upon a time, many years ago, there were two brothers; one was rich and the other was poor. It was Christmas time and the poor one had nothing left in his house to eat. So he went to ask his brother for a little meat to take home to his family. The rich brother was a mean man; he said, 'I will give you this ham if you do one thing for me. Take it to the Devil!' The poor man agreed and went on his way with the ham.

On his return through a wood the poor man met an old, old man with a long white beard, and greeted him with the words, 'Good evening old man.'

'Where are you going?' asked the old man.

'Oh, I've got to see the Devil, if only I could find him, because I'm taking him this ham.'

'Ah, the Devil is very fond of ham,' said the old man, 'but make sure he gives you something for it. Ask him for the old hand-mill he keeps by his door.'

'What do I need a hand-mill for?' asked the poor man.

'Bring it to me,' was the reply, 'and I will show you how to use it.'

Then the old man pointed to a door hidden in the roots of a tree and said, 'Knock on the door and you will find the Devil.'

The poor man knocked and went in. The Devil was there and was very pleased to see the ham. 'You can have it in exchange for that old hand-mill by the door,' said the poor man. The Devil did not want to part with his hand-mill, but finally he agreed.

Back in the forest the old man showed the poor man how to use the hand-mill. 'And remember,' said the old man, 'when you want it to stop you must say "Grind no more, little mill" three times.'

At home that evening the poor man placed the mill on his table and said, 'Grind me a Christmas feast little mill.' At once out came dishes, knives, forks, a big roast turkey, Christmas pudding and lots more besides. The poor man and his family had a wonderful feast.

As the weeks went by the poor man's cottage became a fine new house, and inside was everything the poor man had ever wanted. People got to hear of this wonderful mill, and one day the rich brother too heard the story.

Being mean and greedy he wanted the mill for himself. 'I could grind things to sell and become very rich,' he thought. So one night he came and stole the hand-mill. Early next morning he took it with him on one of his ships and sailed away.

When he was far out to sea he gathered all the empty sacks he could find and said, 'Now mill, grind me salt.' The mill began to grind and the greedy brother filled up his sacks. 'These sacks full of salt will bring me lots of money when I sell them,' he thought, and his eyes gleamed.

Soon the sacks were full, and the rich brother said, 'All right, you can stop now,' but nothing happened. The mill kept on grinding the salt. 'Stop!' shouted the greedy brother, but he did not know the right words. Salt spilt everywhere, it heaped up higher and higher. Slowly the ship sank under the weight of the salt. Down with it went the greedy man, and the little hand-mill still grinding salt. And there it lies at the bottom of the sea, grinding away, and that is why the sea is salt.

(Dutch legend)

Why Summer Days Are Longer

Long, long ago when the World began, the Sun used to race at great speed across the sky. Each day was only a few hours long. Even in the islands of the South Pacific there was little time to go fishing or hunting, and not enough daylight for people to do all that they wanted. Everyone grumbled that the days were so short.

One day a fisherman called Mani decided that he would teach the Sun a lesson. 'That Sun,' he moaned, 'shoots across the sky so fast that we hardly have time for anything. I shall slow him down so that we can have more light to fish and sail in our boats.' So Mani plaited long ropes together to make a huge net. Then one summer morning, long before dawn, he took his canoe and sailed out into the sea carrying with him his great net. On and on, to the very edge of the World he sailed, to the place where the Sun rose from the ocean. As his boat bobbed on the waves Mani cast his net across the sea and waited to see what would happen.

A great flash of yellow light appeared, the Sun began to rise, and as it did so it got tangled in Mani's net. Mani pulled the ropes as tightly as he could. The Sun was caught! 'Let me out of this net,' bellowed the Sun. 'I have far to go.'

Mani shielded his eyes from the glare and said, 'Oh Sun, why do you race across the sky. Give us more time to do our work!'

The sun shone brilliantly, and the ropes on Mani's net began to burn. 'Let me out of this net,' said the Sun, 'and I will help you.'

Mani did not know what to do. He loosened some of the ropes, the Sun rose higher and shone more brightly. Mani felt the burning heat on his skin, and his hands which held the net seemed to be on fire. 'Let me go,' said the Sun. 'I will stand still and let the earth travel round me. That way you will get your longer days, but only in the summertime.'

Mani agreed. He let go of the net, and as the Sun shone down once more, he paddled his canoe back to shore. The Sun kept his word. He stands still in the sky and when the earth turns towards him in summer the days grow longer. To this day you can see the ropes of Mani at dawn and at dusk hanging down in rays from the Sun. They remind us of the day when Mani cast his net and made the Sun stand still.

(Fijian folktale)

William Tell

Many years ago high in the mountains of Switzerland lived a hunter named William Tell. The weapon he hunted with was a crossbow. He was the best shot in the land. At this time the Swiss were not a free people, they were ruled by Austrians, and a man named Gessler was made governor of their country. Gessler was a cruel man. He made many harsh laws which the people had to obey. The Swiss people longed to be free, but there was only one of them brave enough to stand up to Gessler—and that was William Tell.

Gessler knew that the Swiss hated him, so he thought of a plan to show them that he was master. 'Bring me the longest pole that you can find,' he ordered his servant, 'then fetch one of my hats. Not the best one I keep for Sunday, but one of my old ones.' When he had brought the hat Gessler ordered the man to place it on top of the pole. 'Now,' said Gessler, 'tell all the people that whoever passes this hat must bow down to it.'

The long pole was planted in the market square and all who passed would bow down to Gessler's hat.

William Tell lived in a small village a few miles out of town. No one had told him of the strange law of bowing to the hat on the pole. One morning he packed his bag with apples, and said to his son, 'Come on, let's go to town and take these apples to your old grandfather.' So William Tell, together with his son Walter, set off. Over one shoulder Tell carried his trusty crossbow.

When they reached the market place in the town a guard shouted, 'Halt! Why did you not bow to the hat of your master?'

'Why should I bow to a hat?' asked William Tell.

'It's the law. That is the governor's hat, and all must bow before it.'

'I am a free man,' said Tell. 'I will never bow down to a hat.'

The soldier tried to seize hold of William Tell, and a crowd began to gather round. All at once there was the sound of trumpets. Through the crowd rode the governor himself, Herr Gessler. The guard told Gessler what had happened, and he looked at William Tell with cold cruel eyes.

'They say that you are the finest shot with the crossbow in all the land,' he growled. 'I have a little test for you. One of these apples can be your target. You have broken the law, but if you hit the target you shall go free. I will place the apple against that tree—on the head of your son.'

'Punish me,' said William Tell, 'but spare my son. He has done you no harm.'

'I am not afraid, father,' said the boy. 'I will stand quite still. I know you can hit the apple.'

The boy walked over to the tree and carefully placed the apple on his head. William Tell took two arrows from his quiver. He put one in his belt, and the other onto his crossbow. With a steady hand he drew the bow back, took careful aim, and shot. There was silence, and then a great cheer, because the arrow shot into the apple and split it in two.

Gessler turned angrily to Tell, 'All right,' he said, 'you can go. But first tell me why you put that other arrow into your belt.'

'If the first arrow had touched even a hair of my son's head, the second arrow would have found your heart,' replied Tell.

Hearing this Gessler ordered his soldiers to seize William Tell. On the way to prison Tell managed to escape. The people rose up against their enemy. After a great struggle Gessler was killed, and in the end Switzerland, led by the example of William Tell, became what it is today, a free country.

(*Swiss legend*)

The Wind and the Sun

One day the Wind and the Sun had a quarrel. In fact they were always quarrelling for if the truth were known the Wind was rather jealous of the Sun. Everyone could see the Sun shining like a golden ball in the sky, but no one could see the Wind. The Wind showed his strength by blowing things about, and he was very proud of all that he could do. On the day of this quarrel he met the Sun at the top of a hill, and each began to boast of his cleverness.

'I,' glowed the Sun, 'bring warmth to the earth. Without me there would be no flowers in the fields or fruits on the trees.'

'And I,' breathed the Wind, 'can blow the leaves from the trees and make the seas roar.'

'No one is stronger than I am,' the Sun beamed. And once more they began to quarrel.

Just then a man came walking by. He was wearing a thick overcoat.

'Let us try a test of strength,' whispered the Wind 'and see which of us can make the man take his coat off. As I am the stronger I am bound to win.'

'We'll see about that—you try first,' glinted the Sun. 'Meanwhile I will wait and hide behind this cloud.'

So the Wind blew down on the man with all his strength. The man pulled his coat around him, so the Wind puffed harder, and the man wrapped his coat even more tightly around himself. The Wind roared and bent the trees, leaves swirled in the air. The man was bent double and his coat tails flapped. The Wind howled down the hill, but still the man kept his coat on. At last the Wind sighed and gave up. 'It's no good,' he puffed. 'It can't be done.'

The Sun peeped out from behind the cloud. 'Now let me try,' he beamed. Slowly the Sun began to shine. The man felt warm, then hot, then hotter still. The Sun beat down with its full force. The man began to sweat, then to unbutton his coat. Finally the heat was too much. The man took off his coat and collapsed under the shade of a tree.

'Who do you think is stronger now, Mr Wind?' glowed the Sun. But there came no answer, just a gentle rustling of leaves as the Wind blew away. And he never argued with the Sun again.

(Aesop)

The Wise Fools of Gotham

Many years ago in England there was a King called John. He was a greedy and unpopular King. He made the people pay heavy taxes and built his castles on their land. Eventually the rich lords and barons got the better of King John and made him sign a charter called the Magna Carta, to guarantee their rights. Once even the common people got the better of the King. Here is how it happened.

King John was travelling through the country looking for a place to build a castle, when he came to a village called Gotham in Nottinghamshire. The people of Gotham were poor and they had little common land for their cows to graze on. It was a custom of the time that, wherever the King passed, the land became forever part of the King's highway. So if the King crossed their common land it would become part of the King's highway, and they would have very little room to graze their cattle. Not only that, but it was rumoured that the King wanted to build a castle there. If that happened, then the common people would be left with no land on which to keep their cows.

So they decided to build a barricade to keep the King and his men out of their fields. They built a barrier of carts, sticks and old pieces of furniture to prevent the King from crossing their land. Then they scattered into the countryside, leaving the village empty until the King's men had gone. King John was angry that he could not cross the villagers' fields because he was forced to travel a long way round. He did not want the common people to get the better of him, so he sent a party of soldiers into the village to punish the people for stopping his progress, and to see whether it was a fit place to build himself a castle. What could the poor people of Gotham do against a band of soldiers armed with swords and spears? The villagers saw the soldiers coming and quickly made their plans. They could never keep the soldiers off their lands by fighting them, but they had another idea.

When the soldiers arrived they could not believe their eyes. The people of Gotham were all busy doing the craziest things. Some of them were rolling cheeses down a hillside. The captain of the troops rode up to them and asked, 'What are you doing here?'

'Ah,' said one of the old men, 'we haven't got any time to go to market today so our cheeses are going by themselves.'

And he rolled another cheese down the hill.

Other villagers were gathered around the pond. The officer rode off to speak to them. They were throwing eels into the water.

'What are you doing?' asked the captain.

'We're killing these eels,' they said.

'How?' asked the soldier.

'By drowning them of course!'

All over the village people were doing the most foolish things. One group of men were holding hands around a bush.

'What are you doing?' asked the officer.

'There's a cuckoo in here, and we're trapping it,' said a man.

'Cuckoo, cuckoo!' said another.

'I think we'd better get out of here men,' said the captain.

So back the soldiers went to the King, to report that a village full of half-wits would not be the best place for the King to have a castle—and how could you punish such crazy people?

The people of Gotham were pleased that their plan had worked. By acting like fools they had fooled the King. And the wise fools of Gotham were left in peace.

(*Traditional English story*)

The Wise Man of Ireland and His Cake

The Wise Man of Ireland was on his travels. He loved nothing more than having a clear sky above the open road before him. It was morning, the grass was green and the birds were singing. Everything in the world was grand. The Wise Man of Ireland would have been very happy but for one thing. He was hungry, which was not surprising since he had not eaten for a whole day.

The Wise Man sat on a rock by the roadside and felt his tummy rumble with hunger. Suddenly he remembered the cake in his pocket. He took it out and unwrapped it, licking his lips. It looked delicious. Just as he was about to take a large bite he saw a band of people coming towards him along the road. They were all carrying shopping bags. As they came near the Wise Man of Ireland held out his piece of cake. 'All men are brothers,' he said, 'would you like to share my cake?'

The group of people stopped. There was a man with a beard and his six children: three sons and three daughters. They looked at the cake and nodded. So the Wise Man divided his cake into eight pieces, and handed seven of them over to the family. There was only enough for a small piece each.

'I am sorry it is so little,' said the Wise Man.

'Oh a gift is never little,' replied the bearded man, as he took a piece of the Wise Man's cake.

The children also took a piece each, and cheerfully gobbled it up. The Wise Man only had a small bit left for himself, and soon it was gone.

When they had all finished the bearded man said, 'Now we have eaten your cake what shall we do with these large parcels of food that we have brought with us? My wife packed them up for our trip to the market.' Sure enough each one of the children, and the bearded man, had a large parcel of food tucked away in their shopping bags. They certainly didn't feel hungry after eating the Wise Man's cake. 'T'would be a pity to waste them,' continued the man, 'perhaps you would share them with us,' he said to the Wise Man. The Wise Man was still feeling very hungry and was pleased to agree.

So each one of them divided their parcel of food into half, and handed it over to the Wise Man. The Wise Man was amazed to see how much food he was getting. The six children and the bearded man waved goodbye to the Wise Man and continued on their way. 'What did I do,' he wondered, 'to get all this lovely food?'

(*Irish folktale*)

The Wise Priest

There was once a priest who was so wise that all the people came to him with their troubles. One Sunday morning, before the church service, three farmers from the parish called to see him.

'Good morning, Father,' they began.

'Good morning, my friends. What can I do for you?'

'Father, the drought is ruining our crops. We have come to ask if you can find a way to make it rain?'

'Why, of course I can, my friends. Nothing is simpler. I know a prayer which will make the rain pour. It has never been known to fail. All we need to do is to get everybody to agree on the same day. When the service is over we will all say the prayer together.'

'Thank you, Father,' said the farmers.

'We are here to help each other,' said the priest.

So the farmers went into the church, and at the end of the service the priest said to his people, 'My friends, the crops are dying in the fields and we need some rain. You have asked my help to end the drought. Now I know a prayer which will bring rain, but you must all agree for it to rain on the same day. Would you like it to rain today?'

'Oh no, Father!' the young men protested. 'That will spoil this afternoon's football match.'

'Do you want it to rain tomorrow, then?'

'Oh dear, no!' the mothers moaned. 'Monday is our washing day. If it rained our clothes would never dry.'

'Well, shall we make it rain on Tuesday?'

'Oh no!' answered a group of farmers. 'We are harvesting the hay on Wednesday and we cannot do that if it rains on Tuesday.'

'Well, do you want it to rain on Thursday, then?'

'Oh no, Father!' said some schoolboys. 'We are going for an outing so it must be dry on that day.'

'Well, shall we have it rain on Friday?'

'Oh no!' said the builder. 'I am tiling a roof, and I must be finished by the weekend.'

'So you want it to rain on Saturday, then?'

'Dear me, no!' said the Mayor. 'I am opening a fair, and I shall not want to get wet.'

'Well, my friends,' declared the priest, 'as you know, my prayers cannot work unless all of you agree to the same day. But, as you do not seem able to agree, I think we shall have to leave the weather, as always, to the will of our Good Lord.'

(French folktale)

Resources

A Checklist of Resources
for Use in Assembly

anniversaries
artwork

ballads
Bible readings
birthdays

children's writing
choral speaking
cooking
crafts
customs

discussion
drama
dressing-up

events
experiments

festivals
films
filmstrips
folkdances
folk songs
friezes

mime
models
movement
music

news
nursery rhymes

objects
outside speakers
overhead projector

pictures
plays
poetry
posters
projects
puppets

questions
quizzes

radio
radiovision
readings
reports

singing games
slides
slide and tape
songs
sound effects
stories

tape recordings
television and video

Resource Books—A Select Bibliography

1 The School Assembly

Assemblies R. Purton (Blackwell)
Assemblies for the Primaries A. G. Patston (Religious Education Press)
Assembly : Poems and Prose R. Brandling (Macmillan)
Assembly Workshop R. Dingwall (Dartman, Longman, Todd)
A Book of Assemblies D. Waters (Bell & Hyman)
Celebrating Together P. Wetz and P. Walker (Dartman, Longman, Todd)
Day by Day R. Purton (Blackwell)
Explorations in Assembly with Children Dorothy J. Taylor (Lutterworth)
Infant Teacher's Assembly Book D. M. Prescott (Blandford)
Junior Teacher's Assembly Book D. M. Prescott (Blandford)
Meeting Points Assembly Book G. L. Pinfold (Longman)
A Morning Assembly Book J. & J. Brimer (Blackie)
The Morning Cockerel Assembly Book M. E. Rose (Hart Davies)
Pause for Thought M. Cheston (Blackie)
Plays for Assembly P. M. Allen (Schofield and Sims)
Primary School Assembly Book F. Dickinson and I. R. Worsnop (Macmillan)
Readings D. Thomson (Cambridge University Press)
School Assemblies for 8–13s D. Prickett (Denholm House)
101 School Assembly Stories F. Carr (Foulsham)
Senior Teacher's Assembly Book D. M. Prescott (Blandford)
Stories for Middle School Assembly D. M. Prescott (Blandford)
Themes and Poems of Worship I. O'Brian (Basil Blackwell)
Think on these Things R. St. L. Broadberry (Nelson)

2 Festivals and Customs

The Autumn Book J. Reeves (Heinemann)
The Christmas Book J. Reeves (Heinemann)
Christmas Customs and Folklore M. Baker (Shire)
Customs and Traditions Joan Sabin (Blackwell)
Days of the Year J. McLellan (Religious Education Press)
Festivals R. Manning-Sanders (Heinemann)
Festivals and Customs P. Morell (Pan/Piccolo)
Festivals and Saint's Days V. J. Green (Blandford)
The Springtime Book J. Reeves (Heinemann)
Stories of Christmas Customs N. F. Pearson (Ladybird)
Stories of Special Days and Customs N. F. Pearson (Ladybird)
The Winter Book E. Gundrey (Methuen)

See Also :
A Hindu Family in Britain P. Bridger (Religious Education Press)
A Sikh Family in Britain O. Cole & W. Owen (Religious Education Press)

Our Buddhist Friends J. Ascott (National Christian Education Council)
Our Christian Friends A. Nicholls (National Christian Education Council)
Our Hindu Friends T. Perry (National Christian Education Council)
Our Jewish Friends M. Clark (National Christian Education Council)
Our Muslim Friends A. Farncombe (National Christian Education Council)
Our Sikh Friends A. Farncombe (National Christian Education Council)
Understanding your Hindu Neighbour Ewan (Lutterworth)
Understanding your Jewish Neighbour M. Domnitz (Lutterworth)
Understanding your Muslim Neighbour M. Iqbal (Lutterworth)

3 Poetry Books

The Book of a Thousand Poems J. M. Macbain (Evans)
A Child's Garden of Verses R. L. Stevenson (Oxford/Puffin)
Collected Poems L. Clark (Dobson)
Common Ground L. Clark (Faber)
Evans Book of Children's Verse H. Sergeant (Evans)
Fancy Free D. Saunders & T. Williams (Evans)
A First Poetry Book J. Foster (Oxford)
Full Swing D. Saunders & V. Oliver (Evans)
I Like this Poem K. Webb (Puffin)
Junior Voices I–IV G. Summerfield (Penguin)
Miracles D. Saunders & V. Oliver (Evans)
Mood and Rhythm I–IV E. Mears (Black)
The Oxford Book of Poetry for Children E. Blishen (Oxford)
Parlour Poetry M. Turner (Michael Joseph)
Passport to Poetry 1–4 E. L. Black, Davies & Stradling (Cassell)
Poems for Assemblies T. G. Daffern (Blackwell)
Poems for the School Assembly D. M. Prescott (Blandford)
Poems for Movement E. J. M. Woodland (Evans)
Poetry and Life I–IV N. Grisenthwaite (Schofield and Sims)
The Puffin Book of Magic Verse C. Causley (Puffin)
The Puffin Book of Salt Sea Verse C. Causley (Puffin)
A Puffin Book of Verse E. Graham (Puffin)
A Puffin Quartet of Poems E. Graham (Puffin)
Rhyme and Rhythm I–IV J. Gibson & R. Wilson (Macmillan)
Selected Cautionary Verses Hilaire Belloc (Puffin)
A Single Star D. Davis (Puffin)
Strolling Players Z. & I. Woodward (Evans)
Times' Delights R. Wilson (Hamlyn/Beaver)
Young Verse J. Watson (Armada Lion)
See Also:
Where's that Poem? Helen Morris (Basil Blackwell)
Blackwell's Poetry Cards (Basil Blackwell)
Macmillan's Poetry Packs (Macmillan)

4   Hymn and Song Books—A Short Selection

Apusskidu (Black)
Come and Praise (BBC)
Faith Folk and Clarity (Galliard)
Faith Folk and Festivity (Galliard)
Hymns for Junior Schools (Oxford)
The Junior Hymn Book (Nelson)
Morning has Broken (Schofield and Sims)
New Orbit (Galliard)
The Oxford Song Book (Oxford)
Singing Together B. W. Appleby & F. Fowler (Oxford)
Something to Sing at Assembly G. Brace (CUP)
Someone's Singing Lord (Black)
With Cheerful Voice (Black)
Note: the *Come and Praise* record (REC 317) and cassette (ZCM 317)
contain 21 items from the song book.

5   Prayers—Useful Anthologies

The Lion Book of Children's Prayers M. Bachelor (Lion)
Prayers for Young People William Barclay (Collins)
Prayers to Use with 8-11s. A. Smith (Denholm House)
Time and Again Prayers J. Cookson & M. Rogers (Oxford)

Music Suitable for Assemblies

Arnold, M.	*Tam O'Shanter Overture*
Bach, J. S.	*Air on the G String* (from *Suite No. 3 in D*), *Christmas Oratorio, Jesu Joy of Man's Desiring* (*Cantata 147*), *Sheep May Safely Graze* (*Cantata 208*), *St Matthew Passion, Toccata and Fugue in D Minor*
Bartok, B.	*The Miraculous Mandarin*
Beethoven, L. van	*Symphony No. 5, Symphony No. 6* (*Pastoral*), *Moonlight Sonata*
Bernstein, L.	*West Side Story*
Berlioz, H.	*Roman Carnival Overture*
Bizet, G.	*Carmen*
Borodin, A.	*Polovtsian Dances* from *Prince Igor.*
Brahms, J.	*Academic Festival Overture*
Britten, B.	*Four Sea Interludes* (*Peter Grimes*), *Noye's Fludde, Young Person's Guide to the Orchestra*
Coates, E.	*Dam Busters' March, Oxford Street, Sleepy Lagoon*
Chopin, F.	*Grand Valse Brilliante, Heroic Polonaise No. 6, Minute Waltz, Nocturne No. 4 in F*
Clarke, J.	*Trumpet Voluntary*
Debussy, C.	*Children's Corner Suite, Clair de Lune, La Mer, Prélude à l'Apres-midi d'un Faune, Prélude Feux d'artifice*
Delius, F.	*On Hearing the First Cuckoo in Spring*
Dohnányi, E.	*Variations on a Nursery Song 'Twinkle, Twinkle . . .'*
Dukas, P.	*The Sorcerer's Apprentice*
Dvorak, A.	*Carnival Overture, Slavonic Dance No. 10, Symphony No. 9* (*New World*)
Elgar, E.	*Enigma Variations, Pomp and Circumstance March No. 1*
Falla, M. de	*Ritual Fire Dance*
Fanshawe, D.	*African Sanctus*
Gilbert and Sullivan	*The Mikado Overture*
Grieg, E.	*In Autumn, Peer Gynt Suite, Piano Concerto No. 1*

Handel, G. F.	*Harmonious Blacksmith, The Entry of the Queen of Sheba* (from *Solomon*), *Messiah* (*Hallelujah Chorus*), *The Royal Fireworks, The Water Music*
Haydn, J.	*Clock Symphony, The Creation, Farewell Symphony, Surprise Symphony*
Holst, G.	*The Perfect Fool, The Planets Suite*
Humperdinck, E.	*Hänsel and Gretel*
Khatchaturian, A.	*Sabre Dance, Spartacus theme*
Kodaly, Z.	*Háry János Suite*
Liszt, F.	*Lieberstraum No. 3*
Mahler, G.	*Symphony No. 5*
Mendelssohn, F.	*Fingal's Cave* (*Hebrides Overture*), *A Midsummer Night's Dream, Violin Concerto*
Mozart, L.	*Toy Symphony*
Mozart, W. A.	*Coronation Mass* (*Zadok the Priest*), *Eine Kleine Nachtmusik, Exultate Jubilate, Horn Concerto No. 4, Magic Flute Overture*
Mussorgsky, M.	*Night on a Bare Mountain, Pictures at an Exhibition*
Offenbach, J.	*Orpheus in the Underworld Overture* (the 'Can Can')
Prokofiev, S.	*Classical Symphony, Lieutenant Kije* (*Troika*), *Peter and the Wolf*
Quilter, R.	*Children's Overture*
Ravel, M.	*Bolero Suite, Daphnis and Chloë, Mother Goose Suite*
Rimsky-Korsakov, N.	*Flight of the Bumble Bee, Sheherazade*
Rodrigo, Joaquin	*Concierto de Aranjuez* ('Guitar concerto')
Rossini, G. A.	*La Boutique Fantasque, Thieving Magpie Overture, William Tell Overture*
Saint-Saens, C.	*Carnival of the Animals, Danse Macabre*
Schubert, F.	*The Trout Quintet*
Sibelius, J.	*Finlandia, Karelia Suite, Swan of Tuonela*
Strauss, J.	*Blue Danube Waltz, Radetsky March, Trisch-Trasch Polka*
Strauss, R.	*Also Sprach Zarathustra* (2001 *theme*) *Don Quixote, Till Eulenspiegel*
Stravinsky, I.	*The Firebird, Petrouchka, Rite of Spring, The Song of the Nightingale*

Tchaikovsky, P.	*1812 Overture, Nutcracker Suite, Swan Lake*
Vaughan Williams, R.	*Fantasia on Christmas Carols, Fantasia on Greensleeves, Wasps Overture*
Villa-Lobos, H.	*The Little Train of Caipira*
Vivaldi, A.	*Concerto for Piccolo, The Four Seasons*
Wagner, R.	*Parsifal (Siegfried Idyll), Tannhäuser Overture*
Waldteufel, E.	*Skaters' Waltz*
Walton, W.	*Belshazzar's Feast, Façade*
Widor, C.M.J.A.	*Organ Symphony No. 5*

Other music suitable for assemblies will include folk songs, good quality pop music, instrumental music from different countries, current musicals, pop cantatas, film and television themes.

Useful Addresses

Amnesty International, Tower House, Southampton Street, London WC2

British and Foreign Bible Society, 146 Queen Victoria Street, London EC4

British Humanist Association, 13 Prince of Wales Terrace, London W8

British Red Cross Society, 9 Grosvenor Crescent, London SW1

Cheshire Foundation, 7 Market Mews, London W1

Christian Aid, 240/250 Ferndale Road, Brixton, London SW9

The Commonwealth Institute, Kensington High Street, London W8

Countryside Commission, John Dower House, Crescent Place, Cheltenham, Glos.

Dr Barnado's Homes, Tanners Lane, Barkingside, Ilford, Essex

Forestry Commission, 231 Corstophine Road, Edinburgh EH12

Friends of the Earth, 9 Poland Street, London W1

Health Education Council, 78 New Oxford Street, London WC1

Help the Aged, 32 Dover St, London W1

Keep Britain Tidy, 37 West Street, Brighton, Sussex

National Dairy Council, 5 John Princes Street, London W1

National Trust, 42 Queens Gate, London SW1

NSPCC, 1 Riding House Street, London W1

Oxfam, 274 Banbury Road, Oxford

Postal Marketing Department, Publicity Division, St Martin's Le Grand, London EC1

Royal National Institute for the Blind, 224 Great Portland Street, London W1

Royal National Lifeboat Institution, 202 Lambeth Rd, London SE1

Royal Society for the Prevention of Accidents, 1 Grosvenor Crescent, London SW1

Royal Society for the Protection of Birds, The Lodge, Sandy, Beds.

RSPCA Education Department, Causeway, Horsham, Sussex

St John's Ambulance Brigade, 1 Grosvenor Crescent, London SW1

Salvation Army, 101 Queen Victoria Street, PO Box 249, London EC4

Save the Children Fund, 157 Clapham Rd, London SW9

Shelter, 157 Waterloo Road, London SE1

The Spastics Society, 12 Park Crescent, London W1

United Nations Information Service, 14/15 Stratford Place, London W1

UNICEF, 46–8 Osnaburgh St. London NW1

War on Want, 467 Caledonian Road, London N7

World Wildlife Fund, 29 Greville Street, London EC1

A Calendar of Festivals and Anniversaries

The following calendar lists the major festivals and events of the year together with suggested themes. Included are festivals which children of various faiths could share with their friends. To this calendar may be added those dates special to your school and your locality.

The Autumn Term

Date	Festivals and Anniversaries	Themes
September		
	The New School Year	Allsorts, Friends, Teamwork, Rules, Knowledge, Courtesy
2	Great Fire of London (1666)	Disaster
6	Oak Apple Day (1651)	Trees
	The Pilgrim Fathers	Travel
7	Grace Darling	Disaster, Courage
14	Holy Cross Day	
15	Battle of Britain (1940)	Peace
21	St Matthew's Day	Bible Stories
23	Autumnal Equinox	Autumn
29	St Michael/Michaelmas Day	Flowers (Michaelmas Daisy)
30	St Jerome's Day	Caring for Animals, Saints
Also:		
Sept/Oct	Harvest Festival	Harvest Festival, Food, Bread, Gifts, Sharing
	The Moon Festival (Chinese)	The Moon
	Jewish New Year (1980 AD = 5741 AM)	Judaism
	Yom Kippur	Jewish Festivals
	Feast of Tabernacles	Jewish Festivals
	Autumn	Autumn
October		
2	Mahatma Ghandi b. 1869	Peace, India
4	Feast of St Francis	Caring for Animals, Saints
12	Columbus discovers America 1492	Travel, Thinking for Yourself
14	Battle of Hastings 1066	
18	St Luke's Day	Bible Stories, Artists
21	Trafalgar Day (1805)	Heroes, Sea
24	United Nations Day	Teamwork
31	Hallowe'en	Hallowe'en
Also:	Divali (Hindu)	Hinduism, Light
	Dussehra (Hindu)	Hinduism, Fire
	Eid-el-Adha (Muslim)	Islamic Festivals

Date	Festivals and Anniversaries	Themes
November		
1	All Saints' Day	Saints
2	All Souls' Day	Prayer
5	Guy Fawke's Day	Fireworks
11	St Martin (Martinmas)	Sharing
14	Prince Charles b. 1948	The Royal Family
22	St Cecilia's Day	Music
25	St Catherine's Day	Fireworks
	Noah's Flood 2348 BC	Water, Disaster, Bible Stories
30	St Andrew's Day	Scotland
	Advent	
Also:	Remembrance Sunday (nearest to 11th Nov.)	Peace
	The Lord Mayor's Show (second Saturday in Nov.)	(Different theme each year)
	Thanksgiving Day (U.S.A.) (last Thursday in Nov.)	U.S.A., Pioneers, Explorers
	Muslim New Year (Hijra) (AD 1980 = 1400 AH)	Muslim Festivals
	Guru Nanak's Birthday	Sikhism
December		
4	Potato first introduced 1586	Food
6	St Nicholas' Day	Gifts
10	Declaration of Human Rights	Freedom, Justice
16	Beethoven b. 1770	Music, Hearing
21	St Thomas/Winter Solstice	Winter
24	Christmas Eve	Christmas
25	Christmas Day	Birthdays
26	St Stephen/Boxing Day	Gifts, Martyrs
27	St John the Evangelist	
28	Holy Innocents' Day	
29	St Thomas à Becket d. 1170	Anger
31	New Year's Eve/Hogmanay	Scotland
Also:	Advent Sunday (four Sundays before Christmas)	Light, Churches, Symbols
	Chanukah (Jewish)	Jewish Festivals, Light

The Spring Term

Date	Festivals and Anniversaries	Themes
January		
1	New Year's Day	Hope, Diaries
4	Louis Braille b. 1809	Seeing
5/6	Twelfth Night	Gifts, Travel
6	Epiphany, Feast of the Magi	Bible Stories
10	Penny Post begun 1840	Letters
25	Conversion of St Paul	Bible Story
	Robert Burns b. 1759, Burns' Night	Writers, Poetry, Scotland
26	Australia Day	Commonwealth, Australia
27	Mozart b. 1756	Music, Talents
Also:	Plough Monday (the first Monday after Epiphany)	Country Customs
	Birthday of Muhammad	Muslim Festivals, Birthdays
	Up Helly Aa–Viking Fire Festival in Lerwick, Shetland (the last Tuesday in January)	Fire, Vikings
Jan/Feb	Chinese New Year	
February		
2	Candlemas Day	Light
5	Vesuvius erupted AD 62	Disaster, Volcanoes
6	Queen Elizabeth II acceded 1952	Commonwealth
	New Zealand Day	New Zealand
7	Charles Dickens b. 1812	Writers, Reading
13	Captain Cook d. 1779	Explorers
14	St Valentine's Day	Friends, Love, St Valentine
15	Galileo b. 1564	Honesty
16	Tutankhamun's tomb discovered 1923	Gold, Egypt
19	Prince Andrew b. 1960	
22	Chopin b. 1810	Music, Piano
23	Samuel Pepys b. 1633	Diaries
	Handel b. 1685	Music
29	Leap Year Day	

Date	Festivals and Anniversaries	Themes
February		
Also:	Guides 'Thinking Day'	Clubs, Guides
Feb/March	Shrove Tuesday	Food (pancakes)
	Ash Wednesday (first day of Lent)	Bible, Temptation
	Holi (Hindu)	Hindu Festivals
March		
1	St David's Day	Wales
2	Concorde's Maiden Flight 1969	Flight
3	Feast of Dolls (Japan)	Dolls, Fashion, Shinto
4	RNLI founded 1824	The Sea, Disasters, Rescue
6	Michelangelo b. 1475	Artists, Colour, Talents
8	International Women's Day	Famous Women
15	Ides of March Julius Caesar assassinated 44 BC	
17	St Patrick's Day	Ireland
21	First Day of Spring	Spring, Growth
22	J.S. Bach b. 1685	Music
25	Annunciation of the Virgin, Lady Day	
30	Van Gogh b. 1853	Artists, Colour, Talents
Also:	Commonwealth Day (second Monday in March)	Commonwealth
March/ April	Mothering Sunday (fourth Sunday in Lent)	Gifts
	Purim (Jewish)	Jewish Festivals
April		
1	All Fools' Day	April Fools
2	Hans Andersen b. 1805	Writers, Reading, Stories
7	World Health Day (UN)	Healing, United Nations
	Wordsworth b. 1770	Flowers (Daffodils), Poetry
14	'Titanic' sunk 1912	Disaster, Sea, Rescue
15	Abraham Lincoln d. 1865	U.S.A., Freedom

Date	Festivals and Anniversaries	Themes
April		
18	San Francisco earthquake 1906	Disaster, Earthquakes
21	Queen Elizabeth II b. 1926	Birthdays, Kings and Queens
	Rome founded 753 BC	
23	St George's Day	England, Dragons, Legends
	Shakespeare b. 1564, d. 1616	Writers, Tudors, Plays
25	St Mark's Day	Bible Stories
30	Walpurgis Night	Night, Superstitions, Fear
Also:	Pilgrimage to Canterbury (Chaucer)	Travel, Pilgrims
	Passion Sunday	Easter, Eggs
	Palm Sunday	Forgiveness
	Maundy Thursday	Bible Stories
	Good Friday	
	Easter Sunday	
	Passover (Jewish)	Jewish Festivals
	Baisakhi (Sikh)	Sikhism

The Summer Term

Date	Festivals and Anniversaries	Themes
May		
1	May Day	May Day
3	Columbus discovers Jamaica 1494	Travel, Explorers
7	Tchaikovsky b. 1840	Music, Dance
8	World Red Cross Day	Red Cross, Healing
	VE Day 1945	Peace
9	J. M. Barrie (Peter Pan) b. 1860	Writers, Reading, Flight
12	Florence Nightingale b. 1820	Healing, Nurses
17	Edward Jenner, discovered vaccination, b. 1749	Scientists
21	Elizabeth Fry b. 1780	Charity, Prisons
29	Mt Everest climbed 1953	Perseverance, Mountains
	Oak-Apple, Royal Oak or Restoration Day (Charles II)	Escape
30	St Joan of Arc burned 1431	Saints, France
Also:	Ascension Day	
	Christian Aid Week	Charity, Hunger, Aid
May/June	Vesak (Buddhist)	Buddhism
	Pentecost (Jewish)	Jewish Festivals
	Whit Sunday	Faith
June		
2	Coronation of the Queen 1953	
5	First ascent in hot air balloon by Montgolfier brothers 1783	Air, Flight
6	D Day landings in Normandy 1944	
7	Death of Muhammad AD 632	Islam
10	Prince Philip, Duke of Edinburgh b. 1921	
13	Lords cricket ground opened 1787	Sports, Cricket
14	Flag Day (U.S.A.) Stars and Stripes adopted 1777	Flags, U.S.A.

Date	Festivals and Anniversaries	Themes
June		
15	World Children's Day	World Family, Babies, Names
	Magna Carta signed 1215	Freedom
16	First woman in space 1963	Flight, Solar System
18	Battle of Waterloo 1815	Heroes, War
21	The Summer Solstice (longest day)	Sun
24	Midsummer Day	Summer
27	Helen Keller b. 1880	Hearing, Seeing
29	St Peter's Day	Bible Stories, Fishing
Also:	Father's Day (around 20th June)	Families
June/ July	Ramadhan (Muslim)	Muslim Festivals
July		
1	Dominion Day, Canada (1867)	Commonwealth, Canada
4	American Declaration of Independence 1776	Freedom, U.S.A.
	Dr Barnado b. 1845	Homes, Charity
11	Robert the Bruce, King of Scotland b. 1274	Perseverence
12	Julius Caesar b. 100 BC	
14	Bastille Day (France)	France
15	St Swithin's Day	Rain, Weather
21	Apollo 11 Moonlanding 1969	Moon, Flight
25	St Christopher's Day	Travel, Saints
29	Defeat of Spanish Armada 1588	
Also:	Sports Days	Sports, Keep Fit
	Swan Upping (last Monday in July)	Birds
	Summer Holidays	Holidays
July/Aug	Rakshabandhan (Hindu)	Families
	End of School Year	Into the Future